Knowing About Language

C000163079

Knowing About Language is an essential and comprehensive introduction to and discussion of the value of linguistics in the secondary and post-16 curriculum. Split into three easily accessible parts, each chapter draws on theoretical and practical reasons for developing language awareness for the teacher and student, the impact of government and institutional policy on teaching and teacher knowledge, and explores recent research about the value of linguistic knowledge to support student attainment. Expert contributors show how recent innovations in linguistics can support language teaching by providing a range of practical ideas that can be used in the classroom.

Knowing About Language is a valuable theoretical, critical and practical guide for the teacher and researcher – and anyone interested in applied linguistics and the study of language in education. Written by authors who are passionate about the value of language study both as a classroom topic and more generally, this book acts as a resource to inform and support teachers in wider aspects of their role by demonstrating the powerfully enabling nature and inherent value of language study and linguistics in secondary and post-16 curricula.

Marcello Giovanelli is Assistant Professor in English Education at the University of Nottingham, UK.

Dan Clayton is a teacher of English Language at the Sixth Form College, Colchester, UK.

NATE

The National Association for the Teaching of English (NATE), founded in 1963, is the professional body for all teachers of English from Primary to Post-16. Through its regions, committees and conferences, the association draws on the work of classroom practitioners, advisers, consultants, teacher trainers, academics and researchers to promote dynamic and progressive approaches to the subject by means of debate, training and publications. NATE is a charity reliant on membership subscriptions. If you teach English in any capacity, please visit **www. nate.org.uk** and consider joining NATE, so the association can continue its work and give teachers of English and the subject a strong voice nationally.

This series of books co-published with NATE reflects the organisation's dedication to promoting standards of excellence in the teaching of English, from early years through to university level. Titles in this series promote innovative and original ideas that have practical classroom outcomes and support teachers' own professional development.

Books in the NATE series include both pupil and classroom resources and academic research aimed at English teachers, students on PGCE/ITT courses and NQTs.

Titles in this series include:

Knowing About Language

Linguistics and the secondary English classroom

Edited by Marcello Giovanelli and Dan Clayton

Routledge
Taylor & Francis Group

LONDON AND NEW YORK

First published 2016
by Routledge
2 Park Square, Milton Park, Abingdon, Oxon OX14 4RN

and by Routledge
711 Third Avenue, New York, NY 10017

Routledge is an imprint of the Taylor & Francis Group, an informa business.

British Library Cataloguing in Publication Data
A catalogue record for this book is available from the British Library.

Library of Congress Cataloging in Publication Data
Names: Giovanelli, Marcello, editor. | Clayton, Dan, editor.
Title: Knowing about language : linguistics and the secondary English classroom / edited by Marcello Giovanelli and Dan Clayton.
Description: Milton Park, Abingdon, Oxon ; New York, NY : Routledge, [2016]
Identifiers: LCCN 2015045916| ISBN 9781138856226 (hardback) | ISBN 9781138856233 (pbk.) | ISBN 9781315719818 (ebook)
Subjects: LCSH: Language awareness. | Second language acquisition. | Applied linguistics–Study and teaching (Secondary) | Language acquisition–Age factors. | Language acquisition–Research–Methodology. | Language teachers–Training of. | Language and education.
Classification: LCC P120.L34 K623 2016 | DDC 410.71/2–dc23LC record available at http://lccn.loc.gov/2015045916

ISBN: 978-1-138-85622-6 (hbk)
ISBN: 978-1-138-85623-3 (pbk)
ISBN: 978-1-315-71981-8 (ebk)

Typeset in Galliard
by Cenveo Publisher Services
Printed by Ashford Colour Press Ltd.

MIX
Paper from
responsible sources
FSC
www.fsc.org   FSC® C011748

Table of contents

List of figures and tables

Figures

Tables

List of contributors

Margaret Berry, now retired, was Reader in English Language at the University of Nottingham. She has published introductory books on systemic linguistics, and articles on systemic functional linguistic theory, context of situation, exchange structure, Theme and Rheme, register variation, and the application of systemic functional linguistics to the teaching of English. She has lectured in China, Australia and Canada, as well as in European countries.

Gavin Brookes is a doctoral researcher in health communication at the School of English, University of Nottingham. He is Editorial Assistant for the *International Journal of Corpus Linguistics* (published by John Benjamins). His doctoral research examines the discursive constructions of diabetes and diabulimia in online health fora.

Ronald Carter is Research Professor of Modern English Language at the University of Nottingham. He has published extensively in the fields of applied linguistics and literature and language in education, and is the author and editor of over 40 books and 100 articles in these fields. Recent publications as author and co-author include *Language and Creativity: The Art of Common Talk* (2015) and *How to Analyse Texts* (2015). He was director of the Language in the National Curriculum (LINC) project from 1989–1992, and was made a life member of NATE in 2008 for his services to English teaching in the UK. In 2009, he was awarded an MBE for services to education.

Billy Clark is Associate Professor in English Language and Linguistics at Middlesex University. His research and teaching interests cover a range of topics in linguistics and linguistic theory. His main focus has been on various aspects of meaning (semantics and pragmatics), mainly within the framework of relevance theory. This has included work on lexical and syntactic meaning, phatic communication, prosodic meaning, multimodality and stylistics. Recent publications include a book, *Relevance Theory* (2013), and a collection edited with Siobhan Chapman, *Pragmatic Literary Stylistics* (2014). He has worked with a number of groups interested in connections between work at school and at university. He is a member of the UK Linguistics Olympiad committee (www.uklo.org) and, with Marcello Giovanelli and Andrea Macrae, coordinates the *Integrating English* project (www.integratingenglish.org).

Dan Clayton teaches A-level English at the Sixth Form College, Colchester, and has examined and moderated for an English examination board, along with writing a number of publications for students and teachers of A-level English Language. He has also worked as Research Fellow on the Survey of English Usage at University College, London, and taught for ten years at St Francis Xavier Sixth Form College in South London, establishing links between linguists and post-16 teachers throughout this time.

Ian Cushing teaches English at secondary and sixth form levels, and holds undergraduate and postgraduate degrees in linguistics and phonetics. He is interested in integrated approaches to language-literature teaching, stylistics and educational linguistics. He co-authored the Cambridge University Press textbook for AQA A-level English Language and Literature and runs courses for the English and Media Centre on A-level English Language. He also sits on the Education Committee for the Linguistics Association of Great Britain and the United Kingdom Linguistics Olympiad committee.

Victoria Elliott is Associate Professor of English and Literacy Education at the University of Oxford. She is a fellow of St Hilda's College. She works with teachers on the PGCE English and the Master's in Learning and Teaching, and teaches qualitative methods to doctoral researchers. She is also an external subject expert for Ofqual. Her research interests include curriculum and teaching of English in secondary schools, classroom discourse, and educational assessment. She has published on these topics in *Journal of Pragmatics, Assessment in Education, The Curriculum Journal* and *Changing English*.

Marcello Giovanelli is Assistant Professor in English Education at the University of Nottingham. He has research interests in educational linguistics, descriptive and pedagogical stylistics, cognitive poetics, and the pedagogies and discourses of English language teaching in the UK. His recent book publications include *Text World Theory and Keats' Poetry* (2013) and *Teaching Grammar, Structure and Meaning* (2014). He has published research in journals such as *Language and Education* and *English in Education*. He is Chair of Examiners for A-level English Language and Literature at an English examination board and a member of the UK Linguistics Olympiad committee.

Angela Goddard is a professor of English Language, a Higher Education Academy National Teaching Fellow, and Chair of Examiners for English Language A-level at an English examination board. She has taught English across the age range from primary schools to higher education, and in universities both in the UK and abroad. She has written and edited many books and articles about English language, including the Routledge *Intertext* series and *How To Analyse Texts* (2015), which recognises the international nature of much contemporary English use. Her research interests include the language of new communication technologies.

Kevin Harvey is Assistant Professor in Sociolinguistics at the School of English, University of Nottingham. His specific research interest is in the area of discourse-based health communication, which includes corpus linguistic and multimodal approaches to health-related discourse. He has published extensively in these areas and is the author of *Investigating Adolescent Health Communication: A Corpus Linguistics Approach* (2013).

Sam Hellmuth is Senior Lecturer in the Department of Language and Linguistic Science at the University of York. She teaches phonetics and phonology at all levels and maintains active research on stress and intonation in dialects of English and Arabic. With colleagues at York, she runs CPD workshops for teachers of English A-level and a resource book of teaching materials is in preparation. Sam is Treasurer of the United Kingdom Linguistics Olympiad committee.

Willem B. Hollmann is Senior Lecturer in the Department of Linguistics and English Language at Lancaster University. His research is mainly in cognitive linguistics, language change and the grammar of regional dialects, with forensic linguistics being a more recent interest. His work has been published in books such as *The Oxford Handbook of Construction Grammar* (2013) and journals such as *Cognitive Linguistics, English Language and Linguistics* and *Studies in Language*.

Richard ('Dick') Hudson is Emeritus Professor of Linguistics at University College London. His research interest lies in theoretical linguistics, but he also has a long-standing interest, which goes back to working with Michael Halliday in the 1960s, in building bridges between academic linguistics and schools. His main publications in this area are a book, *Teaching Grammar: A Guide to the National Curriculum* (1992), a number of chapters, (e.g. 'Grammar Instruction' in the *Handbook of Writing Research*, 2nd edn, 2015) and a series of about a hundred snippets about grammar teaching in the *Times Educational Supplement*.

Jenni Ingram is Associate Professor of Education at the University of Oxford, where she coordinates the mathematics strands of the Master's in Learning and Teaching and of the PGCE. She is a fellow of Linacre College. Her research interests are in the area of classroom discourse, students' understanding of mathematics and classroom pedagogy. She has published on these topics in *Journal of Pragmatics, For the Learning of Mathematics, The Cambridge Journal of Education* and in key texts for PGCE students.

Andrea Macrae is Senior Lecturer in Stylistics at Oxford Brookes University. She teaches stylistics, narratology and cognitive poetics. Her primary areas of research and publication include literary deixis, stylistics of performance, metafiction and pedagogical stylistics. She is also a co-author of the *English Language and Literature A/AS Level for AQA Student Book* (2015).

Jessica Mason is Lecturer in English Language and Literature at the University of Sheffield. She works to bring cognitive linguistics into educational research and is interested in the ways readers connect different literary texts and experiences. She has developed a 'narrative interrelation framework', a cognitive model of intertextuality, focusing particularly on how readers make and understand intertextual references. In 2015, she was awarded the *Terry Furlong Award for Research* by the National Association for the Teaching of English.

Debra Myhill is Professor of Education at the University of Exeter. Her research interests focus principally on aspects of language teaching, particularly the teaching of writing, the role of grammar, and the relationship between talk and writing. She is the author or co-author of several books including: *Talking, Listening, Learning: Effective Talk in the Primary Classroom* (2005), *Using Talk to Support Writing* (Sage, 2010), *The Handbook of Writing Development* (2009) and *Writing Voices: Creating Communities of Writers* (2011).

Felicity Titjen is Course Leader for English Language and Literature at Oldham Sixth Form College and Chief Examiner for A-level English Language and Literature at an English examination board. Her primary teaching interests are in A-level English Language and English Language and Literature. She has contributed to resource books aimed at both students and teachers to encourage and support knowledge and understanding in these key subject areas.

Graeme Trousdale is Senior Lecturer in English Language at the University of Edinburgh. He has research interests in cognitive linguistics (especially construction grammar), historical linguistics and dialects of English in Britain. He is also committed to increasing the visibility of linguistics in the school classroom, particularly via the United Kingdom Linguistics Olympiad. He is the author of *An Introduction to English Sociolinguistics* (2010), the co-author, with Elizabeth Closs Traugott, of *Constructionalization and Constructional Changes* (2013) and the co-editor, with Thomas Hoffmann, of *The Oxford Handbook of Construction Grammar* (2013).

Acknowledgements

The editors would like to thank Alison Foyle at Taylor and Francis for her enthusiasm for this project, and Sarah Tuckwell for her continued advice and guidance during the writing process. An edited collection heavily relies on the quality of its contributors and we are delighted to have received the support of an outstanding group of writers. We would also like to thank the two reviewers of our original proposal for their positive comments on our idea, and NATE for agreeing to adopt the book in their series. We are particularly grateful to Ronald Carter for his support and for writing the foreword to this book.

Marcello Giovanelli
I would like to thank my family for their support during the writing and editing of this book with particular thanks, as always, to Jennie, Anna, Zara and Sophia. I am very grateful to Dan Clayton for all of his work in co-managing what ended up being a larger than expected but very rewarding project. Lastly, my thanks go to Megan Mansworth for supplying some data for one of the chapters and to Jess Mason for her support in the final stages of putting the book together.

Dan Clayton
I would like to thank John Cox, my English teacher at Bishop Wordsworth's School, Salisbury, for spurring my interest in English and for provoking lively debates about the nature of the subject. Thanks are also due to Margaret and Terry Clayton, who despite being a chemist and psychologist respectively, encouraged my study of a soft arts subject. Finally, I would like to thank Marcello Giovanelli for involving me in this project and for his patience in dealing with a newcomer to editing.

Transcription key

(.)   indicates a pause of less than a second
(2)   indicates a longer pause (number of seconds indicated)
((*italics*))   indicates contextual or additional information
[ ]   indicates the start and end points of simultaneous speech

Foreword

Yesterday, today and tomorrow in linguistics and education

(a) Analyse into clauses the following passage. Give the grammatical description of the clauses and show their connection with each other.

In that year (1851) when the Great Exhibition spread its hospitable glass roof over the elms of Hyde Park, and all the world came to *admire* England's wealth, progress and enlightenment, there might *profitably* have been another 'Exhibition' to show how our poor were housed and to teach the admiring foreign visitor *some* of the dangers *that* beset the path of the vaunted new era.

(b) State the grammatical features of the words italicised.

(General Secondary Education paper (1946): English)

....

Every time the question of language surfaces, in one way or another, it means that a series of other problems are coming to the fore: the formation and enlargement of the governing class, the need to establish more intimate and secure relationships between the governing groups and the national-popular mass, in other words to reorganise the cultural hegemony.

(Antonio Gramsci, *Selected Writings* 1985)

During the course of the past fifty or so years the relationship of linguistics to the secondary English classroom has been characterised both by marked challenges and by very distinct progress. There have been different views of the subject of linguistics, different views of the subject of English and different views of what it means to be competent both as a student of English and as a teacher of English. And there have been disagreements and resolutions involving educationalists and politicians of all political persuasions resulting in the development of a national curriculum in which English has remained a core subject. Fifty years may appear to be a long time but change has been continuous and at the time of publication of this book such change is still with us and is the site of continuing contestation and debate.

The positive and forward-looking character of this book together with the arguments, examples and evidence provided by such a high-powered cast list of contributors is its particular strength. Embracing the inevitably oversimplifying character of all book prefaces and summaries of this kind I'd like to begin by briefly highlighting what I see as the nature and character of some of the tensions affecting the place of linguistics in secondary English. I offer an outline of some of these tensions, focusing on past and present disputations, followed by a more inclusive signalling of some key themes for future development.

Instructive pasts and changing presents

Linguistics and language in education

Although united in many ways, there are continuing differences between proponents of language in education and proponents of linguistics in education. On the one hand it is said that attention to language and language development in students is best done implicitly and intuitively, that language is a tool for learning that needs to be nurtured with a full awareness of context, purpose and audience and with due sensitivity to its creative potential. Citing, among others, foundational work in the 1970s and 1980s by Douglas Barnes, James Britton, Nancy Martin and John Dixon, the only really significant insights into language in education, it is argued, have come from those with this orientation. The practice of some linguists has been seen and continues to be seen as too reductive and mechanistic in orientation and overly focused on structure rather than use. There remain reservations about the role of language analysis in the English classroom and whether analysis should precede or ever can lead to greater competence.

On the other hand, there is increasing and ever more convincing research evidence – richly illustrated in this book – to show that contextually sensitive linguistic analysis connected to the best work in the history of language in education can result in marked improvements in language and literacy development. It is argued that goals for language learning and development are best achieved by more explicit and precise linguistic description of the forms and functions of language and that the tools of linguistic science should be deployed to this end.

Both these general positions are inevitably clinal, are more yesterday than today and are united by more than they are divided, but the differences continue to influence thinking and practice. It should be noted that the differences are apparent only in what may be very loosely described as first language contexts of English teaching. In the world of teaching and learning English as a second and foreign language at all levels the part played by linguistics is incontrovertible and largely uncontested and is witnessed over the past fifty years by the massive expansion, ubiquity and success of courses in applied linguistics in colleges and universities world-wide aimed at English teachers.

All who are committed to a language in education viewpoint and to a linguistics in education viewpoint have profound reservations about government-imposed and ideologically-driven curricula in which language is taught and tested in a decontextualised way, reading and writing privileged to the detriment of oracy development and in which the relationship between knowing a metalanguage for English and learning about the subject are seen, unproblematically, as seamless. There is a unity in the suspicion that issues of language only come to the fore for governments when there are deeper anxieties at play about social unity and a need for greater social control. Witness the words of Gramsci at the head of this foreword. Witness too the extract from a GSE English paper from 1946 which bears an uncanny resemblance to current versions of grammar tests at Key Stage 2 and which also underlines the views of many in UK government that performance in language needs to be tested in clean and straightforward ways. The significance of accountability through tests cannot be denied but what can be tested in a clean and neat way is commonly not what is most valued in literacy development in primary and secondary English classrooms or needed in the world of the workplace. The complexity and nuances embedded in many different kinds of spoken and written texts in secondary English teaching cannot easily be tested in the formats or timelines or conditions currently being imposed. Teachers know this; many politicians with their formulaic take on accountability do not. But politicians have the power; teachers do not.

Some of the positions described above have their origins, of course, in differences and distinctions within the world of language sciences. Some branches of linguistics are indeed concerned primarily with theories of language directed mainly at mapping mentalistic and cognitive underpinnings to language structure and remain more psycho-linguistically oriented. Some involve data that are invented or contrived for purposes of illustration. These contrast of course with the more functional approaches to language influenced mainly by the work of Michael Halliday, where the primary concern is to describe how language works in use and in social contexts, is more sociolinguistically oriented, involves empirical data and has a more direct and immediate relevance to secondary English classrooms. The explicitness offered by the best linguistic analyses also means that commentaries on language are retrievable and verifiable by others.

Literature and language studies

Another underlying tension in the domain of secondary English teaching is that between literature and language study. The past here shows sharper oppositions and disagreements that continue to permeate discussions today. The more literary focus underlines the centrality of literature to the English curriculum on account of its primary concern with creative and imaginative uses of language art which, it is argued, can only be fully understood and studied with reference to the sociohistorical contexts in which such language was produced by the poet, novelist or dramatist being studied. By contrast, language study has been seen as ahistorical, too narrow and restrictive, describing texts in an overly mechanistic and unimaginative way and commonly dealing with texts which are essentially ephemeral. It is also argued that language study has little to say about the history of ideas, that it lacks a proper intellectual content, has no real concern with hermeneutics and that it is too focused on language description to the detriment of helping students better understand cultures and human values. These are concerns that need to be more fully addressed, especially by all those interested in the relationship between linguistics, poetics and literature. In the case of literary studies, however, literature is, fundamentally, *made* from language and it is argued that no full account of a literary text (or any text for that matter) can or should be made without systematic attention to the ways in which language works in the text and to the part played by linguistic patterns in an interpretation of meanings and effects.

The growth of English Language and applied linguistics

Such views as these concerning the practice of language studies do, however, seem to take little account of work in linguistics which embraces connections between language and social ideologies, the nature of intercultural communication, sociolinguistic work on language varieties and on world Englishes, sociocognitive research into language creativity and poetics, analysis of language and gender, explorations of language and hermeneutic interpretation as well as the developing interdisciplinarity within applied linguistics which sees ever more courses that connect language and other disciplines such as history, psychology, cultural and media studies. And the exponential growth of corpus linguistics, aided by multi-million word databases, has moved beyond simply providing better evidenced descriptions, invaluable though these are, to describe a much wider notion of communication and social contexts. All these developments and many others have reinforced the linguistic turn in the humanities to the point where language analysis is seen as a mediating component in many disciplines and where language itself becomes not simply a medium but a content to be critically investigated and ideationally explored. Linguistic description has in the past twenty years moved significantly beyond an identification of parts of speech of the kind illustrated in the above GSE paper and now embraces a much fuller concern with how language operates in extended texts beyond the individual sentence and beyond the individual speaking turn. The study of literature which fails to embrace these changes is, many language specialists argue, inevitably attenuated as a result.

The curriculum changes over the past twenty years, which have led to the growth of A-level English Language, and which have also resulted in integrated language and literature programmes in literary and linguistic stylistics are undoubtedly changing this picture today. Some tensions remain that have affected and continue to affect curriculum choices for students in some school English departments and at the transition from school to university English Studies.

Present challenges

Different positions produce debate and the nature and contexts of many debates at the present time are healthier overall than they have ever been. Paradoxically, whatever their respective positions, all concerned today with the subject of English in schools are united in this view. They are also united in their opposition to political interference by all political parties which always seems to result in a narrower curriculum with, as argued above, learning related to what can be more easily tested and with minimal understanding of, if not resistance to, the linguistic and cultural diversity of the contexts in which many teachers teach.

These different positions and tendencies also, of course, affect the professional construction and constitution of the subject and again this can also be for the better. Questions such as: is 'English' literature or language or both? How can they be more inclusively integrated? What are the relationships of English with other curricular subjects? Where do all the recent developments in courses in creative writing fit? Why can't creativity be studied in a wider range of texts and rhetorics beyond the conventional triad of poetry, prose and drama? Can we only really speak properly in terms of literatures in English and of Englishes in the plural? What exactly is a text in the context of English and how do students best pedagogically engage with texts, spoken and written, productively and receptively? What are the values to be promoted in the study of English? Are the values associated with creative writing the same or are they inflected differently? Richmond (2015) offers further valuable perspectives on these current questions in relation to language and literacy in English classrooms.

New tomorrows

English and the political context

There are numerous contradictions in this context. The more schools are given autonomy for managing, including greater freedom to manage teacher education, the greater the accountability and centralised control. The more English teachers strengthen their resolve to resist a narrowing of the curriculum but cannot fully agree on what English is, the weaker they become and the greater the risk that English as a secondary subject becomes fragmented and fractured. The more knowledge about language teachers have the more they can challenge the politicians seeking greater curricular control but who lack linguistic understanding. Such oppositions and contradictions also simply underline, however, a further paradox that those who have the power do not have the knowledge and those who have the knowledge do not have the power.

English language as a subject

From the point of view of academic subjects the lack of consensus about what constitutes English as an academic discipline is both a strength and a weakness.

It is important that the rapid development of English language studies as a degree subject in departments of English is continued, that advances in stylistics are consolidated with due concern for parallel advances in literary and cultural studies, that a wider variety of texts are engaged with beyond the conventional 'literary' texts and that creativity in language is seen as operating in a wide variety of texts.

In secondary schools there is likewise a need for a greater variety of genres and text-types to be studied and developed in both speech and writing. Narrative is a core genre but English teachers in particular can be more fully acquainted with the structure of and creative possibilities inherent in non-fictional texts, in instructional texts, in arguments, reports and recounts and in scientific writing in general. There is also considerable potential for English to be taught more fully to reflect recent advances in corpus linguistics and sociolinguistics.

Linguistics, teacher preparation and teacher development

In the whole domain of teacher development, curricular space is ever more crowded and constrained with ever more demands for coverage of ever more topics. Nonetheless, increasing evidence of the value of formal language study suggests that teachers across all subjects (but especially teachers of English) should be linguistically better informed and better able to understand the complexities of language use. The foundation here is being better able to describe the forms and functions of language and developing a better appreciation of the centrality of language choice in relation to context and audience. In terms of classroom pedagogy, directives and templates have a limited value but the history of English teaching shows that the achievement of competence in any aspect of language comes primarily from creating classroom conditions in which language is an enjoyable and personalised experience, and that learning how to mean is closely connected to learning appropriately how to construct and infer meaning in language in both production and reception.

Being able to analyse language as a teacher is not the same thing as teaching students to analyse language. Pedagogically, becoming more competent in the use of language is complex and involves a balance between experience and analysis of and reflection on language that the profession is still learning more about. For all, however, the increasingly widely practised methods adopted for language study of learner-centred, empirical, data-driven explorations of language in real-world contexts of use provide something close to this balance. What is also increasingly acknowledged and is reinforced throughout this book is that the more knowledge about language we have the better able we are to achieve these aims of fuller 'applied' knowledge in the service of secondary English language and literacy development.

This book

This book charts the developments of yesterday and today with considerable lucidity, with an expansive and catholic view of the many sides to the arguments and oppositions and with a positive view of what tomorrow may hold. There is considerable unanimity among the contributors about what futures may look like and what may need to be done to build upon the advances described in the individual chapters. There is also an appropriate realism about appropriate resolutions.

Even if at times it may feel as if there is regression, the oppositions, contradictions and complexities outlined both in this foreword and in the book do not invalidate the progress made over the past fifty years; indeed they can be positively embraced. The relationship between linguistics and secondary English teaching has come a long way and linguistics has played a key part in identifying issues for further exploration by all English specialists. There are numerous current challenges, pasts to be learned from and tensions to be resolved. Nothing should, however, be allowed to either blunt or blur the kinds of developments, achievements and future visions articulated so cogently and persuasively in this volume.

Ronald Carter, School of English,
University of Nottingham

Reference

Richmond, J. (ed.) (2015) 'The Fight to Recover': Half a Century of Contest over the Curriculum in English, Language and Literacy, 3 to 19, Leicester: UKLA/Owen Education.

Introduction

Marcello Giovanelli and Dan Clayton

Rationale for this book

In the context of very recent, and very rapid, curriculum reform in England, we believe that this is an important and timely book. From 2015, schools and colleges began to teach new GCSE and A-level qualifications, and debates about the nature and content of English as a curriculum subject continue to be at the heart of discussions involving politicians, school leaders, subject associations and those working as teachers in all sectors of education. These discussions are not without controversy. For example, in 2014, sections of the media criticised the prospect of A-level students studying the language of Dizzee Rascal, Russell Brand and Caitlin Moran, with accusations of 'dumbing down' and 'political correctness gone mad'[1] in abundance. What many journalists (and even more online commentators) failed to grasp was that these texts – and many others like them – had for many years been staple parts of English Language syllabuses: not analysed as literature but as texts that demonstrate the rich range of language available to modern users in all its written, spoken and digital forms. The furore also demonstrated that for many, the study of English has been, and will always be, the study of English literature; as a consequence language study has struggled to justify its status and value. Interestingly, as we write (September 2015), the decision to discontinue an A-level qualification in Creative Writing has re-ignited age-old debates about the cultural and pedagogical value of aspects of 'English', what should be made available for secondary and Post-16 students to study, and who should be making those decisions. The struggle to claim a place as part of the English curriculum it seems is destined to continue.

This scenario is familiar to those who have advocated both the usefulness of explicit language work in the English classroom, and the value of linguistic knowledge more generally to the English teacher in understanding and supporting the skills of speaking, listening, reading and writing. Too often caught up in political and ideological debates, the position of language work in schools in particular has never been secure. But, as a subject, 'English Language' or 'Linguistics' inherently lends itself to the study of new and exciting topics and progressive teaching and learning methodologies. For example, the advent of new technologies and their affordances including their available meaning-making resources, methods of inter-action and forms of representation have allowed 'English' to be more than just the study of words and print-based texts. And, advances in portable recording equipment and large collections of data in the form of language corpora have meant that it is possible to develop models and frameworks that allow for the systematic analysis of spoken language. Furthermore, linguistics has become truly interdisciplinary; linguists have built innovative and mutually beneficial links with cognitive science, sociology, psychology, anthropology and literary studies. This interdisciplinarity has resulted in detailed theoretical models and practical meth-odologies to explore language in all its multitude of forms.

In schools and colleges, the growth of A-level English Language as a post-16 qualification has contributed to the popularity of both English Language and Linguistics at undergraduate and postgraduate levels. This has led to increased dialogue between the sectors with higher education programmes owing much to the value attached to language work at Key Stage 5 and the dedication and commitment of A-level teachers to provide high-quality teaching to encourage students to want to continue their studies. In addition, the current focus in higher education on demonstrating impact as part of the Research Excellence Framework (REF) has meant that more and more value is being placed on academics establishing and building connections with school English and work-ing with teachers to develop collaborative teaching and learning approaches and to support transition. Indeed there is a long history of academics leading programmes designed to bridge the gap between the sectors and support research-led investigative language work in schools, most notably the Schools Council Programme in Linguistics (1964–71) and the Language in the National Curriculum project (1989–92). But there have also been others, and many of the contributors in this volume have played and continue to play important roles in building bridges between school and university-level study and in influencing both policy and practice in the classroom.

In putting together this book, we have drawn on the issues discussed above to provide what we feel is a much-needed acknowledgement and discussion of the value of linguistics in the secondary and post-16 curriculum. It offers a theo-retical background to the history and practice of the subject in the light of government initiatives and policies, and draws on research in linguistics to support English language teachers in both their teaching and their wider peda-gogical concerns. Each of the chapters in this book also argues, whether directly or indirectly, for the central place of linguistics in teachers' pre- and in-service development. However, as well as the *what* and the *why*, this book highlights ways in which recent innovations in linguistics can support language teaching in schools and sixth form colleges by providing a range of practical ideas that can be used in the classroom and which demonstrate *how* theory might be turned into practice. We are delighted to have secured contributions from a wide field of teachers and researchers, all of whom have extensive experience of working in secondary, further and higher education.

Knowing about language

In 'Linguistics and the teaching of English', Michael Halliday (1967: 83) suggested that language work in schools broadly fell into one of three types:

1   the *productive*: concerned with developing skills and competences in speaking, listening, reading and writing;
2   the *descriptive*: concerned with learning about the content of the subject, for example the structures and uses of English;
3   the *prescriptive*: a form of 'linguistic table manners' that urges conformity and the uptake of desired ways of speaking and writing.

Unfortunately, well over one hundred years of language work in schools has to a large extent been overshadowed by debates about the place and value of formal grammar teaching in schools and the relative value of different varieties of English together with discussion as to whether or not such work provides some impact or measurable output and therefore can be justified as part of the curriculum. Several of the chapters in this book draw on these productive and prescriptive debates. However, much of the really interesting and valuable work in linguistics allows researchers and teachers to explore more revealing questions about attitudes, competences, psychologies, social interactions, individuals and communities; that is, the descriptive study both of language as a system and of the people who use it.

To undertake such descriptive work with students in their classrooms, teachers clearly need to have linguistic knowledge and be able to apply it in ways that encourage students to understand and investigate the subject. And, they also need access to resources and research to support their continuous professional development. However, linguistics as a discipline is not only useful in as far as it allows teachers *explicitly* to use that knowledge in teaching aspects of the subject itself; we also believe that it has an inherent value as a resource to support teachers more *implicitly* in understanding their professional capacity in the classroom and beyond. This is a crucial point and one that is addressed through each of the chapters in this book, particularly those in Part III. This point and the distinction between these two kinds of explicit and implicit knowledge are emphasised by Carter (1982: 8) who argues for the value of 'linguistics as a foundation for classroom language teaching'. By this, Carter proposes that in the broadest sense, knowledge about linguistics provides a pedagogical foothold from which a teacher is able to understand the processes of speaking, listening, reading and writing that occur in the classroom. In turn the teacher is able to use this knowledge to inform planning, teaching and learning, develop a common metalanguage for the classroom, make decisions about teaching design and methodology, and understand the wider historical and political contexts surrounding debates about the nature of English, all of which permit and facilitate discussion as knowledgeable stakeholders with curriculum and policy-makers.

We are aware that this book follows in a line of others that have approached the subject of linguistics and schools. Over thirty years ago, contributors to a book that has greatly influenced our planning for and writing of this present volume, *Linguistics and the Teacher* (Carter 1982), argued for greater prominence and importance to be given to the place of linguistics and language study in the curriculum. More recently, other multi-author volumes have promoted, celebrated and analysed the role of language work in schools and the value of linguistics as a discipline to teachers, including from several international perspectives (see for example the chapters in Denham and Lobeck 2006, 2010; Locke 2010; and Ellis and McCartney 2011). We hope that this volume extends the discussion and provides teachers and researchers with further opportunities to reflect both on how advances from linguistics might be integrated into the classroom, and on how fruitful dialogue might continue to take place between secondary and higher education colleagues.

We are also aware in that in planning, writing and editing this book, we would be doing so in the context of various definitions that have come to refer to the study of language amongst native users, for example, *language awareness, knowledge about language, language study,* and *linguistic knowledge.* Whilst there are motivations, and histories, for using these terms, we have intentionally adopted the term *linguistics* to refer to all aspects of the field covering language as a system, the study of its users, and as an underlying set of principles of thinking about communication and the construction of meaning. Equally, we have not distinguished between *applied linguistics* and *linguistics* as we think that linguistics taught and used well by the professional practitioner is an inherently applied subject.

Organisation of the book

This book is organised in three parts. For each chapter, we asked contributors to explore the place of linguistics and linguistic knowledge from within their specific area of expertise and interest. We were, however, conscious that this should not just be a book that imparts knowledge about linguistics without a clear focus on how its application might be useful to the teacher. Therefore, each contributor not only outlines some area of specific linguistic knowledge but frames this in a way that foregrounds its application in the service of understanding history and policy (Part I chapters), developing ideas, activities and resources for classroom activities (Part II chapters), and addressing wider pedagogical and professional concerns (Part III chapters). In all cases, contributors make a strong case for applying topics, ideas and research from the field of linguistics to educational study and practice.

In Part I, each of the contributors examines the theoretical, historical and political background to teaching language within the English curriculum in UK schools. They draw on theoretical and practical reasons for developing language awareness for the teacher and student, the impact of government and institutional policy on teaching and teacher knowledge, and recent research about the value of linguistic knowledge to support student attainment.

In Chapter 1, Marcello Giovanelli argues for the teacher as a kind of applied linguist. Outlining the subordinate status of language work in schools, Giovanelli's chapter focuses on an analysis of a noticeboard banning certain words and phrases which recently appeared in a secondary school, and which received a great deal of attention in the national press. He argues that its content and sentiment provide a rich springboard for various kinds of descriptive and analytical work and also open up important questions about the perception and given status of language varieties. Drawing on James Paul Gee's notions of *primary* and *non-primary* theories of language, Giovanelli argues that linguistic knowledge can be an invaluable tool for the teacher to support inclusion and non-discrimination, building on rather than stigmatising the considerable assets and implicit knowledge that students bring into schools, and allowing them to study these in a focused and explicit way.

The relationship between policy and practice is the focus of Richard Hudson in Chapter 2. Hudson traces how these interrelate by describing some of the ways that centralised decision-making can pan out in the day-to-day reality of schools and classrooms. He discusses how government policy, professional practice, the economics of publishing and the assessment system all impact on whether policies get actualised in the classroom. In particular, he emphasises how teacher professional development, often ignored in the density of official documentation, is crucial to its successful implementation. While highlighting the significant nature of recent changes in the National Curriculum as the motivation for a renewed interest in grammar teaching, Hudson acknowledges that much work still needs to be done to ensure a fully coherent language pedagogy in schools.

In Chapter 3, Debra Myhill draws extensively on the literature surrounding grammar teaching and its effect on students' writing to offer a convincing and principled argument for language work in schools. Myhill identifies the frustrations imposed by a dominant discourse of grammar that has been centred on notions of correctness and rules. Arguing that explicit knowledge of language as a system can give students access to understanding different genres, registers and styles of writing, Myhill sees the grammatical choices that writers make as inherently meaningful and as part of a range of meaning-making resources that allow deliberate choices to be made with particular interpretative effects in mind. Myhill's chapter also highlights the substantial body of work being undertaken in the United States and Australia in the Systemic Functional Linguistics tradition (see also Margaret Berry's chapter in this book), suggesting that these offer the potential for a further body of empirical studies on the relationship between the explicit teaching of grammar and development in writing.

In Part II, the emphasis of each chapter is on how research in a particular linguistic field might be useful to the teacher in the classroom. In this part, each contributor outlines a specific area of linguistics, drawing on recent research findings and suggesting how teachers might use these to develop students' awareness of language and their analytical skills. In many cases, these chapters are based explicitly on case studies and work with schools and colleges that contributors have undertaken.

In Chapter 4, Andrea Macrae opens Part II by exploring the powerful potential of rigorous language-focused analysis to improve students' sensitivities to texts. Macrae outlines the central principles of stylistics as an applied linguistic discipline and methodology, arguing that despite the fact that stylistics tend to focus on literature, the skills behind such analyses are useful for all kinds of texts (in fact, stylisticians call into the question the very notion of *literariness*). Macrae shows how the guiding principles of stylistics are at the very heart of the latest version of the Secondary English National Curriculum, and while some of the activities she describes will already be familiar to English teachers and researchers, she carefully outlines how stylistics allows students to both explore language topics and develop their understanding of a text in more nuanced and less impressionistic ways.

In Chapter 5, Billy Clark considers the ways in which language creates meanings, not in abstract and theoretical ways, but when it is employed in genuine interaction between people: the field of pragmatics. Drawing initially on the work of Paul Grice, Clark examines how teachers can make use of pragmatics to draw on students' understanding of the language around them, offers a range of teaching ideas linked to both the creation and interpretation of meaning, and then moves on to look at more recent neo-Gricean approaches. Throughout, Clark shows the importance of students making sense of how language intersects with the social contexts and environments that they inhabit, illustrating that meaning making is an active process for students to engage in.

In Chapter 6, Dan Clayton explores the often-heated debates that exist in a discussion of the ways in which language changes and varies: from person to person, community to community and area to area. Drawing on his experience as an A-level English teacher, he looks at the ways in which such debates and discussions can be scrutinised in the classroom and the light that these arguments shed on the social dimensions of language use. Looking at regional dialects and sociolects, as well as recent technologies, he argues that students benefit from examining the ways in which some forms of English make use of non-standard vocabulary and grammar to convey meanings, and how the study of non-standard English both enriches their understanding of the diversity of English and allows them to examine what makes Standard English what it is.

In Chapter 7, Ian Cushing and Sam Hellmuth open up the rich and varied fields of phonetics and phonology. Arguing from the outset that the study of how we make and perceive sounds is inherently interesting, they provide a range of detailed ideas for classroom exercises covering areas such as child language acquisition, accents and dialects, and language change. Starting with introductory work at Key Stage 3, they provide some clear focus on how speech can be transcribed and represented on the page, before moving into more investigative work for older students. The chapter puts 'phon' concepts at the heart of English teaching: a refreshing focus, given the recent sidelining of so much spoken language across the secondary curriculum.

In Chapter 8, Dan Clayton focuses on the changing face of language in an era of digital communication, arguing that students whose lives are now increasingly lived online should be at the forefront of exploring and analysing how language is being changed and shaped both by and around them. Taking Computer-Mediated Communication (CMC) as the main focus of the chapter and using examples from Twitter, text messaging and online discussion forums, he examines how students can learn about the connections between language and identity. Referring to the work of Erving Goffman and applying it to online communication, he argues that the study of digital texts opens up a range of linguistic possibilities and should be at the very core of language study throughout the secondary English curriculum.

The last three chapters in Part II are linked by the fact that they are all relatively new fields of linguistics, not to those writing the chapters but in all likelihood to most who are outside the fields themselves. What all of these chapters share is a focus on applying new ideas from these fields of linguistics to English teaching in ways that will enthuse and inspire many teachers. In Chapter 9, Graeme Trousdale introduces readers to the field of cognitive linguistics and explains what it offers as a way of thinking about language and the world. Trousdale outlines how cognitive linguists see continuities between language and other domains of human cognition and learning, how grammatical structures are in themselves meaningful and how language as a whole can be viewed as a usage-based system, influenced both by our species-specific capacities and by our interaction with others in the social world. Trousdale draws on a range of text types, including political and literary discourse to demonstrate how teachers might use ideas from cognitive linguistics to support the study of language change and variation, and the analysis of texts in the classroom.

In Chapter 10, Gavin Brookes and Kevin Harvey explain the revolutionary impact that corpus linguistics has had on the study and processing of language data in higher education and look at how advances made in the field could be of use in the secondary classroom. Opening with some clear introductions to three key corpus tools, *frequency*, *keywords* and *concordance*, they offer examples of how teachers can construct or select their own corpora for use in the classroom and outline the many uses that these can be put to. Using examples from literary and legal texts, as well as a host of other accessible data extracts, they illustrate the power of corpus analysis to offer a new way of exploring language in the classroom.

Chapter 11's focus is on forensic linguistics. Here, Willem B. Hollmann outlines some detailed case studies in which language analysis has been used to solve crimes or identify contested authorship. Drawing on examples that will pique the interest of many secondary students, Hollmann explains the fundamentals of forensic linguistics, its wider uses in law enforcement and its practical applications in the classroom. The chapter, like the two others preceding it, offers readers the chance to consider how advances in linguistics outside the classroom can be incorporated into new and inspiring ways to involve students in the detailed study of language.

In Part III, contributors address the question of teacher knowledge and professional development, considering ways in which research in linguistics can be used to support, develop and allow practitioners to reflect on the broader aspects of their practice. These chapters draw on research related to developing and promoting quality classroom interaction, reading and writing skills, on initiatives in initial teacher education and in-service continuous professional development, and on the relationship between school and higher education programmes in English language and linguistics, with a specific focus on A-level English Language.

Chapters 12, 13 and 14 all focus on how knowledge of linguistics could support teachers in developing students' abilities in the core curriculum skills of speaking and listening, reading and writing. In Chapter 12, Victoria Elliott and Jenni Ingram write within the context of work that has been undertaken looking at the function and use of 'wait time' in the classroom and at the structure of classroom discourse. Drawing on both established research and their own data, they outline how advice to teachers on improving classroom interactions has tended to advocate the development of questioning strategies rather than encouraging teachers to consider the impact of extended silence. They argue convincingly that teachers who are aware of the positive benefits of silence when questioning can reduce the likelihood of student non-response and provide support for more detailed answers to improve the quality of dialogue within the classroom.

Jessica Mason, in Chapter 13, draws on her own research at the interface of cognitive linguistics and education to explore the class reader and reading practices in schools. Mason uses her own corpus of classroom transcripts derived from two complete class reader units involving Key Stage 3 classes and her 'narrative interrelation framework' to argue that an understanding of ways that people make connections across texts in their engagement with literature would be of real benefit to the teacher setting up classroom reading activities. Central to Mason's discussion is what she perceives as a dislocated relationship between reading inside and outside of the English classroom. Since research has shown demonstrable cognitive and social benefits of reading for pleasure, Mason's suggestions for how in and out of school reading can be more closely related are of considerable interest to the teacher. Her chapter demonstrates how an applied knowledge of cognitive linguistics could support practitioners in designing lessons and offer them a conceptual framework and metalanguage to reflect on reading practices in their classrooms.

In Chapter 14, Margaret Berry follows a long line of research within Systemic Functional Linguistics on classroom practice in a discussion of how teachers can utilise key principles of SFL to support the development of students' writing. Outlining an overview of some key concepts, Berry shows how the view of language as a set of resources from which students can make choices offers a coherent and flexible pedagogical model for the classroom. Researchers interested in the application of Systemic Functional Linguistics in classroom contexts have traditionally emphasised both its contextually sensitive nature and its capacity to support students to understand and access different genres of writing, and Berry shows, through detailed discussion of examples of classroom work, the potential for Systemic Functional Linguistics to be a useful resource for teachers to support the development of students' writing repertoires.

Chapters 15 and 16 can be viewed as a pair since they both explore how teachers develop their linguistic knowledge in the service of pedagogical practice. In Chapter 15, Marcello Giovanelli explores some issues related to linguistic subject knowledge and Initial Teacher Education (ITE). Drawing on a case study involving students taking a Postgraduate Certificate in Education (PGCE), Giovanelli shows how the fact that the majority of pre-service English teachers are from non-language/linguistics backgrounds means that there is more often than not an acute need for ITE providers to offer substantial support to beginning teachers. In the context of more explicit language-focused work in the National Curriculum and the growth of A-level English Language at post-16 as well as the changing nature of ITE provision and the lack of official subject enhancement programmes, Giovanelli calls for an explicit and coherent programme of professional development in language study for teachers at all stages of their career.

Felicity Titjen's focus in Chapter 16 is on how such continuous professional development can be of use to the experienced teacher both in its direct impact on subject knowledge and career progression, and as a way of understanding the dynamics of the workplace in more general terms. Framing her chapter within the notion of a 'community of practice', Titjen traces the impact of her own experiences taking a master's degree in English Language and working as a senior examiner in A-level English Language for a national awarding body on her role as a classroom teacher. She outlines the benefits that these have provided for her and shows some of the ways in which teachers can continue to develop themselves professionally. Titjen also argues that this knowledge has, for her, provided an important theoretical lens through which to understand teachers' practices and interactions in the workplace.

Angela Goddard's Chapter 17 completes this book with a discussion of several issues related to the identity of English Language as a school and university subject. Goddard reviews recent developments in the post-16 curriculum in the context of cross-phase transition both from key stage to key stage within the secondary school and as a continuum of language work from primary school to undergraduate study. She highlights important aspects of the identity of 'English Language' as part of a suite of 'Englishes' in what is a complex and sometimes frustrating picture in higher education with considerable grey areas surrounding subject names, intellectual identities and questions of value. In her final comments, Goddard emphasises how the truly interdisciplinary nature of English Language as a subject could sit at the heart of a more forward-looking and integrated curriculum of the future.

Our intention in putting this volume together is to provide a resource that stands as a valuable theoretical, critical and practical guide for the teacher and researcher, and indeed anyone interested in applied linguistics and the study of language in education. We are passionate about the value of language study both as a classroom topic, and more generally, as a resource to inform and support teachers in wider aspects of their role. We hope that each of the following chapters demonstrates the powerfully enabling nature and inherent value of language study and linguistics in secondary and post-16 curricula.

Note

1   See for example press coverage such as this: www.dailymail.co.uk/news/article-2622038/
    Now-A-level-Brandspeak-Controversial-plans-mean-language-comedian-rapper-Dizzee-
    Rascal-new-exam.html

References

Carter, R. (ed.) (1982) *Linguistics and the Teacher*, London: Routledge.

Denham, K. and Lobeck, A. (eds) (2006) *Language in the Schools: Integrating Linguistic Knowledge into K-12 Teaching*, New York, NY: Routledge.

Denham, K. and Lobeck, A. (eds) (2010) *Linguistics at School: Language Awareness in Primary and Secondary Education*, New York, NY: Cambridge University Press.

Ellis, S. and McCartney, E. (eds) (2011) *Applied Linguistics and Primary School Teaching*, Cambridge: Cambridge University Press.

Halliday, M. (1967) 'Linguistics and the teaching of English', in J. Britton (ed) *Handbook for English Teachers: 2. Talking and Writing*, London: Methuen, pp. 80–90.

Locke, T. (ed.) (2010) *Beyond the Grammar Wars: A Resource for Teachers and Students on Developing Language Knowledge in the English/Literacy Classroom*, London: Routledge.

Part I

Language and linguistics in the secondary school

Theoretical, historical and research-based perspectives on the English curriculum

Chapter 1

The value of linguistics to the teacher

Marcello Giovanelli

Introduction

In this chapter I provide theoretical, professional, and I hope moral justifications for the value of linguistics to the secondary English teacher. By *linguistics*, I mean an awareness of how language works in terms of its structures, systems and uses across a range of communicative practices and products. By *value*, I mean the extent to which this awareness is deemed to be an important part of the curriculum as part of a broadly integrated notion of English on an equal footing with the study of Shakespeare, or nineteenth-century novels, or the media and so on. But, I also want to argue that knowledge about linguistics is important and valuable for the teacher as an educator, regardless of the academic field within which he or she works, as a way of understanding the ways that people and ideas about them are represented through language and other meaning-making resources. I argue that a teacher can be a kind of *applied linguist*, responsible for promoting a more inclusive educational environment that utilises the considerable language resources that students themselves have. In this chapter, I therefore promote both a broad and functional view of linguistics, beyond some of the narrow working parameters that have typified discourses about language study over the last one hundred years, particularly those that have explored value simply in terms of a teacher being able to improve students' grammatical knowledge.

This chapter begins by providing a brief sketch of the origin, nature and identity of curriculum English and the historical privileging of 'literature' over 'language', offering some comment on the debates that have surrounded language work in schools, and highlighting its largely undervalued status. Then, drawing on a text that appeared as part of a story on language use in schools in the UK press, I suggest two important ways that linguistics can be valuable to the teacher. First (and as the chapters in Part 2 of this book show), I demonstrate how a teacher can use linguistic knowledge as a powerful tool for facilitating meaningful and genuinely insightful descriptive language work in the classroom. Second, and drawing on James Paul Gee's work in the area of social and cultural approaches to language and literacy, I argue that a teacher is an applied linguist in a much broader sense by drawing attention to how a linguistically informed teacher might use linguistics to make more readily available implicit values and representations of individuals and groups. I end with a note of caution but also with a firm call for optimism in briefly considering both some external and internal barriers to improving teachers' knowledge.

Linguistics, language and schools: a brief sketch

The subordinate status of language study in schools and at the heart of the English curriculum has a long history dating back to the nineteenth century where the teaching of English literature was viewed as a mechanism for civilising the working classes, providing a strong sense of moral purpose, and for both building and upholding society values (Poulson 1998). In the early part of the twentieth century, there were two major movements that helped to strengthen the position of English literature as English teaching *per se*. The first was the 1921 Newbolt Report (Board of Education 1921) which, following the First World War, sought to re-establish a national identity by promoting the importance of national literature as a vehicle for teaching universal truths and acceptable ways of looking at the world. Although the report authors also emphasised that all students should have explicit teaching in their mother tongue, I have argued elsewhere (Giovanelli 2014: 10–11) that this second sentiment largely amounted to a narrow deficit and prescriptive view of language study that aimed to draw attention to right and wrong ways of speaking and writing. Effectively, the study of high-quality literature to support teachers was emphasised as socially and morally valuable, whereas language work was seen merely as utilitarian and instructive.

The second movement grew naturally from the ethos of The Newbolt Report and gave a shape to literature as a school discipline and to the literature-as-English paradigm. This influence is most evident in the epistemologies advanced by F. R. Leavis (1932, 1979) and his students whose thinking prescribed a certain kind of literature study (only certain authors were considered as being part of the canon) through the practice of close and systematic criticism. This *Leavisite* view of literary criticism as a powerful civilising and stabilising force revolutionised English teaching in higher education as well as in schools (see Hilliard 2012 for a detailed discussion). Consequently, the study of literature was viewed for many years as the exclusive cornerstone of the English curriculum (Thompson 1969, 1975). In contrast, philology, which had been the primary focus of language work at the turn of the century all but disappeared in the face of fervent support for literature teaching. Where grammar teaching did remain, it was largely centred on teaching children to label parts of invented and decontextualised sentences; unsurprisingly a body of research found that this had very little benefit (Macauley 1947; Cawley 1958; Harris 1962). Together with the lack of real interest at the interface of linguistics and education up until the early 1960s (Hudson and Walmsley 2005), this meant that language work in schools was marginalised and any consequent notion of value in linguistic knowledge for the teacher was downplayed to the point that it was seen as negligible, if worth anything at all.

However, in the mid-seventies, another influential government report, *A Language for Life* (DES 1975), demonstrated how much had changed in the perceived value of linguistically informed work since the middle of the century (Burgess and Hardcastle 2013: 5). Known as 'The Bullock Report', after the chair of the committee that produced it, its main recommendations included the requirement for schools to have a policy for language across the curriculum, the inclusion of knowledge about language in education as a part of initial teacher training, and the establishing of a national centre for language and education (DfE 1975: 515). The Bullock Report explicitly attaches value to language work in much broader terms than simply the knowledge of grammatical terminology. Indeed a different kind of 'English', driven by educationalists with backgrounds in the psychology and sociology of education and centred on the role of language as an important tool for learning the development of the individual in the classroom (see for example Britton 1970), had been gathering momentum since the early to mid 1960s. In turn, an important government-funded programme, Schools Council Programme in Linguistics and English Teaching, led by Michael Halliday had run from 1964–71 and had foregrounded the value of students being able to explore their own language in their own terms. This programme attached great importance to teachers' own confidence in, and knowledge of, language both as a system and as a pedagogical tool in the classroom (Halliday 1967). The programme, arguably the most important development in language education work in English schools, produced substantial teaching materials for primary and secondary levels (see McKay *et al.* 1970; Doughty *et al.* 1971), and influenced a later series of books aimed at teachers and teacher educators which explored aspects of language work in classroom contexts. These included volumes on children's language in school (Thornton 1974) and outside it (Rogers 1976), accents and dialect (Trudgill 1975), language varieties in schools (Richmond 1982) and the language of literature (Carter and Burton 1982). A further important movement, the National Congress on Languages in Education (NCLE), was established in the mid seventies to promote a coherent approach to language work through *language awareness*, a term that encompassed the exploration of language across subjects and varieties, including learning of and about languages other than English (Donmall-Hicks 1997; and see also Hawkins 1984).

The later Kingman Report (DES 1988) positioned a language pedagogical framework around discrete levels of language analysis, modes and genres, language development, and historical and geographical variation. It also provided the impetus for the Language in the National Curriculum (LINC) project, which began in September 1989 and involved the production of teaching materials and dissemination of these together with specific training across regional centres (see Carter 1990; Bain *et al.* 1992). However, the materials were pulled just as they were about to be made available for teachers on the basis that they were not suitable for use with children in the classroom. Despite being funded by the government, the right-wing press and ministers believed that the materials promoted exactly the kind of inquiry-led and descriptive approach to language study that compromised their desire to make such work more prescriptive and geared towards standards and notions of correctness (see Sealey 1994 for a discussion of the press coverage of the project and its suppression). Even if LINC was not valued by the government that had commissioned it, its legacy was to enthuse teachers with the possibility of genuinely engaging language work in their classrooms, and it can be no surprise that the unofficial dissemination of the materials among networks of teachers coincided with the rapid growth of A-level English Language throughout the 1990s and 2000s.

More recently of course, the value attached to language work in schools and consequently the expectations and demands on teachers' linguistic knowledge have been, in functional and utilitarian terms, evident in the content and pedagogies promoted by the primary literacy and secondary national strategies (Clark 2010). Equally, the latest round of GCSE reform (for teaching from September 2015) has seen the removal of spoken language study from examination specifications, a move which is all the more surprising given that it had been a fairly new addition (from 2010 specifications). This kind of work had provided a welcome opportunity for students to explore discourse strategies, interaction, registers, contexts and the influence of new technologies on communicative practices in ways which gave a valuable introduction to AS and A-level study. For those not moving into the Sixth Form, it at least meant that all students were required to complete some descriptive language work. It could be argued that despite a renewed focus on grammar at Key Stage 2, the latest reforms at Key Stages 3 and 4 fail to provide a coherent pathway from Key Stage 2 to Key Stage 5 work, and may also mean that many students will not do any meaningful language-based study across their five years in secondary school.

Promoting value: The teacher as applied linguist

Linguistics in the classroom

Figure 1.1 reproduces the text from a noticeboard that was put up by a senior leadership team in a south London school in 2013. The noticeboard attracted a great deal of coverage in the right-wing press in 2013 since the school had decided that certain words (presumably that were being used frequently by students) ought to be banned. This story was one of a number of similar and high profile reports that appeared at the time around the use of language in schools (see English and Marr 2015: 210–17 for detailed discussion of two others).

In classroom terms, the text offers plenty of opportunities for students of all ages to explore meaningful and complex issues around standard and non-standard forms, registers, language varieties, attitudes to language, the institutional power of schools, language change, creativity in language and so on. Clearly a teacher

```
┌─────────────────────────────────────────────┐
│                Banned Words:                  │
│                                               │
│        COZ              AINT                  │
│                                               │
│        LIKE             BARE                  │
│                                               │
│        EXTRA            INNIT                 │
│                                               │
│    YOU WOZ    and    WE WOZ                   │
│                                               │
│    Beginning sentences with BASICALLY         │
│                                               │
│      Ending sentences with YEAH               │
│                                               │
└─────────────────────────────────────────────┘
```

Figure 1.1 Banned words

with knowledge of these areas of language study would be able to guide students towards engaging with some of these issues, and draw attention to the inherent problems with attempting to undertake this kind of language policing. This in turn could lead to a critical examination of the attitudes of the producers of this text towards various concepts such as dialectical variation, compressions, informal registers, speech and writing, and how varieties of language are clearly appropriate in some contexts and not in others. And, the text could be analysed to explore how the institutional power of the school is actualised in specific choices around language and text design. The following gives merely a flavour of the types of focus that could be explored at various levels of language analysis.

Lexis and semantics

The analysis of some of the individual 'Banned Words' provides a way in to exploring different kinds of language use and aspects of language change and variation. For example, the use of 'bare' as an adverb meaning 'very' was commonplace in the fourteenth century and is therefore a good example of how words come in and out of common parlance. Equally, the common use of 'innit' as a tag question and the use of quotative 'like' as a dialogue introducer (see Tagliamonte and Hudson 2000) are both key features of spoken discourse and are markers of solidarity in interaction particularly among younger speakers. And, the sentence adverb 'basically' to modify and present a speaker's stance towards a state of affairs also occurs frequently in speech (see O'Keefe *et al.* 2007: 45).

Syntax

The fact that 'aint' exists in many dialects, but not in Standard English, where 'I am' has no contracted negated form (compare how 'you are' becomes 'you aren't') would provide a fascinating opportunity to explore regional variation. On the noticeboard itself, the use of the nominalisation 'Banned Words' instead of a clause either in the active voice 'We have banned these words' or the passive voice 'These words have been banned' offers the potential to explore why grammatical constructions in themselves are meaningful and are exploited by writers and speakers.

Pragmatics

The text allows for a wide range of discussions around the notions of power behind authorship and the likely audience and contexts of reception. In this example, the school's institutional power means that students are likely to treat the warnings seriously.

Discourse and graphology

Finally, the ways in which text design coheres with lexical, syntactic and pragmatic aspects is available for analysis. This might include comments on colour (in the original, 'Banned Words' is in an emphasised yellow font against a red background while the remainder of the text is in white) and on how the positioning of the school's logo and name represent authority.

I would argue that the linguistically informed teacher is able to tap into a range of language issues using a text – and an accompanying press story – that is interesting and engaging. Furthermore, language use in school is an area that is of real interest to young people that they would be motivated to explore. Indeed recent research in sociolinguistics has highlighted how teenagers view language as a marker of social identity that works in tandem with identity-forming *resources* such as hair styles, clothing, gestures and cultural activities and practices among their peers as part of a broad and multi-faceted semiotic system (Bucholtz 2011). Consequently, they are acutely aware of, and willing to explore and discuss, their own language use and how it is perceived by others (Willoughby *et al.* 2015).

Linguistics, ideology and 'discourse'

I want to suggest that there is another, and arguably more important, reason why knowing about language is essential for the teacher as an educator. The teachers whose classrooms include the kind of work that I have been describing above have effectively been supporting their students (at whatever level) in undertaking some quite sophisticated critical discourse analysis, unlocking and discussing how aspects of power, performativity, identity and constraints are actualised and realised through close attention to linguistic form and function. However, what seems clear to me is that in doing this kind of work the teachers are also likely to have gauged for themselves very quickly and explicitly that this text projects a rather uncomfortable way of seeing the world. In its conflation of a range of linguistic issues, the text represents a group (here the student body) as users of an inherently 'Bad English'. However, it ignores some of the most fundamental principles of language in use: how context informs the use of different registers and varieties of language; that some language choices are more likely to be made in speech rather than in writing; and that Standard English is simply one of many dialects of English, and that other dialects are not inferior in any way, shape or form. It promotes a deficit rather than an asset-based model both of language and of its users.

This 'Bad English'/'let's ban those words'/'students shouldn't be speaking and writing like that' mindset is part of what Gee (2012) calls a *discourse*, a way of 'behaving, interacting, valuing, thinking, believing, speaking, and often reading and writing' (2012: 3); in short, it is a way of constructing and acting out the world as one believes it ought to be. As Gee argues, every language user is a user of potentially many different *discourses* and a member of the communities that use them, speaking, acting and viewing the world in different ways. Each of these belief systems develops from theories that users have regarding what 'counts as a "normal" person and the "right" ways to think, feel and behave' (2012: 4). Gee points out that such theories can be either *overt* in that they have been discussed and explicitly outlined, or *tacit* in that they have often been accepted without due consideration or engagement (2012: 13). In either case, a theory may be *primary* in that it is based on an individual's own reading, research or engagement with other professionals in a direct manner, or *non-primary* in that it has just been accepted from less-direct sources (Gee 2012: 17).

Clearly those world-views that are grounded in primary theories are more likely to have been well considered and are probably more ethically sound. Read in Gee's terms, the 'Bad English' discourse is likely to be based on a non-primary theory and is probably tacit for the majority of those who subscribe to it. Through the lens of a linguistically informed opinion (or primary theory), much of what it stands for can be rejected. Despite being underpinned by what were probably good intentions, the widespread banning of non-standard forms and expressions, many of which are genuinely common features of spoken language, contradicts research which shows that schools taking an asset-based approach to children's own language are likely to impact positively on student learning (Cummins 2000). A linguistically informed teacher might understand how language use is so intrinsically tied to a sense of identity, and that identities are often for children constructed in terms of the two distinct spaces of home and school (Mayall 1994; Alldred *et al.* 2002). That teacher would be wary of the potential to stigmatise students' ways of speaking and their identities and backgrounds, and consequently construct school space as exclusive and discriminatory against certain groups. Furthermore, that teacher might know that for many children, imposing ways of speaking could mean that they would automatically reject the linguistic norms set up by the school in favour of their own code, leading to discrimination, exclusion and disenfranchisement (MacRuairc 2011).

It should be evident from my discussion that I believe that any teacher having a primary theory of language as a reference point might think and approach the issue faced in Upper Norwood in a different way within their school community. They would also no doubt understand how a perceived problem around use of appropriate register could be the basis for some informed discussion about code-switching between home and school spaces and the different language practices required in both settings. They would recognise the inherent relationship between language and identity, and would be sensitive to the practices of all groups of students. And, crucially, they would consider how what we know about language might solve the problem faced by the school regarding supporting students in making appropriate choices of register rather than setting up a simple 'good/bad' dichotomy. In fact we might say that a teacher with some knowledge of linguistics would not put the noticeboard up in the first place.

Some issues for teachers

The discussion above may make it seem as though developing a linguistic toolkit to support practice is straightforward when in fact there have been many barriers to teachers becoming linguistically informed. These are not only the external ones relating to the kind of top-down policy-making I discussed earlier in this chapter, but can be internal ones too. As Hudson (2010) argues, many teachers simply feel de-skilled when asked to undertake any language work in the classroom, and the research literature gives many examples of issues from anxieties about subject knowledge (Watson 2012), uncertainties around language pedagogies (Bell 2015; Watson 2015) and unrealistic awareness of one's own capabilities and capacities to take on language work (Sangster et al. 2013). It is still the case that the majority of teachers coming into English classrooms are literary rather than linguistically trained, have a strong motivation for wanting to work with literature in their classrooms (Ellis 2003) and believe in the transformational power of reading literature in developing children's imaginative, linguistic and social skills (Goodwyn 2002, 2010). On the other hand, I have recently shown (Giovanelli 2015) how empowered and enabled teachers can feel they are when they take on language teaching, and a number of studies have argued for the benefits of teachers using linguistic theory to explicitly support the planning of teaching and learning activities in the classroom (see for example Macken-Horarik 2009; Myhill 2000; Myhill et al. 2012; Ingram and Elliott 2014; Giovanelli and Mason 2015; Giovanelli 2016).

Two other barriers are worth mentioning here. The first is the persistent idea that language work is simply the study of the grammar of Standard English (for example Heffer 2010; Gwynne 2011) and consequently uninteresting and/or simply about prescription, correctness and maintaining standards. The second is the belief that language work is too difficult and linguistics too abstruse a subject to have appeal to teachers and their students at school level. I hope in my analysis and discussion of the 'Banned Words' text to have shown that the kinds of discussions that language work can promote are interesting, inherently accessible and incredibly important to both students and teachers and that there is a real value in all members of a school community being able to engage in these sorts of discussions. Equally, the 'too difficult' argument seems to me to do little more than patronise teachers and their students; for a fascinating account of what can take place in classrooms with some fairly complex ideas, I would urge readers to refer to Ruth French's account of using systemic functional linguistics as a teaching tool in a primary classroom in New Zealand (French 2010).

Conclusion

In this chapter I have argued that in effect every teacher could and probably should be an applied linguist, and most certainly an educational linguist (see Brumfit 1997), drawing on what is best known from the academic field of linguistics to support a range of learning and teaching needs both in the classroom and beyond. Writing about linguistics and teacher education, Michael Halliday (1982: 14–15) argues that linguistics is both uncomfortable and subversive in destabilising some of the prejudices that we hold about language and society, and forcing us to change viewpoints and belief systems: 'it is there behind the lines, underlying our classroom practices, and our ideas about children, and about learning and reality' (p.15).

In summary then, I hope to have shown that the value of linguistics to the teacher is in using explicit knowledge about language both as a springboard for practical classroom work and in enabling all members of a school community to be overtly and critically aware of how and why language is used in particular contexts.

References

Alldred, P., David, M. and Edwards, R. (2002) 'Minding the gap: People and young people negotiating relations between home and school', in R. Edwards (ed.) *Children, Home and School: Regulation, Autonomy or Connection*, London: Routledge, pp. 120–36.

Bain, R., Fitzgerald, B. and Taylor, M. (1992) *Looking Into Language: Classroom Approaches to Knowledge About Language*, London: Hodder.

Bell, H. (2015) 'The dead butler revisited: Grammatical accuracy and clarity in the English primary curriculum 2013–2014', *Language and Education* 29(2): 140–52.

Board of Education (1921) *The Teaching of English in England* (The Newbolt Report), London: HMSO.

Britton, J. (1970) *Language and Learning*, Harmondsworth: Penguin.

Brumfit, C. (1997) 'The teacher as educational linguist', in L. van Lier and D. Corson (eds) *Encyclopaedia of Language and Education, Volume 6 Knowledge About Language*, Dordrecht: Kluwer, pp. 163–72.

Bucholtz, M. (2011) *White Kids: Language, Race, and Styles of Youth Identity*, New York, NY: Cambridge University Press.

Burgess, T. and Hardcastle, J. (2013) 'Englishes and English: Schooling and the making of the school subject', in A. Kent (ed.) *School Subject Teaching: The History and Future of the Curriculum*, 2nd edn, London: Routledge, pp. 1–28.

Carter, R. (1990) 'Introduction', in R. Carter (ed.) *Knowledge about Language and the Curriculum: The LINC Reader*, London: Hodder and Stoughton, pp. 1–20.

Carter, R. and Burton, D. (1982) *Literary Text and Language Study*, London: Edward Arnold.

Cawley, F. (1958) The difficulty of English grammar for students of secondary school age', *British Journal of Educational Psychology* 28: 174–6.

Clark, U. (2010) 'The problematics of prescribing grammatical knowledge: the case in England', in T. Locke (ed.) *Beyond the Grammar Wars: A Resource for Teachers and Students on Developing Language Knowledge in the English/Literacy Classroom*, London: Routledge, pp. 38–54.

Cummins, J. (2000) *Language, Power and Pedagogy*, Clevedon, OH: Multilingual Matters.

DES (1975) *A Language for Life* (The Bullock Report), London: HMSO.

DES (1988) *Report of the Committee of Inquiry into The Teaching of English Language* (The Kingman Report), London: HMSO.

Donmall-Hicks, G. (1997) 'The history of language awareness in the UK', in L. van Lier and D. Corson (eds) *Encyclopaedia of Language and Education, Volume 6 Knowledge About Language*, Dordrecht: Kluwer, pp. 21–30.

Doughty, P., Pearce, J. and Thornton, G. (1971) *Language in Use*, London: Edward Arnold.

Ellis, V. (2003) 'The love that dare not speak its name? The constitution of the English subject and beginning teachers' motivations to teach it', *English Teaching: Practice and Critique* 2(1): 3–14.

English, F. and Marr, T. (2015) *Why Do Linguistics?: Reflective Linguistics and the Study of Language*, London: Bloomsbury.

French, R. (2010) 'Primary school children learning grammar: rethinking the possibilities', in T. Locke (ed.) *Beyond the Grammar Wars: A Resource for Teachers and Students on Developing Language Knowledge in the English/Literacy Classroom*, London: Routledge, pp. 206–29.

Gee, J. P. (2012) *Social Linguistics and Literacies: Ideology in Discourses*, 4th edn, New York, NY: Routledge.

Giovanelli, M. (2014) *Teaching Grammar, Structure and Meaning: Exploring Theory and Practice for Post-16 English Language Teachers*, London: Routledge.

Giovanelli, M. (2015) 'Becoming an English language teacher: Linguistic knowledge, anxieties and the shifting sense of identity', *Language and Education* 29(5): 416–29.

Giovanelli, M. (2016) 'Text World Theory as cognitive grammatics: A pedagogical application in the secondary classroom', in J. Gavins and E. Lahey (eds) *World-Building: Discourse in the Mind*, London: Bloomsbury Academic, pp.109–26.

Giovanelli, M. and Mason, J. (2015) '"Well I don't feel that": Schemas, worlds and authentic reading in the classroom', *English in Education* 49(1): 41–55.

Goodwyn, A. (2002) 'Breaking up is hard to do: English teachers and that LOVE of reading', *English Teaching: Practice and Critique* 1(1): 66–78.

Goodwyn, A. (2010) *The Expert Teacher of English*, London: Routledge.

Gwynne, M. (2011) *Gwynne's Grammar: The Ultimate Introduction to Grammar and the Writing of Good English*, London: Idler Books.

Halliday, M. (1967) 'Linguistics and the teaching of English', in J. Britton (ed.) *Handbook for English Teachers: 2. Talking and Writing*, London: Methuen, pp. 80–90.

Halliday, M. (1982) 'Linguistics in teacher education', in R. Carter (ed.) *Linguistics and the Teacher*, London: Routledge, pp. 10–15.

Harris, R. (1962) *An Experimental Enquiry into the Functions and Value of Formal Grammar in the Teaching of English, with Special Reference to the Teaching of Correct Written English to Children Aged Twelve to Fourteen*, Unpublished PhD thesis, University of London.

Hawkins, E. (1984) *Awareness of Language: An Introduction*, 2nd edn, Cambridge: Cambridge University Press.

Heffer, S. (2010) *Strictly English: The Correct Way To Write And Why It Matters*, London: Random House.

Hilliard, C. (2012) *English as a Vocation: The Scrutiny Movement*, Oxford: Oxford University Press.

Hudson, R. (2010) 'How linguistics has influenced schools in England', in K. Denham and A. Lobeck (eds) (2010) *Linguistics at School: Language Awareness in Primary and Secondary Education*, New York, NY: Cambridge University Press, pp. 35–48.

Hudson, R. and Walmsley, J. (2005) 'The English Patient: English grammar and teaching in the twentieth century', *Journal of Linguistics* 43(3): 593–622.

Ingram, J. and Elliott, V. (2014) 'Turn taking and "wait time" in classroom interactions', *Journal of Pragmatics*, 62: 1–12.

Leavis, F. (1932) *New Bearings in English Poetry: A Study of the Contemporary Situation*, London: Chatto & Windus.

Leavis, F. (1979) *For Continuity* and *Education and the University*, Cambridge: Cambridge University Press.

Macauley, W. (1947) 'The difficulty of grammar', *British Journal of Educational Psychology* 17: 153–62.

McKay, D., Thompson, B. and Schaub, P. (1970) *Breakthrough to Literacy: The Theory and Practice of Teaching Initial Reading and Writing*, Harlow: Longman.

Macken-Horarik, M. (2009) 'Navigational metalanguages for new territory in English; the potential of grammatics', *English Teaching: Practice and Critique* 8(3): 55–69.

MacRuairc, G. (2011) 'They're my words – I'll talk how I like! Examining social class and linguistic practice among primary-school children', *Language and Education* 25(6): 535–59.

Mayall, B. (1994) 'Children in Action at Home and School', in B. Mayall (ed.) *Children's Childhoods Observed and Experienced*, London: The Falmer Press.

Myhill, D. (2000) 'Misconceptions and difficulties in the acquisition of metalinguistic knowledge', *Language and Education*, 14(3): 151–63.

Myhill, D., Jones, S., Lines, H. and Watson, A. (2012) 'Re-thinking grammar: the impact of embedded grammar teaching on students' writing and students' metalinguistic understanding', *Research Papers in Education*, 27(2): 139–66.

O'Keefe, A., McCarthy, M. and Carter, R. (2007) *From Corpus to Classroom: Language Use and Language Teaching*, Cambridge: Cambridge University Press.

Poulson, L. (1998) *The English Curriculum in Schools*, London: Cassell.

Richmond, J. (1982) *The Resources of Classroom Language*, London: Edward Arnold.

Rogers, S. (1976) *They Don't Speak Our Language*, London: Edward Arnold.

Sangster, P., Anderson, C. and O'Hara, P. (2013) 'Perceived and actual levels of knowledge about language amongst primary and secondary student teachers: Do they know what they think they know?', *Language Awareness* 22(4): 293–319.

Sealey, A. (1994) 'Language and educational control: The construction of the LINC controversy', in D. Scott (ed.) *Accountability and Control in Educational Settings*, Cassell: London, pp. 121–36.

Tagliamonte, S. and Hudson, R. (2000) '*Be like* et al. beyond America: the quotative system in British and Canadian youth', *Journal of Sociolinguistics* 3(2): 147–72.

Thompson, D. (1969) *Directions in the Teaching of English*, Cambridge: Cambridge University Press.

Thompson, D. (1975) *What to Read in English Literature*, Lanham, MD: Rowman and Littlefield.

Thornton, G. (1974) *Language, Experience and School*, London: Edward Arnold.

Trudgill, P. (1975) *Accent, Dialect and the School*, London: Edward Arnold.

Watson, A. (2012) 'Navigating "the pit of doom": affective responses to teaching grammar', *English in Education* 46(1): 21–36.

Watson, A. (2015) 'Conceptualisations of "grammar teaching": L1 English teachers' beliefs about teaching grammar for writing', *Language Awareness* 24(1): 1–14.

Willoughby, L., Starks, D. and Taylor-Leech, K. (2015) 'What their friends say about the way they talk: The metalanguage of pre-adolescent and adolescent Australians', *Language Awareness* 24(1): 84–100.

Chapter 2

The impact of policy on language teaching in UK schools

Richard Hudson

Introduction

I start with a statement of the obvious: that the impact of any policy decision, taken top-down by the authorities, will also be heavily influenced (bottom-up) by the situation that existed in schools before the change was launched. In other words, education may allow evolution, but it can never allow revolution for the simple reason that it has to be implemented by teachers, most of whom trained and practised under the previous regime. This is not to say that policy changes are a waste of time: they can have a major impact, but only if teachers not only have time to adjust their thinking and their practice, which may take generations, but are also motivated, either by carrots or by sticks, to apply the new policy. The result of the change may be different from what the policy-makers had in mind; it may be 'watered down' (a negative evaluation) by teachers, but equally it may be implemented in imaginative and productive ways by teachers who find the strengths of the new policy and combine them with the strengths of what went before to produce 'a remarkable melange of old and new ... teaching' (Cohen and Loewenberg Ball 1990: 331). In the light of this principle, it is unreasonable to expect any policy to have the full impact intended by the policy-makers. On the other hand, we might expect policy to have some measurable impact, so there is an important general question about how to maximise this impact. After all, there is no point in having good policy if it has no impact.

This principle applies as clearly to language teaching as it does to any other area of teaching, and indeed we shall see that, in some respects, recent policy has had remarkably little effect on teaching and learning. This chapter does not try to establish principles even for language teaching (for which see Spolsky and Hult 2008) let alone for all areas and kinds of education (Bell and Stevenson 2006; Coffield et al. 2008; Cohen and Loewenberg Ball 1990) but has much more specific goals: to look at the effect of policy on one particular area of education – language education, and more specifically, the teaching of first-language English – in one particular country – the UK, and even more specifically, England. Of course, it may be that some of my conclusions will generalise, but that is a different issue.

The principle also means that history matters. If you want to implement a policy, it is essential to understand the status quo before the policy is introduced; and if you want to understand a policy's impact, or lack of impact, it makes sense to look for historical precedents. True, we can't wind history back, so we are where we are; but deciding what to do next requires an understanding of why we are here, rather than where we would like to be. The search for explanation can take us surprisingly far back in time.

Henry VIII and *Lily's Grammar* of Latin in English

Seen from the twenty-first century, Henry VIII is surprisingly relevant, and the story of his grammar of Latin provides an interesting contrast with more recent policy initiatives. The facts are well known and well documented (Gwosdek 2013). In the Renaissance, as in the Middle Ages, the heart of education was the teaching of Latin, and fluency in both speaking and writing Latin was the first goal of teaching. By modern standards, the method was dreadful: the much-criticised 'grammar-translation' method, concentrating on systematic and explicit learning of grammar and translation exercises. It was because of this emphasis on grammar that schools founded at that time were so often called 'grammar schools'.

However, grammar teachers faced both a challenge and an opportunity. The challenge was how best to teach the grammar of Latin to novices who knew only English, and knew nothing about grammar. The solution required a grammar book – a systematic presentation of the facts of Latin written in English. The problem was not a lack of such books, but a surfeit: every grammar teacher wrote his own, and confusion threatened. The opportunity was printing, which allowed the production of multiple copies – not only a copy for the teacher, but also individual copies for the pupils. When applied to the existing multitude of hand-written texts, inconsistencies simply multiplied and became more obvious.

The opportunity offered by printing was not lost on King Henry, keen to unify his kingdom and to assert his power over the church (which had till then controlled the contents of school teaching). There was one dominant grammar, which was popularly called *Lily's Grammar* although its author, William Lily (the first headmaster of St Paul's School in London), had died twenty years earlier. This grammar already had a very high profile because of its association with prominent scholars – not only Lily (who had introduced the teaching of Greek to London), but also the super-star Renaissance scholar, Erasmus of Rotterdam, who wrote a preface for the grammar. Henry may not have actually commissioned this grammar book, but he certainly authorised it for exclusive use throughout his realm. This was in 1542, a few years before he did the same for the Book of Common Prayer.

The introduction of a uniform grammar for the teaching of Latin in grammar schools by Henry VIII's decree became part of his educational policy and a means to ensure control over teaching in grammar schools, a privilege once held exclusively by the Church. This measure became an important part of the king's political control of education and reform in the interests of religious uniformity after the Reformation (Gwosdek 2013: 122).

Furthermore, Henry decreed that only one printer should have the monopoly for this book at any one time, which guaranteed enthusiastic competition among printers for this lucrative contract. The combination of law and commerce kept *Lily's Grammar* in place as the only permitted grammar of Latin in English for an astonishing 350 years, until it was replaced by Kennedy's Latin Primer, which also survived for over a century.

Lily's Grammar was enormously influential, a clear example of policy having a major impact on practice; for instance we know that it was the grammar from which the young Shakespeare learned Latin (from age seven), and similarly Isaac Newton and William Wordsworth. This was partly because of the legal sanctions threatening any grammar teacher who used any other book:

> ... we will and commaunde, and streightly charge al you schoolemaisters and teachers of grammer [sic] within this our realme, and other our dominions, as ye intend to auoyde our displeasure, and haue our fauour, to teache and learne your scholars this englysshe introduction here ensuing ... and none other, ...
>
> (Gwosdek 2013: 157)

But after Henry's death, why should a school teacher worry about his displeasure? And why would teachers continue to favour this book in the very different political circumstances of eighteenth-century England? The simple answer is that we don't know, but the publishing monopoly, which continued for centuries, must have played a significant part, as must the simple inertia created by a firmly established text, which allows a teacher to teach exactly as he himself was taught.

Lily's Grammar is a model of what can be achieved given a combination of academic quality (Lily and Erasmus), commercial pressures and political will, but it also served as a model for the first published grammar of English (Bullokar 1586) – another unintended by-product of Henry's policy. Inevitably, the study of English gradually acquired a higher profile, from being a means to the end of learning Latin, to being an end in itself. But of course it was only in the nineteenth century that English was recognised as a subject either at school or at university (Applebee 1974; Hudson and Walmsley 2005). Until the introduction of universal education, including literacy in English, the teaching of English was not a matter of public policy.

Public examinations and publishers

Governments between Henry VIII and Margaret Thatcher had a hands-off policy regarding the content of what was taught, to contrast themselves proudly with more centralised education systems such as the French. Government policy tended to control the provision of schooling rather than its content. By the early twentieth century, government policy was carried out by the Board of Education, which later became first the Ministry of Education and eventually the Department for Education. Although the Board did not control the content, it did take an interest in it and in 1921 it produced the first important report on the teaching of English, The Newbolt Report (Board of Education 1921). This is a remarkable document not only for the quality of its recommendations but also for its lack of impact, illustrating admirably the general principle that policy needs to be supported by pressure. Here is a small selection of its 105 recommendations (Board of Education 1921: 348–60):

1   That every teacher is a teacher of English because every teacher is a teacher in English ...
2   That it is the business of the ... School to teach all its pupils to speak standard English, and that the scientific method of doing this is to associate each sound with a phonetic symbol.
3   That the schools should not aim at the suppression of dialect, but at making the children bi-lingual.
4   That oral work is the foundation upon which proficiency in the writing of English must be based.
5   That the sounds of spoken English should be scientifically taught.
6   That time might be saved in the study both of Classics and of Modern Languages (including English) by the adoption of a uniform grammatical terminology ....
7   That during the period 16–18 some study of the growth and development of the English language would be preferable to a course in Old English.

This document also reveals the relatively low status of English compared with science and foreign languages, and its recommendation that this status should be raised ('That the Senior Teacher of English should be allowed the same powers of direction as are usually given to the Senior Teacher in Mathematics, Science or Modern languages' p. 351) has certainly been implemented, in contrast with many of the recommendations listed above, which are still waiting for action nearly a century later.

As for the content, this was left to two other institutions which broadly reflected the interests of teachers and the educated public, rather than those of government as such: publishers and the universities. Publishers saw schools as a major market for their books, and especially for textbooks. Textbooks were typically written by schoolteachers, who naturally presented a summary of what they themselves had learned at school and university, so textbooks reflected the state of play in universities. At the start of the twentieth century, the standard textbook was by J. C. Nesfield (Nesfield 1900), and contained a great deal of detail about English grammar, combined with an extraordinarily dry summary of historical relations between English and other languages. (Compare the comments in The Newbolt Report about the history of English being preferable to Old English.) But as the century progressed, language disappeared from undergraduate English degrees (Hudson and Walmsley 2005) so university influence on language textbooks also dwindled to nothing. By the middle of the century, the market was dominated by the numerous works of Ronald Ridout, whose 500 textbooks exceeded 90 million sales. In contrast with Nesfield, these books presented very little systematic grammar though they included prescriptive grammar exercises, and nothing on the history of English. As their popularity attested, they were in tune with the mood of the time, and helped to consolidate the view that English teachers had very little content to teach.

The other influential institution was the universities, which created and controlled the public examinations for the schools. Since most children left school without taking any public examination (other than the 11+ examination for entry to grammar schools), the influence of the universities was initially confined to the academic 25 per cent of the population who attended grammar schools. (Although independent schools were and are independent of government control, they tend to take the same public examinations.) The universities set up the examination boards which from 1951 ran the General Certificate of Education, with its examinations at Ordinary level and Advanced level and, from 1965, the Certificate of Secondary Education for the non-academic until this was merged twenty years later with the Ordinary level examination to form the new, and continuing, General Certificate of Secondary Education – the GCSE. The Advanced examinations continue. During this period, the links between examination boards and universities became increasingly tenuous, so in essence it was the examination boards, rather than the universities, that determined the content not only of the examinations but also of the school teaching leading up to them.

Of most relevance to the present chapter is the place of formal grammar teaching in the Ordinary level English Language exam. In the early days, there was always an optional question on grammatical analysis. For instance, the 1962 English paper set by the JMB (one of the examining bodies) included the following questions (Keith 1999):

1 State the part of speech of each of the underlined words in the sentences below ...
2 In five of the six sentences below there is an error of grammar or expression. Write out the sentences, correcting the faulty ones as economically as possible, ...
3 Make up seven sentences, each at least seven words long, using the words underlined below as indicated. ...
4 State the kind and function of each of the clauses underlined in the following sentences, and then shorten each clause into a phrase with the same meaning ...

But thanks to a complex combination of circumstances (see Hudson and Walmsley 2005), by 1962 the teaching of grammar was terminally ill, and within the next few years even this optional question was abandoned by all the examination boards – a change dictated not by official policy but presumably by market pressures from the teaching profession. At least secondary English teachers were increasingly disenchanted with the teaching of grammar, for which they had had no training at university and which seemed pointless; so the examination boards followed the mood of the time by dropping the grammar question. Meanwhile, however, grammar teaching remained popular among primary teachers so as late as 1975 a survey reported that 82 per cent of all nine-year-olds spent at least half an hour per week on grammar and punctuation exercises (Philp 1994).

It is easy to look back on the centuries of hands-off policy as a halcyon period for teachers, in which they only taught what they knew and found interesting, with little external constraint from official policy, and were generally supported, rather than constrained, by both publishers and university-led examination boards. No doubt reality was somewhat different, at least to the extent that a school's senior management would develop policy on what should be taught; and no doubt the result of this freedom was sometimes less good for the pupils than for the teachers.

One positive aspect of this freedom from government control was the possibility of developing innovations led by teachers. One particularly impressive example was the Advanced level examination in English Language, which has had an enormous impact on the teaching of English. (A-level examinations take up the last two years of secondary schooling, as a preparation for university.) This examination started in the early 1980s in two geographical centres, Manchester and London, each dominated by the local university's examination board. The underlying ideas stemmed from a university initiative driven by two influential linguists, Randolph Quirk and Michael Halliday, both based in UCL, who not only launched the modern study of English language in British universities, but also saw its potential relevance for schoolteachers. However it was schoolteachers, inspired by these ideas, who drove the new examination from the grass roots and persuaded the examination boards to adopt it. Since the 1980s, the number of entries for English Language at A-level has increased steadily, and in 2012 for the first time they equalled the number of candidates for French, German and Spanish combined. The A-level course demands its own teaching methods and knowledge base, but of course most of the teachers also teach English at lower levels where there are sometimes opportunities for applying these skills (Giovanelli 2015). Paradoxically, then, what is arguably the most important positive change in English teaching during this period happened because government policy was to have no policy on what should be taught.

The National Curriculum

One of the most enduring legacies of the Thatcher government (1979–90) was the National Curriculum, introduced as a matter of government policy through the Education Act of 1988. For the first time ever, government policy would include the content of the whole curriculum, including English – a revolutionary step indeed, and not one to be expected from a Conservative government, least of all from one committed to reducing the size of the state. Equally paradoxically, one of the main achievements of the Conservative-Liberal Democrat coalition government of 2010–15 was to subvert the revolution by allowing more than half of state-funded schools (academies and free schools) to ignore the National Curriculum.

The National Curriculum needed, and received, a great deal of careful planning, and nowhere more so than in the subject area of English. This was recognised as particularly troublesome, and one of the main areas of concern was in the teaching of grammar. The government launched a series of discussion papers called *Curriculum Matters* (DES 1984), the first of which was devoted to English. This introduced the idea that English teachers should teach 'knowledge about language', a phrase which triggered a great deal of disagreement. In particular, should it include knowledge about grammar? The issue was so contentious that the government set up two inquiries which produced The Kingman Report (DES 1988) and The Cox Report (DESWO 1989).

Both reports supported the general idea of teaching knowledge about language, building on the ideas of university linguistics:

> Courses should not be watered down linguistics. They should, however, be informed by principles and insights drawn from linguistics – for example, the idea that language in all its diversity can be approached in a non-prescriptive, non-judgmental way and that it is possible to treat systematically and objectively an aspect of human life which is often the focus of emotive and prejudiced reactions.
>
> (DESWO 1989: 6.13)

Moreover, they also supported the teaching of grammar, but again insisted that this should be informed by modern linguistics:

> For grammar to be of relevance to English teaching, it should be:
>
> 1 a form of grammar which can describe language in use;
> 2 relevant to all levels from the syntax of sentences through to the organisation of substantial texts;
> 3 able to describe the considerable differences between written and spoken English;
> 4 part of a wider syllabus of language study....
>
> (DESWO 1989: 4.28)

Thanks to these reports, the idea of grammar as a tool for studying ordinary language rather than as a prescription for 'correct usage' has found its way into the National Curriculum, where it sits reasonably comfortably alongside the idea that schools should teach children Standard English without proscribing non-standard varieties.

However, The Cox Report also recognised that teaching about language is not easy for English teachers who have themselves never received such teaching whether at school or at university:

> The kind of exploratory, data-based teaching about the forms and functions of language which is proposed in this Report requires teachers who are confident in their ability to handle the material and apply it to well-chosen and stimulating examples. Our proposals therefore have serious implications for teacher training programmes and for those who develop teaching materials as well as for the teachers themselves.
>
> (DESWO 1989: 4.27)

The Kingman Report had made a similar recommendation which persuaded the government to fund a large-scale project (Language in the Curriculum, or LINC) which ran for three years (1989–92) and provided training for a large number of English teachers (Carter 1996). In many ways this was very successful in supporting major changes in the teaching of English, so that teachers became much more confident in talking about topics such as dialect variation, historical change, genre differences and child language. The one topic it did not address, however, was grammar.

Another official policy decision that affected English teaching was the decision by the Labour government to launch the Literacy Strategy in 1998 (Stannard and Huxford 2007), which later turned into the Primary Strategy and was joined by the Secondary Strategy before being abandoned altogether in 2011. The 'strategies' were nationally centralised attempts to change teaching practice directly. On the one hand, they prescribed teaching practice in great detail (notably through the primary 'literacy hour', broken down into precisely timed sections for different kinds of activity); but on the other hand the strategies also provided a great deal of in-service training for teachers (including, in this case, a very limited coverage of formal grammar).

As for the National Curriculum itself, since its launch in 1981 there have been four different curriculum statements for English, but all of them have included some grammatical knowledge. For example, the 1999 version includes this:

Language structure

7 Pupils should be taught:

    a. word classes and the grammatical functions of words, including nouns, verbs, adjectives, adverbs, pronouns, prepositions, conjunctions, articles
    b. the features of different types of sentence, including statements, questions and commands, and how to use them [for example, imperatives in commands]
    c. the grammar of complex sentences, including clauses, phrases and connectives.

(DfEE/QCA 1999: 57)

But – and this, I shall argue, is a crucial gap – until recently there was nothing in official policy to persuade teachers to comply with the curriculum. What if teachers were not 'confident in their ability to handle the material'? Why should they expose themselves to ridicule from possibly better-informed students by teaching grammar?

In summary, the National Curriculum has had a major impact on what teachers are expected to teach, which is now much clearer and more uniform than it used to be. And thanks to the many major changes mentioned earlier – the A-level in English Language, the LINC programme and the Primary and Secondary Strategies – most primary teachers and some secondary English teachers have much more confidence in handling knowledge about language in its less technical aspects. But formal grammar is still work in progress.

A number of research reports suggest that secondary English teachers, typically trained in literature, remain to be convinced that they could or should teach grammar (Giovanelli 2015; Watson 2015). They doubt their ability to teach it because they themselves have never been taught grammar; but they have also heard many negative things about grammar being dry, difficult, incompatible with creativity and pointless, so they also remain to be convinced that grammar deserves a place in the curriculum alongside literature. Fortunately for these teachers, it is easy to avoid grammar altogether in secondary English, because there are no public tests of their pupils' knowledge of grammar, nor do school inspectors check on whether it is being taught. With so few incentives to bite the bullet, it would not be surprising to find that the official policy has been quietly ignored. And this does in fact seem to be the case, to judge by an audit of the grammatical terminology known by school leavers in 1987 (just before the National Curriculum was introduced) and later repeated in 2009 (Alderson and Hudson 2013). This audit consisted of a very simple test in which incoming first-year undergraduates were asked to find examples of various named grammatical categories (e.g. 'preposition' or 'auxiliary verb') in a presented sentence. The results showed that school leavers actually knew less grammatical terminology in 2009 than their counterparts had known in 1987, which suggests strongly that at least that part of the National Curriculum had had absolutely no positive effect at all.

But the latest version of the National Curriculum (dated 2013) is different. This puts even more emphasis on grammar, thanks to a three-page appendix on grammar for primary schools, and an associated fourteen-page glossary. But crucially it has been introduced at the same time as the 'SPaG test' – a national test of spelling, punctuation and grammar. This is currently taken by every pupil in Year 6, and from 2017 a similar test will be taken by every pupil in Year 2. This is partly a test of practical skills but it also tests explicit knowledge of grammar. Because this is a national test, and each school reports its results to government, schools for the first time see a practical benefit of teaching about grammar, as well as the educational benefits promised by new, and strong, evidence that explicit discussion of grammar improves children's writing (Jones et al. 2013; Myhill and Jones 2014; and see also Myhill in Chapter 3 of this book).

Between them, the new curriculum, the SPaG tests and the new research underpinnings for grammar teaching are likely to have a noticeable effect on English teaching, though as yet this expectation is only supported by anecdotal evidence. To judge by comments and discussions among secondary teachers, children are leaving primary school with a significant amount of grammatical knowledge; and publishers are investing in grammar courses for both primary and secondary pupils. An optimistic grammarian could reasonably hope that sensible grammar teaching is on its way back. On the other hand, there are still serious impediments to this change: secondary English teachers are still by and large both anxious about grammar and reluctant to teach it; university degrees in English still ignore language; English teachers still do not collaborate with their colleagues in foreign languages, where grammatical knowledge is an obvious shared topic and resource; and of course official policy can change with the colour of the government. So nothing can be taken for granted in the area of grammar teaching.

I have focused on grammar because this is such a clear example of how government policy is just one part of a complex of teacher knowledge and attitudes, the sticks and carrots of examinations and the economics of publishing, so policy alone may have very little effect on teaching. Creating policy is easy, but (in the absence of a king's dreaded displeasure) implementing it is very hard.

References

Alderson, J. C. and Hudson, R. (2013) 'The metalinguistic knowledge of undergraduate students of English language or linguistics', *Language Awareness* 22(4): 320–37.

Applebee, A. (1974) *Tradition and Reform in the Teaching of English: A History*, Urbana, IL: National Council of Teachers of English, http://eric.ed.gov/?id=ED097703 (last accessed 12 March 2015).

Bell, L. and Stevenson, H. (2006) *Education Policy: Process, Themes and Impact*, London: Routledge.

Board of Education (1921) *The Teaching of English in England (The Newbolt Report)*, London: HMSO.

Bullokar, W. (1586) *A Pamphlet for Grammar*, London: Bollifant.

Carter, R. (1996) 'Politics and knowledge about language: The LINC project', in R. Hasan and G. Williams (eds) *Literacy in Society*, London: Longman, pp. 1–28.

Coffield, F., Edward, S., Finlay, I., Hodgson, A., Spours, K. and Steer, R. (2008) *Improving Learning, Skills and Inclusion: The Impact of Policy on Post-Compulsory Education*, London: Routledge.

Cohen, D. and Loewenberg Ball, D. (1990) 'Relations between policy and practice: A commentary', *Educational Evaluation and Policy Analysis* 12(3): 331–8.

DES (1984) *English from 5–16, Curriculum Matters 1*, London: HMSO.

DES (1988) *Report of the Committee of Inquiry into The Teaching of English Language (The Kingman Report)*, London: HMSO.

DESWO (1989) *English 5–16 (The Cox Report)*, London: HMSO.

DfEE/QCA (1999) *The National Curriculum: Handbook for Primary Teachers in England*, London: DfEE and QCA.

Giovanelli, M. (2015) 'Becoming an English language teacher: Linguistic knowledge, anxieties and the shifting sense of identity', *Language and Education* 29(5): 416–29.

Gwosdek, H. (2013) *William Lily's Grammar of Latin in English: An Introduction of the Eyght Partes of Speche, and the Construction of the Same*, Oxford: Oxford University Press.

Hudson, R. and Walmsley, J. (2005) 'The English patient: English grammar and teaching in the twentieth century', *Journal of Linguistics* 41: 593–622.

Jones, S., Myhill, D. and Bailey, T. (2013) 'Grammar for writing? An investigation into the effect of contextualised grammar teaching on student writing', *Reading and Writing* 26(8): 1241–63.

Keith, G. (1999) 'Noticing Grammar', in *Not Whether but How: Teaching Grammar in English at Key Stage 3 and 4*, London: QCA, pp. 22–32.

Myhill, D. and Jones, S. (2014) 'Language as putty: Framing a relationship between grammar and writing', in A. Goodwin, L. Reid and C. Durrant (eds) *International Perspectives on Teaching English in a Globalised World*, London: Routledge, pp. 144–55.

Nesfield, J. C. (1900) *Outline of English Grammar: In Five Parts*, London: Macmillan.

Philp, A. (1994) 'English grammar in British schools, 1960–1990', in R. Asher (ed.) *Encyclopedia of Language and Linguistics*, Oxford: Pergamon, pp. 1127–31.

Spolsky, B. and Hult, F. (2008) *The Handbook of Educational Linguistics*, Oxford: Blackwell.

Stannard, J. and Huxford, L. (2007) *The Literacy Game: The Story of the National Literacy Strategy*, London: Routledge.

Watson, A. (2015) 'Conceptualisations of "grammar teaching": L1 English teachers' beliefs about teaching grammar for writing', *Language Awareness* 24(1): 1–14.

Chapter 3

The effectiveness of explicit language teaching

Evidence from the research

Debra Myhill

Introduction

The question of whether there is a place for explicit language teaching, specifically grammar teaching, in the language curriculum has been a long-running and still largely unresolved debate, and one about which there have been extensive publications (see for example: Tomlinson 1994; Sealey 1999; Hudson 2004; Myhill and Watson 2014). In general, the quality of this debate has been somewhat impoverished by predetermined positions or political agendas. It is a highly politicised topic in Anglophone countries, with policy-makers commonly conflating grammar with accuracy and correctness in language use, and tending to equate mastery of grammar with standards, including moral standards (see Cameron 1995). Indeed, in the summer of 2011, following the street riots in England, the London *Evening Standard* published an article directly linking the riots to young people's inability to speak 'correctly'. This is not restricted to the UK: in New Zealand, Elley *et al.* (1975: 3) noted the tendency to see 'strong doses of English grammar as a cure for some of our educational ills'. Within the professional community, there is a parallel history of opposition to grammar teaching as counter to creativity, or even harmful (Braddock *et al.* 1963). Much of this debate, both politically and professionally, is predicated upon a view of grammar as fundamentally about rules, be that grammar to eradicate the errors in language use, or grammar through its emphasis on rules as stifling creativity and freedom of expression. The consequence of this is that the intellectual agenda has concentrated more on claim and counter-claim, with research studies designed more to proving or disproving the efficacy of grammar teaching than to developing a coherent theoretical view of language in the curriculum, or to pursuing a body of programmatic studies which cumulatively build knowledge about how children learn grammar and how learning about grammar may support their capability as language users. In the light of this, this chapter sets out to discuss the role of explicit grammar teaching in the language curriculum and to present an overview of the research evidence addressing this.

Knowledge about grammar

Explicit language teaching in its broadest sense encompasses a wide variety of activities including how to read, developing comprehension skills, literary criticism, letter shaping and handwriting, spelling, the process of writing, digital literacies, and multimodality. To an extent, it is hard to think of anything that might happen in an English or Language arts classroom which is not, in some way, explicit language teaching. In general, however, discussions about explicit language teaching have tended to refer to the value of linguistics or grammar in the curriculum. It is this that this chapter takes as its focus of attention. In this section, the knowledge which constitutes 'grammar knowledge' is considered.

Tacit (implicit) and explicit knowledge

The general concepts of tacit and explicit knowledge draw from learning theory more broadly, rather than specifically being about language and grammar, but they are of central importance to thinking about the role of grammar in language learning. Tacit knowledge is that knowledge which we possess but cannot verbalise (Polanyi 1966; Collins 2001), such as for example, how we stay afloat when we are swimming, or how we recognise someone's face. In contrast, explicit knowledge can be verbalised and explained to another person, such as factual information or skills which can be explained, such as how to cook a particular food. Tacit knowledge is frequently learned through experience and social interaction, and through observation and practice. Ryle (1945) described tacit knowledge as 'know-how' compared with the 'know-that' of explicit knowledge. In terms of grammar, all language users have an immense and sophisticated stock of tacit knowledge which we learn from a very early age. Very small babies can discriminate the phonemes of their own language from those of other languages before they even have the words to describe this. Similarly, toddlers who say 'I goed' or 'I wented' reveal tacit knowledge of the regular formation of the past tense, and older toddlers who have mastered 'I went' have developed tacit knowledge of irregular past tense formations: but of course they cannot articulate this knowledge. In fact, what children learning to talk develop is tacit knowledge of the deep rules of their mother tongue: for example, in English, not just tense forms, but also word order, agreements and a host of other principles. Fluent language users often know what is correct but cannot always explain it: as a PhD supervisor of many second-language speakers, I am often unable to explain why we use articles or prepositions in the way we do in English, but I would never make a mistake in their usage. This complex tacit knowledge of grammar is developed through meaningful social interactions in contexts where language and action are inter-related.

Tacit language knowledge, however, is not confined to talk: young children also develop tacit knowledge of written text through their experiences as readers. When my eldest granddaughter was about three-and-a-half, she was at the scribble writing stage of writing development. One day she made a scribble and said 'That's says Elizabeth [her name]'; she then wrote a smaller scribble and said 'That says Lia' [her little sister's name]. She then told me that 'Lia' was shorter than 'Elizabeth' because Lia was smaller than her – although the logic was wrong, what she was showing was emerging tacit knowledge about words and their link to meaning. Similarly, Frankie, an early years writer, shows his emerging knowledge of how you build a relationship with the reader (Fisher *et al.* 2010), with positioning adjectives ('amasing') and the direct address to the reader ('If you look closely'), which represent tacit knowledge, most likely drawn from reading experiences:

> This is the nisy amazing longleat. There are some very cheeky monkeys there. If you look closely you mite see some juicy fruit and a grey rhino. Because it has ascaped. I hope he dosent see gumdrop or mr old caste or Black Horace.
> (Fisher *et al.* 2010: 13)

The issue of tacit and explicit knowledge is central to the debate about the role of grammar in the language curriculum, though few have expressed it in this way. The strongest professional argument against grammar teaching has always been that explicit knowledge is not necessary because we have so much tacit knowledge. When we write a sentence, we don't consciously think about the need for a subject and a verb, or about the positioning of a subordinate clause: as Elley *et al.* (1975: 99) put it, 'it is highly debatable whether many students, or professional writers for that matter, are aware of the choices they make when generating new sentences'. The argument, therefore, is that tacit knowledge, gained through meaningful interactions is the real driver of language growth. This argument, however, assumes that all language learners have tacit knowledge upon which to draw. With writing especially, this is not always the case. Despite the strong relationship in English between oral and written language, writing is not 'speech written down' (Perera 1987: 17), and children who do not read much or who are learning English as an additional language may not have the appropriate tacit models of 'writerly' language in their repertoire. Equally, young learners may be asked to write genres in school which they have not read: for example, persuasive texts such as letters of complaint or campaign material, and academic or scientific writing. In these cases, explicit grammar teaching creates new explicit knowledge which equips learners to fulfil the demands of the task. Where the curriculum requires analysis of written texts, as in the study of literature in secondary schools, explicit grammar teaching develops new explicit knowledge to support such critical analysis.

Knowledge of grammar as a system

One strand of explicit grammatical knowledge is knowledge of language as a system. Curiously, the contested history of grammar teaching has been preoccupied with whether learning grammar improves learners' attainments in reading and writing, but there has been no serious consideration of the value of grammatical knowledge in its own right. Yet, in every jurisdiction, the school curriculum determines what bodies of knowledge are valued and, in most cases, this is not simply on utilitarian grounds, but on a cultural judgement about what constitutes a broad and balanced education. Knowing the periodic table or the history of medieval England are unlikely to be *useful* knowledge to most adults, yet they may well be *valuable* knowledge. Grammatical knowledge of the structure of your own language could very plausibly be argued as equally valuable knowledge. In subject English in many Anglophone countries the teaching of literature and literary analysis is accompanied by the use of literary metalanguage, the figures of speech, such as metaphor, enjambement, caesura and such similar. This, like grammar, is an abstract metalanguage but its place in the curriculum has been largely unquestioned. In England, at least, this may be because the university education system tends to separate English Literature and Linguistics, and the dominant route into becoming an English teacher is the English Literature route (Shortis and Blake 2010). As a consequence, teachers' beliefs about the value of grammar and of literary metalanguage are paradoxical (Wilson and Myhill 2012), and underlying these paradoxical beliefs is a lack of confidence in linguistic subject knowledge counterweighted by greater confidence with literary metalanguage. This is pithily summed up by a teacher in one of our research projects who, in an interview, explained that she did not teach the word 'preposition' in the lesson observed because it was too hard, but was nonetheless quite comfortable teaching children the term 'caesura'. She reflected that:

> I'm completely confident with making my writing effective … completely confident in making my writing effective and to suit purpose and audience and all the stuff … But then there's something about, maybe it's just because of my bad experiences, I don't feel as confident talking about the differences between … a complex and a compound and all the rest of it … I can teach caesura and enjambement much better than I can subordinate clauses and complex sentences.

Of course, linguists over time have described grammar as a system differently and with different theoretical assumptions. There is, however, widespread agreement that the work of a linguist is to describe grammar as it is used, not to prescribe how it should be used. From an educational perspective, the theoretical thinking under-pinning Halliday's development of Systemic Functional Linguistics (SFL) is interesting because in describing language as a system, Halliday (1978) attends to both the structures of language and how they make meaning. As a functionally-oriented theory of grammar, SFL attends to how language operates at word, sentence and text level and is sensitive to context and the ways in which meanings shift subtly, or not so subtly, according to the context in which they are used. In addition to the traditional metalanguage of word classes and syntax, SFL contributes new ways of describing language according to its metafunctions, *the ideational, the interpersonal and the textual* (Halliday 1978). Derewianka and Jones (2010: 9) note the difference between a view of grammar as an abstract system against which accuracy can be determined and the Hallidayan view of language 'as a resource, a meaning-making system through which we interactively shape and interpret our world and ourselves'. Arguably, curriculum knowledge about grammar as a system could usefully incorporate both knowledge of grammar as structure and of grammar as choice (Carter and McCarthy 2006), enabling learners to appreciate that grammar knowledge can help them understand not only what structures are evident in a text but also that as language users we have choices of which grammatical structures best suit our meaning-making purposes. Functional approaches to grammar have developed considerable currency in Australia, New Zealand and the United States, a phenomenon which is explored in more depth later in this chapter.

Research evidence of relationships between explicit grammar teaching and learner outcomes

Research meta-analyses

Ironically, there are almost as many meta-analyses of the effect of explicit grammar teaching on students' learning as there are empirical studies. One of the earliest, by Braddock *et al.* (1963) came to the conclusion that the formal teaching of grammar had a negligible beneficial effect and, because it displaced other teaching about composition from the curriculum, he argued it had 'a harmful effect on the development of original writing' (1963: 37). Hillocks (1984) came to a similar conclusion, and his later review with Smith (Hillocks and Smith 1991) reiterated the view that there was no evidence for a beneficial effect. In England, in the light of the greater emphasis on grammar in the National Literacy Strategy, the government-funded EPPE reviews (Andrews *et al.* 2004a; 2004b) found no evidence of any benefits of grammar teaching on writing instruction, although they did note there was more robust evidence on sentence-combining, which will be discussed more specifically later in this chapter. Graham and Perin (2007) did not set out to focus on grammar but on evidence of instructional strategies which raise learner outcomes in writing: nonetheless, their meta-analysis reports a negative effect for 'the explicit and systematic teaching of the parts of speech and structure of sentences' (2007: 21). Such a succession of meta-analyses over such a period of time and representing research from several continents might seem pretty conclusive but, in looking more closely at the empirical studies and at more recent research, a different conclusion might be drawn.

Empirical studies

Despite the large number of meta-analyses on the same topic, the evidence base for their conclusions is very small. Indeed, Andrews *et al.* drew attention to both the poor quality of the research and its age (Andrews *et al.* 2006: 51) and, in the end, used only three studies to inform their findings (Bateman and Zidonis 1966; Elley *et al.* 1979; Fogel and Ehri 2000). The expressions 'formal grammar teaching' and 'traditional grammar instruction' recur throughout these meta-analyses, in general referring to teaching which involves learners in labelling and parsing sentences and in undertaking grammar exercises – the goal of such teaching seemingly being to be able to correctly identify word classes and syntactical structures, and in some cases to identify error and correct it. This kind of formal instruction was often de-contextualised from the rest of the language-teaching curriculum and, given contemporary understanding of how learning is socially constructed in meaningful contexts, it is perhaps not surprising that the results of decontextualised formal instruction were not positive.

Significantly, however, the Fogel and Ehri (2000) study was conceived from a different position: they investigated whether or not explicit grammar instruction would help their students manage the switch from Black English Vernacular (BEV) to Standard English (SE) in their writing. Thus the impetus for their study was a recognised writing need in their students. Their study had three treatment groups: 1) natural exposure to SE in the classroom plus texts in SE; 2) natural exposure plus explicit instruction in strategies to support use of SE; and 3) natural exposure, explicit instruction, and guided practice and feedback in transforming BEV to SE. It was treatment group 3 which showed the strongest effect, although the group sizes are small. What Fogel and Ehri did which, at the time of the meta-analyses, seems unique was to make a connection for the learners between the grammar point and their own writing needs: the guided practice 'clarified for students the link between features in their own nonstandard writing and features in SE' (Fogel and Ehri 2000: 231). The idea that teaching might somehow make a connection between grammar and writing or grammar and reading is central to the study by Fearn and Farnan (2007). They note that grammar policy in the US is dominated by requirements to identify and define, and that literature and writing are taught separately from each other. In contrast, their study set out to consider the impact on students' writing of teaching where 'grammar and writing share one instructional context' (2007: 16), focusing on grammar taught during writing classes. They too found a positive effect and argued that 'the more powerful influence' of explicit grammar teaching is realised when 'students' attention is focused on using grammar to think about writing' (2007: 11).

In sentence-combining students are shown through exercises how to put simple sentences together to create more syntactically complex sentences, and one major weakness is that the measure of success, the effect size, is commonly whether children have created more complex sentences or whether their writing has evidence of more complex sentences. There is no evaluation of the effectiveness of the sentences used, just their presence. This is founded on a view that syntactical maturity is a marker of writing quality, but as Crowhurst (1980) demonstrated, there is no clear relationship between these. This may be because sentence-combining focuses upon syntactical manipulation, rather than upon the purposes and effects in specific writing tasks of different kinds of syntactical choices. The benefits of sentence-combining, reported in the meta-analyses, seem clear until the evidence is studied more closely. There were a flurry of studies on sentence-combining in the US in the 1980s (O'Hare 1971; Daiker *et al.* 1978; Hake and Williams 1979; Hillocks and Mavrogenes 1986), although there has been relatively little since. Sentence-combining could be claimed as an instructional approach which develops learners' tacit grammatical knowledge, as it eschews using the explicit syntactical metalanguage relevant to the activity.

Grammar as meaning-making

The empirical evidence, therefore, seems conclusive. There is no positive benefit of explicit and de-contextualised grammatical instruction on learners' competence as language users, with or without the use of grammatical metalanguage. However, informed by a functionally-oriented theorisation of grammar, and noting that those studies which seem to indicate positive outcomes (Fogel and Ehri 2000; Fearn and Farnan 2007) located the grammar teaching within the teaching of writing, or with a direct emphasis on an identified learning need, there is an emerging body of new research suggesting real benefits of explicit grammar teaching. Our own research (Myhill *et al.* 2012) took as a starting point that explicit grammar teaching should be incorporated within the teaching of writing, and that the grammar selected for attention should be relevant to the genres being taught or identified learning needs. This approach was based on a pedagogy that was theoretically grounded in functionally-oriented understandings of grammar, and thus sought to make connections for learners between grammatical choices and meaning-making in their own writing. So, for example, in a sequence of lessons on the teaching of narrative, attention might be given to how character description can be built up through well-crafted noun phrases, or how the choice of first or third person voice creates different viewpoints and different narrative possibilities (see Jones *et al.* 2013). A randomised controlled trial showed a positive benefit of this approach on learner outcomes (Myhill *et al.* 2012; Jones *et al.* 2012). A subsequent smaller-scale study demonstrated that the approach benefits weaker writers (Myhill 2013): in this study, the grammar focuses were particularly targeted towards the identified needs in struggling writers' narratives. A more recent study (Watson *et al.* 2014) looked at older writers aged fifteen to sixteen and the demands of the national qualification, GCSE (General Certificate of Secondary Education), where students are tested for writing and for reading comprehension. This study, therefore, looked not only at writing, but whether the focus on grammar would support the students' response to the reading comprehension questions. As with the previous studies, this study reported a statistically significant positive impact of the approach, with a stronger impact on reading than writing. This may be because learning gains are faster in responding to reading than the more demanding activity of writing.

Detailed analysis of sub-scores on the reading comprehension responses provides further evidence of the impact of this approach. The examination rewards students for information retrieval, inferential comprehension and language analysis: the analysis of scores indicate that there were no statistically significant differences between the intervention and control groups on information retrieval and comprehension, but the language analysis responses produced the significant differences.

This attention to explicit grammar teaching set within a functionally-oriented frame of reference is not limited to the UK. In the United States, there is an interest in 'rhetorical grammar' (Micciche 2004; Hancock 2009), which adopts a similar functionally-oriented lens: however, the research in this area is largely theoretical, rather than empirical. At the same time, the work of Schleppegrell, in the US, adopts an SFL lens to consider language learning, particularly second language learning (see, for example, Schleppegrell 2010, 2011, 2012). Likewise in Australia, there is a substantive and growing body of classroom-based research using the affordances of systemic functional linguistics, which is also showing benefits (Derewianka and Jones, 2010; Macken-Horarik *et al.* 2011; Jones and Chen, 2012), although as yet there are no statistical studies here. Derewianka (2012: 129) argues that whilst traditional, prescriptivist models of grammar tended to privilege classical texts, functional approaches are intrinsically concerned with language differences instantiated in context: for example, examining how language is used in different curriculum subjects. The work of Macken-Horarik and her team has looked particularly at the concept of grammatical thinking, arguing that SFL enables students to develop the capacity to think grammatically about language and to understand its power as a meaning-making resource (Macken-Horarik 2011).

Collectively, this body of work, perhaps for the first time in the past sixty years, is focusing not on simplistic 'what works' research, but on trying to understand how grammar can support language development, how children learn to think grammatically and what pedagogies facilitate this learning.

Conclusion

It is important to theorise how explicit teaching of grammar relates to students' language learning. It is not simply fostering their capacity to use grammatical metalanguage and apply it in their own language use: it is developing metalinguistic understanding. Arguably, the failure to consider and conceptualise metalinguistic understanding in earlier studies of the value of grammar in the curriculum is their collective fundamental flaw. Both in the context of learning to read and learning to write, we know that metacognition is a key skill (Kellogg 1994; Baker 2008), and metalinguistic understanding, the capacity to think explicitly about language as an artefact, is an important subset of metacognition. Drawing on psychological, sociological and linguistic disciplinary discourses, we have defined metalinguistic understanding as 'the explicit bringing into consciousness of an attention to language as an artefact, and the conscious monitoring and manipulation of language to create desired meanings grounded in socially shared understandings' (Myhill 2011: 250). Explicit teaching of grammar focuses on language as an artefact, bringing to consciousness, or to 'meta-awareness', how language is shaping meaning in different texts and different social contexts. Earlier in this chapter, the distinction between tacit and explicit knowledge was considered; but another relevant distinction, particularly in the context of writing, is the distinction between tacit and explicit knowledge, and automated processes. In becoming writers, learning requiring explicit knowledge becomes automated over time – for example, shaping letters, using punctuation, structuring sentences and so on. The vast majority of spelling executed by proficient writers is automated. But when there is a 'problem', what is unconscious and automated becomes the locus of conscious attention – at this point, it is metalinguistic knowledge which helps to regulate transitions between conscious and unconscious activity and to inform decision-making (Myhill and Jones, 2016).

What then can we deduce from this review of evidence about the value of explicit grammar teaching? It remains true that historically there has been little evidence of its value, but equally it is not a field that has been characterised by rigorous or systematic research. More recently, there is a clear emerging body of research signalling real benefits of explicit grammar teaching when the teaching is grounded in meaningful language-learning contexts. That this research is international, drawing on different educational jurisdictions, lends weight to its evidence. But there is scope for more research in this area, both studies which rigorously investigate the impact of this teaching on students' capacity as language users, and studies which explore the nature of students' thinking about grammar and how that transfers into their thinking about text. In education, evidence is best when it derives from a cumulative body of work, rather than over-relying on one study, and that body of work is now beginning to flourish.

References

Andrews, R., Torgerson, C. J., Beverton, S., Freeman, A., Locke, T., Low, G., Robinson, A. and Zhu, D. (2004a) 'The effect of grammar teaching (sentence combining) in English on 5 to 16 year olds' accuracy and quality in written composition', London: EPPI-Centre, Social Science Research Unit, Institute of Education.

Andrews, R., Torgerson, C. J., Beverton, S., Freeman, A., Locke, T., Low, G., Robinson, A. and Zhu, D (2004b) 'The effect of grammar teaching (syntax) in English on 5 to 16 year olds' accuracy and quality in written composition', London: EPPI-Centre, Social Science Research Unit, Institute of Education.

Andrews, R., Torgerson, C. J., Beverton, S., Freeman, A., Locke, T., Low, G., Robinson, A. and Zhu, D. (2006) 'The effect of grammar teaching on writing development', *British Educational Research Journal* 32(1): 39–55.

Baker, L. (2008) 'Metacognitive development in reading: Contributors and consequences', in K. Mokhtari and R. Sheorey (eds.) *Reading Strategies of First and Second-Language Learners: See How They Read*, Norwood, MA: Christopher-Gordon, pp. 25–42.

Bateman, D. R. and Zidonis, F. J. (1966) *The Effect of a Study of Transformational Grammar on the Writing of Ninth and Tenth Graders*, Champagne, IL: National Council of Teachers of English.

Braddock, R., Lloyd-Jones, R. and Schoer, L. (1963) *Research in Written Composition*, Urbana, IL: National Council of Teachers of English.

Cameron, D. (1995) *Verbal Hygiene*, London: Routledge.

Carter, R. and McCarthy, M. (2006) *Cambridge Grammar of English*, Cambridge: Cambridge University Press.

Collins, H. M. (2001) 'Tacit Knowledge, Trust and the Q of Sapphire', *Social Studies of Science* 31(1): 71–85.

Crowhurst, M. (1980) 'Syntactic Complexity and Teachers' Quality Ratings of Narrations and Arguments', *Research in the Teaching of English* 14: 223–31.

Daiker, D. A., Kerek, A. and Morenberg, M. (1978) 'Sentence-Combining and Syntactic Maturity in Freshman English', *College Composition and Communication* 29(1): 36–41.

Derewianka, B. M. (2012) 'Knowledge about language in the Australian curriculum: English', *Australian Journal of Language and Literacy* 35(2): 127–46.

Derewianka, B. and Jones, P. (2010) 'From traditional grammar to functional grammar: Bridging the divide', Special Issue of *NALDIC Quarterly*, Reading: 6–15.

Elley, W. B., Barham, I., Lamb, H. and Wyllie, M. (1975) 'The role of grammar in a secondary school Curriculum', *New Zealand Council for Educational Studies* 10: 26–41.

Elley, W. B., Barham, I., Lamb, H. and Wyllie, M. (1979) *The Role of Grammar in a Secondary School Curriculum (Educational Research Series No 60)*, Wellington: New Zealand Council for Educational Research.

Fearn, L. and Farnan, N. (2007) 'When is a verb? Using functional grammar to teach writing', *Journal of Basic Writing* 26(1): 1–26.

Fisher, R., Jones, S., Larkin, S. and Myhill, D. A. (2010) *Using Talk to Support Writing*, London: Sage.

Fogel, H. and Ehri, L. C. (2000) 'Teaching elementary students who speak black English vernacular to write in Standard English: Effects of dialect transformation practice', *Contemporary Educational Psychology* 25: 212–35.

Graham, S. and Perin, D. (2007) 'A meta-analysis of writing instruction for adolescent students', *Journal of Educational Psychology* 99(3): 445–76.

Hake, R. and Williams, J. M. (1979) 'Sentence expanding: Not can, or how, but when', in D. A. Daiker, A. Kerek and M. Morenberg (eds) *Sentence-Combining and the Teaching of Writing*, Conway, AR: L&S Books, pp. 134–46.

Halliday, M. A. K. (1978) *Language as Social Semiotic: The Social Interpretation of Language and Meaning*, London: Edward Arnold.

Hancock, C. (2009) 'How linguistics can inform the teaching of writing', in R. Beard, D. A. Myhill, J. Riley and M. Nystrand (eds) *International Handbook of Writing Development*, London: Sage, pp. 194–208.

Hillocks, G. (1984) 'What works in teaching composition: A meta-analysis of experimental treatment studies', *American Journal of Education*, 93(1): 133–70.

Hillocks, G. and Mavrogenes, N. A. (1986) 'Sentence combining', in G. Hillocks (ed.) *Research on Written Composition: New Directions for Teaching*, Urbana, IL: National Council of Teachers of English, pp. 142–6.

Hillocks, G. and Smith, M. (1991) 'Grammar and usage', in J. Flood, J. Jensen, D. Lapp and J. Squire (eds) *Handbook of Research on Teaching the English Language Arts*, New York, NY: Macmillan, pp. 591–603.

Hudson, R. (2004) 'Why education needs linguistics', *Journal of Linguistics* 40(1): 105–30.

Jones, P. T. and Chen, H. (2012) 'Teachers' knowledge about language: Issues of pedagogy and expertise', *Australian Journal of Language and Literacy* 35(2): 147–72.

Jones, S. M., Myhill, D. A. and Bailey, T. C. (2012) 'Grammar for writing? An investigation into the effect of contextualised grammar teaching on Student Writing', *Reading and Writing* 26(8): 1241–63.

Jones, S. M., Myhill, D. A., Watson, A. and Lines, H. E. (2013) 'Playful Explicitness with Grammar: A Pedagogy for Writing', *Literacy* 47(2): 103–11.

Kellogg, R. T. (1994) *The Psychology of Writing*, Oxford: Oxford University Press.

Macken-Horarik, M., Love, K. and Unsworth, L. (2011) 'A grammatics "good enough" for school English in the 21st century: Four challenges in realising the potential', *Australian Journal of Language and Literacy* 34(1): 9–23.

Micciche, L. (2004) 'Making a case for rhetorical grammar', *College Composition and Communication* 55(4): 716–37.

Myhill, D. A. (2011) '"The Ordeal of deliberate choice": Metalinguistic development in secondary writers', in V. W. Berninger (ed.) *Past, Present, and Future Contributions of Cognitive Writing Research to Cognitive Psychology*, New York, NY: Psychology Press/Taylor Francis Group, pp. 247–74.

Myhill, D. A. (2013) *Raising the Attainment of Weaker Writers*, www.pearsonschoolsandfecolleges.co.uk/AssetsLibrary/SECTORS/Secondary/SUBJECT/EnglishAndMedia/PDFs/SkillsforWriting/S715Raisingtheattainmentofweakerwriters Guide-webpageversion.pdf (last accessed 8 June 2015).

Myhill, D. A., Jones, S. M., and Wilson, A. C. (2016) Writing conversations: fostering metalinguistic discussion about writing, *Research Papers in Education* 31(1): 23–44.

Myhill, D. A. and Watson, A. (2014) 'The role of grammar in the writing curriculum: A review', *Journal of Child Language Teaching and Therapy* 30(1): 41–62.

Myhill, D. A., Jones, S. M., Lines, H. E. and Watson, A. (2012) 'Re-thinking grammar: The impact of embedded grammar teaching on students' writing and students' metalinguistic understanding', *Research Papers in Education* 27(2): 1–28.

O'Hare, F. (1971) *Sentence Combining: Improving Student-Writing Without Formal Grammar Instruction*, NCTE Research Report No 15, Urbana, IL: National Council of Teachers of English.

Perera, K. (1987) *Understanding Language*, London: NAAE.

Polanyi, M. (1966) *The Tacit Dimension*, Chicago, IL: University of Chicago Press.

Ryle, G. (1945) 'Knowing how and knowing that'. *Papers from the Aristotelian Society* 46: 1–16.

Schleppegrell, M. J. (2010) 'Supporting a "reading to write" pedagogy with functional grammar', *NALDIC Quarterly* 8(1): 26–31.

Schleppegrell, M. J. (2011) 'Supporting disciplinary learning through language analysis: Developing historical literacy', in F. Christie and K. Maton (eds) *Disciplinarity: Functional Linguistic and Sociological Perspectives*, London: Continuum, pp. 197–216.

Schleppegrell, M. J. (2012) 'Systemic functional linguistics: Exploring meaning in language', in J. P. Gee and M. Handford (eds) *The Routledge Handbook of Discourse Analysis*, New York, NY: Routledge, pp. 21–34.

Sealey, A. (1999) 'Teaching primary school children about the English language: A critique of current policy documents', *Language Awareness* 8(2): 84–97.

Shortis, T. and Blake, J. (2010) 'Who's prepared to teach school English? The degree level qualifications and preparedness of initial teacher trainees of English', London: CLIE.

Tomlinson, D. (1994) 'Errors in the research into the effectiveness of grammar teaching', *English in Education* 28(1): 20–6.

Watson, A., Myhill, D. A. and Newman, R. (2014) *Grammar at GCSE: Exploring the effects of a contextualised grammar pedagogy on reading and writing at KS4*, http:// qualifications.pearson.com/content/dam/pdf/GCSE/English%20Language/2015/ teaching-and-learning-materials/Grammar_at_GCSE_Technical_Report_DC.pdf (last accessed 8 June 2015).

Wilson, A. C. and Myhill, D. A. (2012) 'Ways with words: Teachers' personal epistemologies of the role of metalanguage in the teaching of poetry writing', *Language and Education* 26(6): 553–68.

Part 2

Applying linguistics in the classroom

Chapter 4

Stylistics

Andrea Macrae

Introduction

Stylistics is an approach to reading and analysing texts that concentrates on the relationships between language and interpretative effects. The focus tends to be literary: the texts analysed are often works of literature, the kinds of interpretations explored and developed are of a richness and complexity more commonly afforded to literary reading, and some of the aspects of language analysed occur more densely in literature and so are usually considered to be prototypically 'literary'. However, stylistics works according to the principles that the literariness of language is scalar, and that though discourse is conventionally categorised as either literary or non-literary, this categorisation depends upon prevailing cultural norms and values (including institutionally authorised reading practices), and so shifts over time (Carter 1997: 113). Stylistic analyses of texts categorised as non-literary are just as fruitful as stylistic analyses of literary texts, and bringing both together is ideal. Stylistics offers students an accessible means of investigating how language in texts of all kinds works, and helps students to engage with the characteristics of different genres and discourses, as well as with the contexts governing the systems of their differentiation. Stylistic investigations of the interpretative effects of features of language in particular texts and contexts facilitate a better understanding of the workings of those language features more generally and a more sophisticated appreciation of the ways in which the communicative functioning of those language features is governed by discourse contexts (cultural, social and cognitive).

The practice of stylistics helps students draw explicit links between linguistic details and interpretative effects. As Carter writes, '[p]ut in a crude way, stylistic interpretation involves a process of making equations between, or inferences about, linguistic forms and the meaning contracted by the function or operation of these forms' in a discourse context (1997: 200). Stylistics gives students tools that directly contribute to a range of skills needed in studying English within the National Curriculum. At Key Stage 3, students are required to 'understand increasingly challenging texts through … making inferences and referring to evidence in the text'. They must learn how to 'read critically through … knowing how language, including figurative language, vocabulary choice, grammar, text structure and organisational features, presents meaning'. Students need to develop abilities in 'discussing reading, writing and spoken language with precise and confident use of linguistic and literary terminology'. At Key Stage 4, students are required to become competent in 'identifying and interpreting themes, ideas and information', 'exploring aspects of plot, characterisation, events and settings, the relationships between them and their effects', and 'seeking evidence in the text to support a point of view, including justifying inferences with evidence'. They need to become able to 'make an informed personal response, recognising that other responses to a text are possible and evaluating these' (DfE 2014b). All of these skills require an understanding of relationships between language and interpretation, between textual cues and inferred meanings. Stylistics empowers students to recognise and describe linguistic elements and the inferences they draw, to articulate and deepen interpretations and to understand relationships between texts and effects. With stylistics, students can analyse a text, explain and develop their own interpretative responses, and account for aspects of the responses of others.

This chapter provides an overview of stylistics, its practice and its principles. Most of the chapter is devoted to illustrating four methods of stylistic analysis. First, I demonstrate how cloze procedure can be effectively employed in the service of close stylistic analysis of the integrated effects of lexical, grammatical and other linguistic choices. I then model an analysis of foregrounding, investigating the language features which appear prominent through their fit with, or deviation from, patterns and conventions. A less comprehensive, more focused kind of stylistic analysis follows, directing attention towards one stylistic feature felt to be dominant in the ways in which the text makes meanings available to the reader. I then introduce textual intervention (Pope 1995) as a further means of stylistic analysis. Given that students are required at Key Stages 3 and 4 to read 'a wide range of fiction and non-fiction' and to 'mak[e] critical comparisons across texts' (DfE 2014b), a range of text types will be drawn upon throughout these sections, illuminating some of the particular advantages of stylistic analysis across genres. Finally, I describe some of the main tenets underlying these and other stylistic approaches before outlining some useful resources for teachers to support the use of stylistics in the classroom.

Cloze procedure

Cloze procedure involves blanking out some of the words of a text and suggesting what could fit in the blanked out spaces. The process encourages students to infer the themes and tone of the text and make predictions on that basis, and to think about how co-textual segments shape and constrict possible meanings. Cloze procedure can also be done one line or sentence at a time, each segment of text revealed in turn, to allow students to build an understanding of the semantic direction and grammatical patterns of the text, and to reflect on the successive build-up of cues determining that understanding (see Canning and Simpson 2012 for an example).

Here is the opening section of T. S. Eliot's 'Preludes', with lines numbered and suggestions for words to be blanked out italicised.

I

1   The winter *evening* settles down
2   With smell of steak in passageways.
3   Six o'clock.
4   The burnt-out ends of smoky *days*.
5   And now a gusty *shower* wraps
6   The grimy scraps
7   Of withered *leaves* about *your* feet
8   And *newspapers* from vacant lots;
9   The showers *beat*
10   On broken blinds and chimney pots,
11   And at the corner of the street
12   A lonely cab-horse *steams* and stamps.

13   And then the lighting of the *lamps*.

The extract could be presented as a whole (with the italicised words blanked out) or could be presented line by line. For reasons of space, only two blanked out spaces will be explored here: the extract is analysed more fully later in this chapter, using an alternative stylistic approach.

Students should be encouraged to reflect on both which textual cues lead them to the suggestions they make and the semantic and grammatical consequences of their suggestions for the rest of the line (and beyond). Suggestions for the blanked out word in line one, following 'The winter', might include the adverb 'slowly', or the nouns 'season', 'snow', 'wind' or 'sun'. Each of the nouns is related to the semantic field of weather, evoked by 'winter', and each makes 'winter' a pre-modifying adjective (though you could debate whether or not 'winter' + 'season', for example, constitutes a compound noun). If students opt for reading 'winter' as an adjective, it can be useful to ask them what might lead them to reject other nouns sometimes modified by 'winter', such as 'cold', 'ice', or perhaps 'solstice', 'fashions', 'holiday', etc. (the relative frequency and familiarity of these collocations varying across different sociocultural groups). Students could think about the constraining grammatical effects of the definite article, and the need for tense and number agreement with the verb 'settles'. The constraining semantic significance of the verb phrase 'settles down' can also be explored. For example, whereas the notion of 'ice' settling down clashes with schema of the nature of ice and how it is formed, 'snow' often collocates with the verb to 'settle'. 'The winter sun settles down' could imply a degree of personification, while 'The winter holiday settles down' requires more effort to construct meaningful interpretations.

The alternative suggestions could be ranked for semantic clarity and richness. Students might be encouraged to reflect on whether and why they might allow for more unusual, non-standard grammatical constructions and figurative language within poetic texts, which can lead on to a discussion of genre conventions.

Students might also expect sound patterning to be a priority in the composition of poetry, and could argue that 'season', 'sun' and 'snow' fit because each alliterates with 'settles' and adds to the consonance of the 'n' sound repeated across the line. 'Wind', on the other hand, repeats the first syllable of 'winter', includes the 'n' consonance and offers further assonance in the repetition of the 'i' sound. Some students might prefer 'season' in favour of 'snow' in anticipation of an iambic metrical scheme (this expectation being more likely if the students are given the whole extract at once).

Further into the poem, in line 7, the second blanked out word could prompt suggestion of a variety of possessive pronouns – their, his, my, for example. If they have been given the whole extract, students might reasonably try to link the feet to the cab-horse of line 12, it being the only explicitly mentioned being/ object with 'feet' (of a sort) in the extract. This can open up a discussion of clause relationships. Lines 5 to 12 comprise one sentence. On one hand, the coordinating conjunction 'and', in line 11, and the indefinite article 'a' together present the horse as new information. On the other hand, it is conceivable that the clause which precedes the semicolon at the end of line 8 is introducing or 'setting up' the subject(s) of the proceeding lines.

As Carter advises, use of cloze procedure in class can benefit from careful management of 'the number of words deleted', attention 'to the relative multivalency of the chosen items, [and] to the linguistic competence of a group' (1997: 173). Giving students some initial practice with the process, using shorter texts or extracts with greater degrees of predictability, can be a helpful introduction to the method.

Stylistic analysis of foregrounding, deviation and parallelism

Cloze procedure can be useful for exploratory analysis of a text and development of linguistic and grammatical understanding. However, a more comprehensive and systematic kind of stylistic analysis is possible through investigation of foregrounding, deviation and parallelism. A foregrounded feature is one which is perceived by a reader to be more prominent than others. This relative salience is usually due to that feature paralleling with or deviating from others. *Parallelism*, within this approach, refers to the repetition of features, creating patterns which stand out from the rest of the text, just as the dots of a polka dot pattern stand out from the background colour behind it. *Deviation* is defined as departure from a norm, convention, system or pattern internal to the text (e.g. a poem's rhyme scheme, a text's overarching metaphorical conceit) or external to the text (e.g. the standard grammatical system, conventional spelling, symbolic tropes common across a genre, etc.). Imagine, for example, a polka dot pattern in which one dot is larger, or a different colour from the rest, or a star shape, or missing. The interpretative significance of foregrounded features is explained by two hypotheses within stylistics. Firstly, readers interpret paralleled structures as having meaningful semantic connections, and so look for and construct those connections. This is Short's 'parallelism rule' (1996: 14). Secondly, Leech (1970) proposes the notion of 'cohesion of foregrounding' whereby readers look for meanings which make sense of a text's array of foregrounded features altogether. The foregrounded features are implicitly connected by a web of meaning, eliciting interpretations which can integrate their effects.

Foregrounding can operate at all of the levels of language as delineated within the DfE Key Stage 5 subject content for English Language (DfE 2014a). Table 4.1 lists the language levels and offers examples of kinds of foregrounding that can function at each level.

The language levels can provide a structure for a thorough analytical procedure: students can take a text and work through the levels systematically, examining the kinds of foregrounding at work in the text at each level. However, in order to maintain a focus on the relationship between language and effects, going beyond linguistic description, it is important that the analysis is grounded in and proceeds from interpretation. The beginnings of this kind of analysis of 'Prelude I' (intact, without blanked out words) are illustrated in Figure 4.1. Here, my initial interpretative impressions are outlined at the top, and foregrounded features are annotated, with the related/resultant interpretative effects in italics. The extract is only the first part of the poem, and so there is little scope

Table 4.1 Foregrounding at each language level

Phonetics, phonology and prosodics: how speech sounds and effects are articulated and analysed	Irregular representation/use of phonemes (e.g. semi-phonetic representation of accent), sound patterning
Lexis and semantics: the vocabulary of English, including social and historical variation	Irregular lexical form or function (e.g. neologisms, functional conversion); inconsistent/paradoxical meaning relations (e.g. metaphor, oxymoron, hyperbole)
Grammar (including morphology): the structural patterns and shapes of English at sentence, clause, phrase and word level	Transgression of norms of order and function (e.g. subject-verb inversion, adjective-noun inversion, enjambement, syntactic elision/deletion), deviation from norms of morphological structuring (e.g. irregular use of suffixes/prefixes, altered word boundaries)
Pragmatics: the contextual aspects of language meaning	Contravention of communicative norms re. context or participant relations (e.g. irony, sarcasm, rudeness, obscurity)
Discourse: extended stretches of communication within different genres, modes and contexts	Deviation from conventions of medium and discourse situation (e.g. beginning *in medias res*, mixing registers)

for themes to evolve, but a rich assortment of initial impressions is available. Investigating the foregrounding, deviation and parallelism in the text can help to account for and enhance some of these early interpretations.

Figure 4.1 offers only an initial sketching out of analytical thoughts about the extract, presenting just a few of the ways in which textual features are foregrounded through parallelism and deviation in order to illustrate this stylistic method, but full accounts of more detailed stylistic analyses of 'Prelude I' can be found in Short (1982) and Short (1996).

Attention to foregrounding, deviation and parallelism in literary texts can provide an avenue for enabling students to articulate and extend their linguistic understanding and for encouraging explicit consideration of relationships between features and effects, and between dynamic, integrated inference and holistic interpretation. Analysis of foregrounding, deviation and parallelism in non-literary texts can be equally insightful, however. For example, this kind of analysis of Emmeline Pankhurst's 'Freedom or Death' speech delivered in Connecticut in 1913 (available on various political and historical websites, as well as that of the *Guardian* newspaper) would draw out the way in which binaries run throughout her speech and are made prominent by parallelism. This pattern of binaries is set up by the title and its premise, but dominates at the level of discourse (where parallels are drawn between England and America, revolutionary men and revolutionary women, the rights of slaves and the rights of women, etc.), and at the level of syntax, where what is *not* the case is often introduced first, through negation, followed by what *is*, by comparison. Deviation within syntactic parallelism also creates cohesion and foregrounding within most paragraphs; syntactic patterns are established through repetition of structures two or three times, only for that structure to then be deviated from slightly to foreground (by that deviation) a paragraph's climactic point. The distribution and pragmatic rhetorical functions of the frequent pronoun use are also marked: 'we' women are distinguished from 'you', the American audience constructed as sympathetic, and 'them', the other(ed), unsympathetic Americans and British people. Emmeline Pankhurst's personal presence and the immediacy of the discourse situation (in speaking directly to her present audience) is also foregrounded by repeated use of the first person pronoun in self-reference and the second person pronoun in address and by repetition of other deictic elements (words which signal the relationship between the speaker and the context of utterance). Here is the opening of the speech:

> Mrs Hepburn, ladies and gentlemen: Many people come to Hartford to address meetings as advocates of some reform. Tonight it is not to advocate a reform that I address a meeting in Hartford. I do not come here as an advocate, because whatever position the suffrage movement may occupy in the United States of America, in England it has passed beyond the realm of advocacy and it has entered into the sphere of practical politics. It has become the subject of revolution and civil war, and so tonight I am not here to advocate

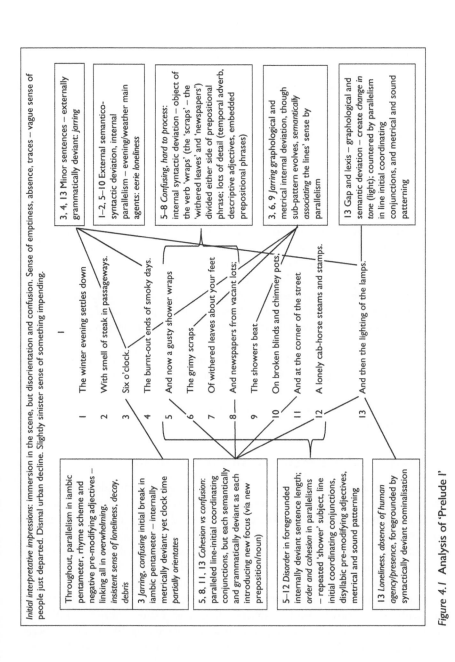

Initial interpretative impressions: immersion in the scene, but disorientation and confusion. Sense of emptiness, absence, traces – vague sense of people just departed. Dismal urban decline. Slightly sinister sense of something impending.

I

1 The winter evening settles down
2 With smell of steak in passageways.
3 Six o'clock.
4 The burnt-out ends of smoky days.
5 And now a gusty shower wraps
6 The grimy scraps
7 Of withered leaves about your feet
8 And newspapers from vacant lots;
9 The showers beat
10 On broken blinds and chimney pots,
11 And at the corner of the street
12 A lonely cab-horse steams and stamps.
13 And then the lighting of the lamps.

3, 4, 13 Minor sentences – externally grammatically deviant: *jarring*

1–2, 5–10 External semantico-syntactic deviation, internal parallelism – evening/weather main agents: *eerie loneliness*

5–8 *Confusing, hard to process:* internal syntactic deviation – object of the verb 'wraps' (the 'scraps' – the 'withered leaves' and 'newspapers') divided either side of prepositional phrase; lots of detail (temporal adverb, descriptive adjectives, embedded prepositional phrases)

3, 6, 9 *Jarring* graphological and metrical internal deviation, though sub-pattern evolves, *semantically associating* the lines' sense by parallelism

13 Gap and lexis – graphological and semantic deviation – create *change in tone* (light); countered by parallelism in line initial coordinating conjunctions, and metrical and sound patterning

Throughout, parallelism in iambic pentameter, rhyme scheme and negative pre-modifying adjectives – linking all in overwhelming, *insistent sense of loneliness, decay, debris*

3 *Jarring, confusing* initial break in iambic pentameter – internally metrically deviant: yet clock time *partially orientates*

5, 8, 11, 13 *Cohesion vs confusion:* paralleled line-initial coordinating conjunctions, but each semantically and grammatically deviant as each introducing new focus (via new preposition/noun)

5–12 Disorder in foregrounded internally deviant sentence length; *order and cohesion* in parallelisms – repeated 'shower' subject, line initial coordinating conjunctions, disyllabic pre-modifying adjectives, metrical and sound patterning

13 *Loneliness, absence* of human agency/presence, foregrounded by syntactically deviant nominalisation

Figure 4.1 Analysis of 'Prelude I'

woman suffrage. American suffragists can do that very well for themselves. I am here as a soldier who has temporarily left the field of battle in order to explain – it seems strange it should have to be explained – what civil war is like when civil war is waged by women. I am not only here as a soldier temporarily absent from the field at battle; I am here – and that, I think, is the strangest part of my coming – I am here as a person who, according to the law courts of my country, it has been decided, is of no value to the community at all; and I am adjudged because of my life to be a dangerous person, under sentence of penal servitude in a convict prison. So you see there is some special interest in hearing so unusual a person address you. I dare say, in the minds of many of you – you will perhaps forgive me this personal touch – that I do not look either very like a soldier or very like a convict, and yet I am both.

The passage opens with a suggestion of a shared time ('tonight') and place ('Hartford'), along with a negation, 'not to advocate reform', Pankhurst contrasting her purpose with that of her 'many' predecessors, whilst introducing (through that negation) the notion of reform. 'I am ... here', 'I ... come' and 'my coming' then together occur eight times in these opening sentences. The verb 'come' encodes a deictic directionality from a place away from the address-ees towards them, and 'here' encodes an immediate and shared spatial context. The final paragraph returns to this stress on immediacy and a shared space and context, opening with 'here I am', followed by three instances of 'I come'. The passage thus opens and closes with a stress on a sense of kinship and together-ness. There is much more to analyse even within these first few lines (the battle and journey metaphors used for the suffrage movement itself, the transitivity, the negation, etc.), contributing to this sense of kinship and creating several other strands of theme and effect. Stylistic analysis facilitates identification of these foregrounded elements and understanding of their integrated functioning to create particular rhetorical impact.

Stylistic analysis focusing on the dominant

Stylistic analysis of foregrounding, deviation and parallelism provides a means for a fairly comprehensive study of a text and the ways in which it makes meanings available to the reader. An alternative, more targeted approach is a stylistic analysis of the dominant – that is, of the linguistic feature which appears to dominate the workings of the text. Analysis of the dominant involves detailed investigation of the particular occurrences and functions of that feature in the text, often with comparison of uses of that feature in language more broadly (including in other texts).

Within Emmeline Pankhurst's 'Freedom or Death' speech, negation is arguably the (consistently) dominant linguistic feature, along with other modalised hypothetical grammatical structures (such as 'if' clauses). Leech (1983: 101) describes negative sentences as having 'a special purpose' in that a negative structure entails the positive counterpart, and markedly foregrounds its absence. A stylistic analysis of negation in the speech would investigate each of the tens of instances of grammatical negation and explore the co-text – what in particular is being negated and with what particular effects.

Students can be encouraged to seek out and compare other texts – literary and non-literary – which use grammatical structures of negation. For example, comparing works such as Edna St. Vincent Millay's 'If I, being born a woman, and distressed', Pablo Neruda's 'I do not love you except because I love you', Mary Elizabeth Frye's 'Do not stand at my grave and weep', and Stevie Smith's 'Do not!', 'Not waving but drowning' and 'I do not speak' can illustrate the different ways in which the linguistic strategy is employed to contribute to the communication of various themes. Students could perhaps go further to explore different texts which use conditional modalised structures to construct possible scenarios as Pankhurst does at several points in her speech, comparing, for example, Pankhurst's modalised embedded narratives with those of Rudyard Kipling's 'If' and his 'The Road not Taken'. Pankhurst's speech could also be compared with Kennedy's 1961 'Ask not what your country can do for you' speech, sections of which are dense with negation, or with Martin Luther King's 1963 'I have a dream' speech, which contains an interesting range of negations and conditional and hypothetical structures (not least its framing 'dream').

A stylistic analysis of the dominant in Linton Kwesi Johnson's poem 'Sonny's Lettah' (1979) would address the effects of its presentation of accent and dialect, which in the case of this text involves all of the levels of language. 'Sonny's Lettah' is a popular Key Stage 4 text and is available online at the British Library's Poetry Archive, which also usefully includes a recording of the poet reading his poem. Students first encountering this poem – especially when encountering it on the page without hearing it read – often report confusion and alienation, and associate its semi-phonetic spelling with the sub-standard, sub-canonical and a sense of illegitimacy. On second and third readings, and/or on hearing the poem read, students often find it more accessible, and become more engaged, begin to navigate its play with linguistic and structural conventions, and start to appreciate the political significance of its 'non-standard' style, which, arguably, lies most overtly in – is 'dominated' by – its externally deviant orthography.

A stylistic analysis would examine the detail of this semi-phonetic spelling to explore the nature and particular effects of its deviations from standard orthography. Here are lines 20–22 of the poem, as an example of its style:

> It woz di miggle a di rush howah
> wen evrybady jus a hosel an a bosel
> fi goh home fi dem evenin showah

The poem's spelling presents phonetic differences from standard English pronunciation, such as the various elided consonants, cutting the word-ending phonemes /t/, /h/, /d/ and often /ŋ/; the replacement of /θ/ with /t/ or /f/; the changes in vowel sounds such as the replacement of the 'ou' (/au/) of 'ground' with 'u', and of the 'e' ($/ə/$) of 'the' with 'i', for example. At the levels of lexis and grammar, students could investigate the use of 'fi' in the place of the prepositions 'to' and 'for', the use of 'pan' for 'on', and the use of the object pronoun in the place of the subject and possessive pronoun (e.g. 'him' for 'he' and 'his'), as well as the preponderance of present tense verb forms. Students could discuss the ways in which these deviations from standard English lexis and grammar work with the poem's sound patterning – its consequently unusual assonance, consonance and rhyme, along with its metrical schemes – and its other grammatical parallelisms (such as the parataxis in the second half). These explorations can provide a useful springboard for discussion of the ways in which the text negotiates the needs of political protest and the conventions of poetic discourse, the tension between communication and alienation, between a more authentic orthography and readability. The deviant spelling of 'Inglan' can be used to prompt debates around the notion of a 'standard' English, ownership of language, re-appropriations, etc. Add to the discussion the fact that the semi-phonetic spelling differs slightly between the version of the text originally published on the cover of the record on which the poem was first released as a performance, and the version of the text in Johnson's book of collected poems *Inglan Is A bitch*, published a year later (Sebba 1996), and issues around the lack of a standard, 'correct', authoritative written Creole can be explored. This in turn can lead to a contrasting of the preference, within the variety of written Creoles, to represent the sound of pronunciation with the priorities of modern standard English, and/or consideration of the cultural privileging of written literary forms within modern Western culture. The poem provides not only an interesting and engaging way into analysing phonetics within a specific medium and sociopolitical context, but also several avenues for broader linguistic debate.

At the levels of pragmatics and discourse, an alternative focus could be the form of the text and the competing discourse conventions of a poem, a letter and a story. The text's shifts in register are notable, from the rather formal opening, using polite expressions, into the more informally relayed story, and then back to a more formal close, while the storytelling itself invites analysis of its narrative structure. Assuming most students are initially unaware of the political context of the poem, this can be introduced at a tactical point, with a reflective discussion on the ways in which this contextual knowledge influences and develops interpretations of aspects of the poem, such as the presentation of agency, the speaker's evaluation of events, and so on.

As with Pankhurst's speech, further stylistic research and analysis could involve comparison of this text with others using similar techniques. Though use of semi-phonetic spelling to represent accent and dialect is rare in non-literary texts, it has long been employed in fiction and poetry – from William Wordsworth to Irvine Welsh – to portray regional and 'working class' voices (see Blake's survey *Non-standard Language in English Literature* [1981] for a period-based survey). Likewise, register and narrative structures in other letters can be rewardingly compared (including letters within literary texts, such as epistolary novels, Philip Larkin's poem 'Vers de Société', etc.).

Textual intervention

Textual intervention (Pope 1995), or re-creative writing, involves redrafting aspects of a text and critically comparing the interpretative effects created by the original and redrafted versions. It can be a very effective way of drawing attention to and more fully appreciating the interpretative significance of the linguistic nuances of the original text – of exploring the impact of the author's linguistic choices on the meanings available. Textual intervention can be targeted (at particular features and/or effects) or experimental. For example, a targeted intervention into 'Sonny's Lettah' might redraft the poem in Standard English, or use semi-phonetic spelling to represent a different accent and dialect, perhaps re-appropriating the narrative to that of a different kind of political arrest, or might re-order the narrative structure, or might recast the poem in the form of a regular, non-poetic letter. The same story might be told from the perspective of one of the arresting police officers, in the form of a police report, or might be presented as an article by a newspaper journalist. Each of these interventions would alter the sociopolitical implications of the text as a whole through the sum of smaller changes in interpretative effects at word and line level. A more experimental intervention could re-title the poem in various ways, exploring alternatives drawn from or associated with the poem's content (such as 'notn', 'Inglan', 'shame', 'ikkle Jim', etc.) as well as more random variants. The title could be switched with those of Johnson's other poems or with those of other poems of political protest. It could be shortened to 'Sonny' or 'Lettah'. The impact on the text – on what is foregrounded and backgrounded and on the meanings consequently available – could then be explored, which can lead to discussion about the discourse function of titles.

The reflective, comparative element of the textual intervention process is particularly pedagogically valuable. It pushes students to articulate precisely the nature of the linguistic features they are altering, to analyse relationships between these linguistic features and their contexts, and to identify and explain relationships between language and inference.

Principles of stylistic practice

The stylistic analyses of the texts explored in this chapter illustrate just some of the opportunities for learning about language that are possible through stylistics. Likewise, the four methods present a mere snapshot of a wide range of stylistic approaches to texts. Each of these approaches rests on a set of principles broadly shared across the discipline which are useful to keep in mind when doing stylistic analysis:

- Stylistic analysis can be 'applied to all texts, literary and non-literary, in which there are common … textual patterns' (Carter 1997: 113). Indeed, these common textual patterns to some extent undermine the distinction between the literary and non-literary (c.f. Fowler 1981 and Todorov 1981), and attention to textual commonalities (and differences) invites valuable critical reflection on genre constructions and distinctions between discourse types.

- Stylistics operates from the principle that the literariness of language is scalar, and that 'elements of literariness inhere in all constructed texts' (Carter 1997: 114). Even texts aesthetically (under)valued as transient and mundane manifest sophisticated linguistic crafting and complex and subtle interpretative effects worthy of stylistic attention.

- Stylistics views texts as social products, and, though often focused on linguistic minutiae, the overarching objective of analysing and understanding *interpretations* of language fundamentally entails attending to discourse contexts and interpretative communities.

- Stylistics aims to explore and enhance interpretations with explicit reference to language, to facilitate articulation and defence of interpretations on the basis of textual features, and to enable reasoned debates about available interpretations.

- The notion of availability of interpretations relates to the premise that a stylistic approach 'cannot be viewed simply as a recipe for "anything goes" but rather as an aid to recognition that meanings occur only by courtesy of the conditions or systems under which those meanings can be conferred' (Carter 1997: 206).

- Stylistics recognises interpretation as based in the relationship between the reader (in her/his particular sociopolitical context) and the text, thus arguments about the relative 'legitimacy' of interpretations are refocused on how far interpretations are grounded in the text and its relationship to the communally agreed conventions of communication and meaning. Idiosyncratic and personal associations evoked by a text's words and images should not be ignored, but should be recognised as less shared and less directly text-based interpretative possibilities.

Attending to these principles when using stylistics to explore language, reflecting on them, and encouraging student to do the same, will support a theoretically consistent and critically aware practice.

Recommended further reading

Mick Short's *Exploring the Language of Poems, Plays and Prose* (1996) and Paul Simpson's *Stylistics: A Resource Book for Students* (2014) provide particularly clear and systematic coverage of the field of stylistics. Mick Short (2005) also offers a freely accessible introductory online course, with suggested further reading to support progression through the topics. Ronald Carter and Peter Stockwell's *The Language and Literature Reader* (2012) presents key essays across the development of the discipline. For more on the principles of stylistic analysis, see Ronald Carter's *Investigating English Discourse* (1997) and Peter Stockwell's 'A stylistics manifesto' (2002).

References

Blake, N. F. (1981) *Non-standard Language in English Literature*, London: Deutsch.

Canning, P. and Simpson, P. (2012) 'Chicken and egg stylistics: From lexical semantics to conceptual integration theory', in M. Burke, S. Csábi, L. Weeks and J. Zerkowitz (eds) *Pedagogical Stylistics: Current Trends in Language, Literature and ELT*, London: Bloomsbury, pp. 24–44.

Carter, R. (1997) *Investigating English Discourse: Language, Literacy and Literature*, London: Routledge.

Carter, R. and Stockwell, P. (eds) (2012) *The Language and Literature Reader*, London: Routledge.

DfE (2014a) *GCE AS and A level Subject Content for English Language*, London: DfE, www.gov.uk/government/uploads/system/uploads/attachment_data/file/302109/A_level_English_language_subject_content.pdf (last accessed 5 October 2015).

DfE (2014b) *English Programmes of Study (National Curriculum in England)*, London: DfE, www.gov.uk/government/publications/national-curriculum-in-england-english-programmes-of-study (last accessed 5 October 2015).

Eliot, T. S. (2009) *Selected Works*, London: Faber and Faber.

Fowler, R. (1981) *Literature as Social Discourse: The Practice of Linguistic Criticism*, London: Batsford.

Johnson, L. K. (1979) 'Sonny's Lettah', http://www.poetryarchive.org/poem/sonnys-lettah (last accessed 5 October 2015).

Johnson, L.K. (1980) *Inglan Is A Bitch*, London: Race Today.

Leech, G. (1970) '"This Bread I Break": Language and interpretation', in D. C. Freeman (ed.) *Linguistics and Literary Style*, New York, NY: Holt, Rinehart and Winston, pp. 119–28.

Leech, G. (1983) *Pragmatics*, Harlow: Longman.

Pankhurst, E. 2014 [1913] 'Freedom or death', www.emersonkent.com/speeches/freedom_or_death.htm (last accessed 5 October 2015).

Pope, R. (1995) *Textual Intervention: Critical and Creative Strategies for Literary Studies*, London: Routledge.

Sebba, M. (1996) 'How do you spell Patwa?', *Critical Quarterly* 38(4): 50–64.

Short, M. (1982) '"Prelude I" to a literary linguistic stylistics', in R. Carter (ed.) *Language and Literature: An Introductory Reader in Stylistics*, London: George & Unwin, pp. 55–64.

Short, M. (1996) *Exploring the Language of Poems, Plays and Prose*, London: Longman.

Short, M. (2005) *Ling 131 – Language and Style*, Lancaster University, www.lancaster.ac.uk/fass/projects/stylistics/introduction/start.htm (last accessed 5 October 2015).

Simpson, P. (2014) *Stylistics: A Resource Book for Students*, 2nd edn, London: Routledge.

Stockwell, P. (2002) 'A stylistics manifesto', in S. Csábi and J. Zerkowitz (eds) *Textual Secrets: The Message of the Medium*, Budapest: Eötvös Loránd University, pp. 65–75.

Todorov, T. (1981) *An Introduction to Poetics*, Brighton: Harvester.

Chapter 5

Pragmatics

Billy Clark

Introduction

This chapter indicates some ways in which approaches to pragmatics have developed since the work of Paul Grice (1975, 1989) and presents ideas for classroom work based on activities which I have used in undergraduate programmes, as part of a BA programme in English Language at Middlesex University, with AS and A-level students in residential courses on English Language and Linguistics for the Villiers Park Educational Trust, and in workshops at schools.[1] These activities move beyond the work of Grice to reflect more recent developments in pragmatics. They also focus on pragmatic inferences involved in production (speaking, writing, editing, including group work in producing students' own texts) as well as in interpretation. They focus attention on students' own speech and (in particular, here) writing and so demonstrate a broader relevance for work on pragmatics.

Paul Grice's pragmatics

The work of Paul Grice has of course had a very significant influence on later work on pragmatics. His ideas still appear near the beginning of most classroom work on pragmatics at university and he is the main pragmatic theorist to feature in AS/A-level work in English. (Not all university academics are aware that he appears in work at school. I saw one university lecturer being surprised when she introduced 'a philosopher called Paul Grice' to a group of AS and A-level students and one of the students asked her 'Is he the dude with the maxims?'). Focusing on Grice in early work on pragmatics is appropriate for several reasons, including the influence of his ideas on more recent work, the fact that the central idea behind his approach is fairly easy to grasp, and the fun that students can have with examples.

The central idea is, of course, that we can explain how utterances are understood in context (how we can 'mean more than we say') by assuming that communicators are following a set of pragmatic principles when formulating utterances (and also in nonverbal communication, although this was not discussed by Grice). For Grice, the overarching principle is his 'Cooperative Principle' realised by a number of 'maxims'. Put simply, the maxims say that we should say enough but not too much, be truthful, be relevant, choose expressions which are appropriately ordered, and avoid formulations which are unnecessarily obscure, long-winded or 'ambiguous' (Grice uses 'ambiguous' here to mean vague or hard to disambiguate rather than as commonly used by linguists to refer to expressions such as *pen*, *bank* or *bug* which have more than one linguistically encoded meaning).

Two examples of a type often used to introduce Grice's approach are the exchanges in (1) and (2):

(1) Tourist approaching a stranger:
Do you know how I can get to the Tourist Office from here?
Stranger:
a. Walk.
b. First, raise one leg. Put it down a bit in front of the other. Raise your other leg ...
(2) Parent/carer:
How you getting on with your essay?
Student:
The weather's really changeable just now, isn't it?

Students can quickly see that answer (1a) does not give enough information (since the tourist already knows that walking will be involved in getting to the tourist office) and that (1b) gives both too much (since we know we need to move limbs to get there) and too little (since it says nothing about directions). Similarly, students can quickly see that the student's response in (2) is not directly relevant to the question. These exchanges can be used to demonstrate the maxims of quantity (which are about how much information is appropriate) and relation (about being 'relevant') and that utterances which do not observe the maxims at the level of what is said can nevertheless give rise to implicatures which do seem to conform to them (here, that the stranger is being rude, does not want to help, etc., and that the student does not want to talk about her essay).

Beyond Grice

While Grice is a good starting point for work on pragmatics, there are well-known problems with his approach, some of which are often discussed in classroom work, in student essays and in other exercises. University-level work often moves quickly on from Grice to look at more recent work. This is less common at AS/A-level. One aim of this chapter is to suggest ways in which students can be introduced to more recent approaches.

Students usually notice fairly quickly that Grice's maxims are a bit vague and hard to apply confidently to specific examples. Examples (1) and (2) illustrate this since they can be explained with reference either to the maxims of quantity or to the maxim of relation. All three responses seem to be explainable equally well by seeing them as giving either too much or too little information (quantity) or as not being 'relevant' enough (relation). This raises questions about whether all of the maxims are necessary and how the framework might be modified. It also demonstrates that, as Grice acknowledged, he has not defined the term 'relevant' clearly enough. These problems can lead naturally to discussion of more recent work (some suggestions about how to do this are given below).

Another problem, recognised to varying degrees, is that students tend not to share Grice's intuitions about specific examples. Of course, part of the problem is that Grice was living and working in an earlier age and in a particular context. For example, students are unlikely to be aware of the song 'All the nice girls love a sailor' which one of his examples (of overstatement/hyperbole) alludes to. In my experience, students also tend to have intuitions about Grice's examples which lead them in directions not followed by Grice. Very few students recognise quickly, for example, that saying *There is a garage around the corner* can implicate that the garage is likely to be open and able to sell petrol or that saying *I broke a finger yesterday* is likely to implicate that the finger is one of the speaker's own, biologically attached, fingers (memorably, a student once responded to my suggestion that 'you would assume it was the speaker's own finger, wouldn't you?' by telling me that 'sometimes people assume too much').

One example where intuitions do seem to follow the lines suggested by Grice is the famous reference letter for a former student who has applied for a philosophy job:

> (3) Dear Sir, Mr X's command of English is excellent, and his attendance at tutorials has been regular. Yours, etc.

Students tend to recognise quickly that the letter-writer here is implicating that the former student is not very good at philosophy (for Grice, because 'what is said' by the letter is not informative enough about this). Focusing on problems with intuitions can be a useful way to explore Grice's ideas more fully. The variation in intuitions can also be treated as a motivation to consider other approaches to pragmatics.

More recent approaches

AS/A-level specifications encourage a focus on problems with Grice's work but do not require consideration of other approaches. Teachers may decide not to consider other approaches because they perceive them as less accessible (both in that there are fewer sources which discuss them and that the ideas seem less straightforward). However, there are some fairly simple and potentially effective ways of introducing more recent approaches. This can help students to understand both Grice's approach and pragmatics more generally.

A natural step from discussion of questions about the number and nature of maxims is to move on to consider approaches which suggest a different number of maxims. The two most well-known theorists to have taken this approach are Larry Horn (1984, 2004, 2007) and Stephen Levinson (1987, 2000). Both have suggested replacing the maxims with a smaller number of principles. For reasons of space, I consider only Horn's approach here.

Horn proposes two principles. His 'Q', or 'Quantity', Principle says that speakers should provide 'sufficient' information and his 'R', or 'Relation', Principle says that speakers should not say more than is necessary:

(4) Q Principle:
     Make your contribution sufficient;
     Say as much as you can (given R)
(5) R Principle:
     Make your contribution necessary;
     Say no more than you must (given P)

At first glance, this might seem just to restate Grice's quantity maxims and in fact Horn does intend this. He suggests that a large part of what the maxims are designed to explain can be seen to follow from a tension between the need to give enough information and the need not to give too much. He sees the Q Principle as also subsuming two of the maxims of manner ('avoid obscurity' and 'avoid ambiguity') and the R Principle as also subsuming both the maxim of relation and another manner maxim ('be brief'). Horn's overall aim, then, is to simplify the framework and remove some of the unnecessary overlap among maxims.

A natural next step for work with students is to look at a range of examples and consider to what extent Horn's Q and R Principles do indeed provide explanations as effectively as Grice's larger number of maxims do. Key examples for Horn involve what are known as 'scalar implicatures' (because they relate to informational scales, often referred to as 'Horn scales'). Here are some examples:

(6) Billy: How do you think that seminar went?
     Annie: Some of the students seemed to enjoy it.
(7) Billy: Did you see what happened to the biscuits I left out?
     Annie: I ate two of them.
(8) Billy: Do you think Rachida will want a piece of cake?
     Annie: It's possible.

In (6), Billy is likely to assume that (Annie thinks that) not all of the students seemed to enjoy the seminar. In (7), Annie has said that she ate two of the biscuits. If she has eaten three or four or more, her utterance will still be true (if you eat three, you have to have eaten two) but Billy will assume that Annie is communicating that she ate exactly two and no more. In (8), Annie has said that it's possible that Rachida will want some cake. This would also be true if it is certain that she wants some. However, Annie will be taken to communicate that she thinks this is possible and not anything stronger such as that it is probable or certain. Horn explains these interpretations partly by assuming the existence of informational scales. These are sets of expressions ordered with respect to how much they communicate. The words *some* and *all* are on such a scale, since '*all X*' entails '*some X*'. Given this scale, and pragmatic principles (the Q and R Principle for Horn), the choice of an expression lower on a scale implicates the negation of an expression higher on the scale (all other things being equal). So saying that *some* students seemed to enjoy the seminar will be taken to implicate that not all of them did (if Annie thinks they all did, she should have given 'enough' information and said so). Incidentally, discussion of this example might also focus on Annie's choice of '*seemed to enjoy*' rather than '*enjoyed*'. Similar scales apply to numbers (saying you ate two biscuits can implicate that you did not eat more than two) and expressions such as *possible, probable* and *certain*. Horn's and Levinson's approaches are usually termed 'neo-Gricean' since they preserve the general Gricean idea of maxim-like principles which communicators are expected to conform to. By contrast, 'post-Gricean' pragmatic theories are those which do not assume anything maxim-like. The most well-known of these is relevance theory (Sperber and Wilson 1995; Clark 2013) which proposes instead two law-like generalisations about human cognition and communication. Relevance theory emerged partly from discussion of how to define the term 'relevant' and this has led to a fairly common misunderstanding which sees relevance theory as 'reducing the maxims to one'. In fact, while relevance theory preserves the Gricean notion that pragmatic principles constrain interpretations, it does not assume anything maxim-like. Instead, it proposes two Principles of Relevance which state that our general cognitive processes aim for a technically defined sense of 'relevance' and that recognising that somebody is communicating with us raises fairly precise expectations of this kind of 'relevance'.

The definition of relevance is based on the notions of 'positive cognitive effects' and processing effort. Roughly, a cognitive effect is a change in how an individual represents the world (e.g. discovering something new) and a 'positive' effect is one that it is worth having (because it leads to fuller or more accurate understanding of the world). The generalisation about cognition is that we are generally looking for positive cognitive effects. As I walk down the road in the morning, for example, I am on the lookout for things which might be 'relevant' in this sense, e.g. looking for traffic when crossing the road, noticing other people running as I get near my bus stop, suggesting that the bus is approaching, etc. The generalisation about communication is that we have more specific expectations when we recognise that someone makes clear an intention to communicate something to us. Here we expect enough effects to justify the effort involved in deriving them. Returning to example (2), for example, the student's utterance will be relevant if it helps the parent to understand something about how the essay is going. The parent can see that the student could be implicating that she doesn't want to talk about her essay because it is not going well. This interpretation will then meet the parent's expectations of relevance.

Key examples for relevance theory include utterances where we have to infer something which is a matter of degree. If someone is described as *tall*, for example, how tall do we take them to be? The answer for relevance theory is that we infer that they are tall enough for their height to be relevant. This will, of course, be different depending on who we are talking about and in what context. If a basketball player is described as *tall* we will have different expectations from when a jockey is described as *tall*. A particular jockey might be described as *tall* when discussion focuses on him or her as a jockey but as *not tall* in another context.

Here are three other examples:

(9) *(Billy is visiting Annie in her new flat)*
Annie: I'd offer you a cuppa but I'm out of milk.
Billy: I can nip out and get some.
Annie: The shops are a distance from here.

(10) Billy: Do you fancy a toastie?
Annie: I've eaten.

(11) Billy: I'm thinking of going to Orkney next summer.
Annie: I've been there.

In (9), Billy needs to work out how far 'a distance' is. The shops must, of course, be some distance or other from Annie's place and so Billy needs to work out how far. Relevance theory predicts that this will have to be far enough for it to be worth the effort involved in processing the utterance. Here, this must mean further than Billy had previously thought and far enough for him to rethink his offer to go and get some milk. The uses of a past tense form in (10) and (11) are interestingly different. In (10), Annie must be communicating that she has eaten recently enough not to want a toastie, so within the past hour or so. In (11), Annie's utterance will be relevant enough if she has been to Orkney at all and there is no need to think that this was quite recent. These interpretations can be explained on the assumption that Billy has fairly precise expectations about what he should be able to infer from each of Annie's utterances.

A natural step after looking at relevance theory would be to compare explanations of particular examples suggested by this approach with those of Grice, Horn and others.

Uses of the prefixes 'neo-' and 'post-' in describing these approaches provide an interesting example for pragmatics. Technically, all of the approaches just mentioned are 'post-Gricean' since they come after Grice's approach and presuppose his insights. The 'neo-Gricean' approaches are also 'neo-' in that they preserve (or 'renew') some key aspects of Grice's work. While the term 'post-Gricean' could be taken to refer to all of these approaches, in practice it is used to refer only to those which are 'post-but-not-neo-' Grice's work. This could be an interesting example to discuss in class. It would also be useful to discuss use of the 'neo-' prefix in other contexts, e.g. to describe 'neo-liberal' political ideas (this has an added interest, given varying usage of the term 'liberal').

Another direction in thinking about post-Gricean work would be to make explicit connections with work on im/politeness (this formulation is becoming more common, reflecting the idea that all utterances are more or less polite and that politeness and impoliteness raise the same range of issues, about how they are realised, their salience, deliberateness, etc.) The classic source for work on politeness is Brown and Levinson (1987) but ideas developed by Geoffrey Leech (1983) have also been important. Leech thought politeness phenomena so important that a Politeness Principle was required to operate alongside the Cooperative Principle and he suggested a range of new maxims relevant to this: tact, generosity, approbation, modesty, agreement and sympathy. To some extent, Leech's approach can be seen as opposite to those of Horn and Levinson, since he proposed a greater number of principles rather than a reduction.

Another possible focus in moving on from Grice's ideas is another perceived weakness in his approach. This relates to how he makes the distinction between semantics and pragmatics, and what he takes to be the scope of his maxims. Grice assumed that the maxims were involved in working out a subset of implicatures ('conversational' implicatures, which depend on context). Many recent approaches assume that pragmatic principles are also involved in working out explicit content (what Grice called 'what is said'). Consider, for example, the following exchange:

(12) Billy: Do you think Rachida will want to come out with us tonight?
Annie: She's got a bug.

Here Annie can be taken to implicate that she does not think Rachida will want to come out. Grice's approach could explain this with reference to the maxims of quantity or relation. However, Grice said nothing about how we work out what Annie has communicated directly here (what she 'said' in Grice's terms). To work this out, we need to decide who *she* refers to and what sense of *bug* Annie means. It seems clear that pragmatic principles are involved in this. We could, for example, say that Annie's utterance will not be informative enough (or 'relevant') unless we think Annie is referring to Rachida and that the sense of *bug* here identifies a kind of illness. Grice said nothing about this and also did not discuss other kinds of inference we regularly make in working out what he termed 'what is said', such as deciding how 'tall' we are saying someone is in a given context (as discussed above), or recovering ellipsed material (e.g. if I ask you whether Rachida is ill and you reply 'she is'). Looking at inferences involved in recovering 'what is said' is another useful way to develop discussion beyond Grice's initial ideas.

Pragmatics and production

The discussion so far, as with much discussion in pragmatics, has focused on inferences made in understanding utterances. However, it is clear that inferences are also made when formulating utterances. In her very useful textbook, Jenny Thomas (1995: 22) suggests that:

> meaning is not something that is inherent in the words alone, nor is it produced by the speaker alone, nor by the hearer alone. Making meaning is a dynamic process, involving the negotiation of meaning between speaker and hearer, the context of an utterance ... and the meaning potential of an utterance.

While Grice's approach does not come close to what Thomas suggests here, and most of his discussion focuses on what hearers and readers infer, he does make some remarks which suggest a role for inference in production. Here, for example, is his 'general pattern for the working out of a conversational implicature':

> He has said that p; there is no reason to suppose that he is not observing the maxims, or at least the Cooperative Principle; he could not be doing this unless he thought that q; he knows (and knows that I know that he knows) that I can see that the supposition that he thinks that q is required; he has done nothing to stop me thinking that q; he intends me to think, or is at least willing to allow me to think, that q; and so he has implicated that q.
>
> (Grice 1975: 31)

Notice, in particular, the reflexive nature of 'he knows (and knows that I know that he knows)'. It seems clear then that speakers make inferences about the inferences hearers will make (and that hearers make inferences about those speaker inferences). The rest of this chapter presents some activities designed to focus on inferences in production in general and in students' own speech and writing, with a particular focus here on writing.

Noticing inferences when speaking and writing

It is quite easy to help students notice that we make inferences when communicating with each other. This might begin with exercises like the following:

(13) Classroom Exercise: Spoken Communication
   a. Imagine you have just joined a seminar group at university. You missed the first session and have joined in week two. The tutor asks you to look at an example on last week's handout. You realise that you don't have a copy. Which of the following utterances do you think would be the best to use to ask for one?
      i. Excuse me. I'm really sorry but I don't have the handout from last time. Do you happen to have a spare one?
      ii. I haven't got that handout.
      iii. Got a spare copy of the handout? I've not got one.

b. Imagine you are cooking and your friend asks you what kind of sauce you have made. Any of the following three responses would be accurate:
  i. It's a Mornay.
  ii. It's called a Mornay. It's a Béchamel with cheese.
  iii. It's a kind of white sauce with cheese in it.

Which do you think you would choose? How would you decide? What risks are there in making a particular choice? Can you explain the risks by suggesting what your friend might 'infer' based on each one?

These exercises can be used to help students focus on inferences they make more or less consciously whenever they interact with others. They make inferences about how tutors will react to being addressed more or less politely and more or less directly. They make inferences about how much they need to explain particular ideas. In classroom discussions of the sauce example, we have considered the positive effects of presupposing your friend is knowledgeable, the risk of assuming more than they know, the positive effects of explaining something clearly, the risk of suggesting you think they know less than they do, and so on. Of course, these choices have to do with how much information we think is required in the context.

(14) Classroom Exercise: Email Introductions
Imagine you are an academic working in Middlesex University. You need to send an email to an academic you don't know at a university in Canada. The person you are writing to is a professor and her name is Salwa Sarhan. How do you think you would begin your email?

A benefit of this task is that students do not know much about the communicative conventions of academics. They do not know whether or not it is normal to start with 'Dear', whether to use a title and a surname or just a first name ('Dear Professor Sarhan' vs 'Dear Salwa'), and so on. When they imagine themselves formulating an email, they begin to think about inferences we all make more or less consciously when first addressing someone.

Considering examples like this helps students to think about pragmatic inference as something they do all the time, with varying degrees of awareness. Of course, the tasks raise their awareness and are likely to make them more effective communicators in a range of tasks. The next section presents tasks which focus more directly on writing and editing, helping to develop professional communication skills.

Writing and editing

There are many kinds of activities which can help students to explore the inferences involved in production and to think about them when developing their own practice. This section briefly presents exercises I have used in class which can easily be adapted and expanded to suit particular needs. They encourage students to reflect on their own writing, to develop their own written practice, and to become better communicators, while at the same time increasing their understanding of pragmatics. The nature of the specific tasks can, of course, be changed so that students work in a range of writing contexts.

(15) Classroom Exercise: Writing Task
You are late with the submission of an article you agreed to write for a student magazine. The article is due tomorrow. Write an email to the editor explaining why you are late, apologising for this, and asking if it will be OK to submit it one week after the agreed deadline.

Note that this exercise says nothing about pragmatics or inference.

(16) Individual Writing Exercise
Look at the email you wrote for the previous task. Identify one inference your reader (the editor) might make which you think it might be better to avoid. Rewrite your email to make this inference less likely.

At this stage, the student is being encouraged to think explicitly about inferences likely to be generated by the email and to edit the text to adjust the likelihood of a particular inference being made.

(17) Group Writing Exercise
You are a small team of copywriters. You have been asked to write copy for the front page of the website of a local gym. You are free to decide what kind of gym this is, what kind of audience you are aiming for, what the layout of the page will be (how many images, etc.) and anything else which you think is relevant. Before you write the copy, identify ONE inference you would like readers to make and ONE you would not like them to make. Prepare your copy with these aims in mind.

(18) Group Editing Exercise
Swap the copy you prepared previously with members of another group. Look at what the other group have produced. Identify one inference readers might make which you think it would be wise to avoid. Suggest a way of rephrasing the copy to make that inference less likely.

In working on tasks like these, students explore the effects of different kinds of formulations and relate these to inferences readers are likely to make. They then suggest ways to revise the texts and explore the effects of different choices. Here are two versions of possible copy produced for the gym website (these are not actual examples from student work but they illustrate some of the choices students often focus on):

(19) a. GetFitFast is delighted to announce a special offer during the month of July. Membership fees are reduced by 50% during this period. Simply arrange an appointment with one of our advisers to take advantage of this offer.
       b. We're delighted to announce a special offer this month. Membership is half price. Come and talk to us now and we'll help to get you moving.

Students might begin by discussing these two versions in general terms, e.g. pointing out that (19a) is more formal while (19b) is more friendly. Discussion then moves on to the effects of specific choices, such as the choice of the gym name as opposed to the first person plural pronoun as the subject of the first sentence, reference to *the month of July* as opposed to *this month*, 50% as opposed to *half price, one of our advisers* as opposed to *us*, and so on. As students work through these tasks, their communicative abilities develop along with their ability to reflect on and explain their writing choices. As well as developing their written communication skills, students are developing their understanding of ideas from pragmatics and the more general relevance of pragmatics in formal and informal communication.

Conclusion

The presence of work on pragmatics at AS and A-level has been very successful in helping students understand how we understand each other in context and in preparing for work at university. These activities also useful since they develop skills which are drawn on in A-level questions involving transcript analysis and interpretation of reader positioning in written texts. The suggestions in this chapter aim to help teachers move beyond Grice in looking at more recent work on pragmatics, to consider production as well as interpretation, to develop understanding of pragmatics while working on a range of practical tasks, and to develop students' own communicative skills. They also demonstrate the more general relevance of ideas from pragmatics. Students I have worked with have enjoyed this work and their sense of development as professional communicators in a range of contexts.

Further reading

There are lots of useful introductory textbooks on pragmatics. Chapman (2011) is a useful introduction which discusses Grice, neo-Gricean approaches, relevance theory, politeness and impoliteness. Clark (2013) is an introduction to relevance theory which also contains a substantial chapter on Grice and some discussion of neo-Gricean approaches. Thomas (1995) is still a useful introduction to pragmatics, including discussion of Grice and politeness, with a huge number of entertaining and useful examples. Important publications on im/politeness include Culpeper 1996, 2005; Bousfield 2008; Culpeper *et al.* 2003. Clark and Owtram (2012) discusses classroom work on inference and writing.

Note

1 Some of these ideas were presented in a workshop at the National Association for the Teaching of English conference at Stratford in 2013. I am very grateful to participants there for participation and useful feedback and also, of course, to all of the students who have taken part.

References

Bousfield, D. (2008) *Impoliteness in Interaction*, Amsterdam: John Benjamins.

Brown, P. and Levinson, S. (1987) *Politeness: Some Universals in Language Usage*, Cambridge: Cambridge University Press.

Chapman, S. (2011) *Pragmatics*, Basingstoke: Palgrave Macmillan.

Clark, B. (2013) *Relevance Theory*, Cambridge: Cambridge University Press.

Clark, B. and Owtram, N (2012) 'Imagined inference: Teaching writers to think like readers' in M. Burke, S. Czabo, L. Week and J. Berkowitz (eds) *Current Trends in Pedagogical Stylistics*, London: Continuum, pp. 126–41.

Culpeper, J. (1996) 'Towards an anatomy of impoliteness', *Journal of Pragmatics* 25: 349–67.

Culpeper, J. (2005) 'Impoliteness and entertainment in the television quiz show "The Weakest Link"', *Journal of Politeness Research* 1(1): 35–72.

Culpeper, J., Bousfield, D. and Wichmann, A. (2003) 'Impoliteness revisited: With special reference to dynamic and prosodic aspects', *Journal of Pragmatics* 35: 1545–79.

Grice, H. P. (1975) 'Logic and conversation', in P. Cole and J. Morgan (eds) *Syntax and Semantics 3: Speech Acts*, New York, NY: Academic Press, pp. 41–58. Reprinted in Grice (1989: 86–116).

Grice, H. P. (1989) *Studies in the Way of Words*, Cambridge, MA: Harvard University Press.

Horn, L. R. (1984) 'Towards a new taxonomy for pragmatic inference: Q- and R-based implicature', in D. Schiffrin (ed.) *Meaning, Form, and Use in Context: Georgetown University Round Table on Languages and Linguistics*, Washington DC: Georgetown University Press, pp. 11–42.

Horn, L. R. (2004) 'Implicature', in L. R. Horn and G. Ward (eds) *The Handbook of Pragmatics*, Oxford: Wiley-Blackwell, pp. 3–28.

Horn, L. R. (2007) 'Neo-Gricean pragmatics: A Manichaean manifesto', in N. Burton-Roberts (ed.) *Pragmatics*, Basingstoke: Palgrave Macmillan, pp. 158–83.

Leech, G. (1983) *Principles of Pragmatics*, London: Longman.

Levinson, S. C. (1987) 'Minimization and conversational inference' in J. Verschueren and M. Bertuccelli-Papi (eds) *The Pragmatic Perspective*, Amsterdam: John Benjamins, pp. 61–129.

Levinson, S. C. (2000) *Presumptive Meanings*, Cambridge: Cambridge University Press.

Sperber, D. and Wilson, D. (1995) *Relevance: Communication and Cognition*, Oxford: Wiley-Blackwell.

Thomas, J. (1995) *Meaning in Interaction: An Introduction to Pragmatics*, London: Routledge.

Chapter 6

Attitudes to language change and variation

Dan Clayton

Introduction

Language is not a fixed and unchanging object of study, but rather a fluid and diverse means of communication that changes to suit the needs of its users and varies according to its users' identities and situations. Any study of English language at secondary level needs to acknowledge this and recognise the scope for debate about language that exists among users of English. For example, given that new words are added to the Oxford Dictionary every year provoking either a media fanfare of amusement or a hoot of derision, and words such as 'onesie', 'thanx' and 'selfie' were added to the Scrabble dictionary in May 2015, you might imagine that secondary school pupils would be interested to see why those words have been included and what they reflect about the nature of a changing society. Indeed, young people do seem to be profoundly interested in the language around them (Willoughby *et al.* 2015) but perhaps in a more intuitive than linguistic way.

Likewise, if English is not just about the study of books (as argued by Stubbs [1982], among others), then perhaps the discussion of different regional and social varieties of English and the ways that English has spread around the world could be a central feature in the study of our language which is, after all, spoken as well as written.

As this chapter outlines, such questions go to the heart of what makes English Language such a potentially fascinating subject to study and teach at secondary level, but they also identify some of the problems the subject faces as it negotiates the competing demands of government, awarding bodies, students' own experiences and the knowledge and understanding of those who teach the subject.

In this chapter I will look at the places that exist in the secondary English curriculum for students to explore and debate the nature of English and the many different media representations of the English language and its users. I will examine areas such as Standard and non-standard English, the changing nature of English as influenced by such forces as popular culture, immigration and technology, before considering how students and teachers can make use of the language around them to inform their understanding of what language is, why we use it in the ways we do and why it leads to such strong feelings.

In the first section, I will focus on where this topic sits within existing versions of the Key Stage 3 and 4 and A-level English curricula. In subsequent sections, I will look at some of the key debates around Standard and non-standard English and language change respectively, considering how these topics offer teachers the chance to expand and challenge students' knowledge about language, before moving on in the final section to look at how approaches from the field of critical discourse analysis can be used by students to explore the different media representations of variation and change.

The curriculum

At A-level, the study of language change and variation has been central to the philosophy of the subject since its first appearance in 1985 (for more detail see Hawkins 1984; Giovanelli, 2014). The latest incarnation of the AQA English Language A-level lays out its stall as follows:

> Students will study the key concepts of audience, purpose, genre and mode and will explore language in its wider social and geographical contexts. Students will study varieties of English within the British Isles. This part of the subject content also requires students to study social attitudes to, and debates about, language diversity.
>
> (AQA 2015: 14)

The AQA English Language A-level for first teaching from September 2015 encourages students to consider the history, importance and role of Standard English but also the different non-standard varieties associated with wider social and regional use. The specification also encourages a critical discussion of attitudes to variation and change in its 'Language Discourses' section:

> Students will study a range of texts that convey attitudes to language diversity and change. The texts studied will include those written for non-specialist audiences ... Students will explore how texts are produced to convey views and opinions about language issues.
>
> (AQA 2015: 18)

Clearly then, A-level English Language is a natural home for such discussions, but what kind of preparation do students from Key Stages 3 and 4 have for the demands of this? Do students studying English at secondary level encounter any of the ideas around why some forms of English are more highly respected than others, why the written form is generally more prized than the spoken, or how many regional and social forms are denigrated and vilified?

The status of this debate in secondary English is a somewhat vexed one. Between 2007 and 2013, an understanding of the different opinions and attitudes towards non-standard English, regional and individual varieties and the changing nature of English over time was part of the National Curriculum Programme of Study for Key Stage 4. Under the heading of 'Language, structure and variation', the document stated:

> The study of English should include, across speaking and listening, reading and writing
>
> a) spoken language variation and attitudes to use of standard and non-standard forms
> b) the ways in which language reflects identity through regional, social and personal variation and diversity
> c) the differences between spoken and written language in terms of vocabulary, structure and grammar
> d) the importance of sentence grammar and whole-text cohesion and their impact in writing
> e) the development of English, including its development over time, current influences, borrowings from other languages, origins of words and the impact of technology on spoken and written communication
> f) the importance and influence of English as a global language.
>
> (QCA 2007: 96)

Indeed, in the explanatory notes on language and identity for the 2007 Key Stage 4 Programme of Study, specific mention is made of '... accent, dialect, idiolect, lexical change, varieties of standard English such as Creole, occupational variation, and differences in language use according to age or gender'.

Since 2013 however, the new programmes of study have offered a stripped down version of the curriculum and now the only references to different varieties of English appear as 'analysing some of the differences between spoken and written language, including differences associated with formal and informal registers, and between Standard English and other varieties of English' (DfE 2014: 6). While this streamlining reflects a more general reduction in content across documents for the 2013 qualifications (from twenty-two pages in the KS3 Programme of Study in 2007 to six pages in 2013 – not counting the eighteen pages of the latter devoted to a glossary of key grammatical terms), the absence of any reference to the changing nature of English, language's links to identity and attitudes to language use would all suggest that this part of the subject has been sidelined. Coupled to this, a renewed focus on full, closed texts (i.e. not to be taken into the examination) and pre-1914 literature squeezes wider language study out of the picture.

In a review of the Key Stage 4 Programme of Study written by the well-respected educational charity, the English and Media Centre, exactly these concerns were raised.

> The draft makes no requirements for pupils to learn about how language actually works. While they are given some opportunity to reflect on their

own written work, to study grammar and to consider the differences between formal and informal spoken registers, there is little provision made for studying language as a fluid, dynamic medium. Specifically it makes little or no provision for the following:

- A study of the history of English
- Recognition of the changing nature of English across time and across forms and modes of communication
- The discrete study of different forms of spoken language
- Engagement with debates around Standard English and its appropriate use in particular contexts
- Recognition of the many varieties of English in use (there is not even reference to 'dialect' or 'accent')
- Engagement with any aspects of sociolinguistic study.

(McCallum, 2014)

So, if this is the case, where is the space in the Key Stage 3 and 4 curricula to address sociolinguistic topics? It could be argued that the narrow focus on Standard English and the (to some extent understandable) concentration on teaching students to use this prestige form in their written work prevents any genuine discussion or exploration of non-standard varieties. However, it could also be argued that by studying non-standard forms, students might acquire a more fully rounded grasp of the standard and a better understanding of its uses. What is Standard English after all, but a prestige dialect? How can such a dialect be explained and characterised without looking at the other dialects amongst which it sits and from which it was selected? As I have argued elsewhere:

> studying the forms and structures of regional varieties, street slang, text messaging and spoken language alongside the forms and structures of standard English – as a basis for mastering standard vocabulary, spellings, punctuation tricks, style-shifts, rhetorical devices and grammatical patterns – should be seen not as dumbing down, but as a positive move into the real language of real speakers.
>
> (Clayton and Hudson 2010)

Standard and non-standard English

Most discussions of language varieties at this level presuppose an existing understanding of Standard English. But what is Standard English? Trudgill (2001: 117–28) describes it as follows:

> Standard English is often referred to as "the standard language". It is clear, however, that Standard English is not "a language" in any meaningful sense of this term. Standard English, whatever it is, is less than a language, since it is only one variety of English among many. Standard English may be the

most important variety of English, in all sorts of ways: it is the variety of English normally used in writing, especially printing; it is the variety associated with the education system in all the English-speaking countries of the world, and is therefore the variety spoken by those who are often referred to as "educated people"; and it is the variety taught to non-native learners. But most native speakers of English in the world are native speakers of some nonstandard variety of the language ...

If, as Trudgill suggests, Standard English is being taught to the majority of students almost as a second language, perhaps a starting point for any teaching of the dialect should be an acknowledgement of the other varieties that are available and spoken by the majority of UK pupils. As Williams (2007: 401) notes:

> in spite of its high status, research suggests that Standard English is the home dialect of approximately 15% of the population of UK (Trudgill 2001). It is estimated that between 9% and 12% of the population speak Standard English with a regional accent, while RP (Received Pronunciation), the prestigious accent associated with the aristocracy and those who have received a public school education, is the native accent of only 3% of the UK population.
>
> (Trudgill and Cheshire 1999)

Williams (2007: 402) goes on to argue that:

> Most working-class children therefore start school speaking a dialect other than Standard English. In spite of the efforts of linguists to educate the public about the regular, rule-governed nature of NS dialects, the view that such dialects are inferior and full of errors, 'bad' or 'incorrect' English still prevails, even among some speakers themselves.

It would therefore make sense – both from the perspective of teaching Standard English and showing the nature of the rule-governed variations of non-standard varieties – to work in Key Stage 3 on some of the building blocks of Standard English: morphology and syntax. Of course, it does not need to be introduced as such with the somewhat daunting metalanguage, but pupils will already have a grounding in grammatical terminology from their work at Key Stage 2 which involves (among many other things) being able to differentiate between main and subordinate clauses, label pronouns and understand plural rules. If students look at examples of non-standard English such as those listed below, attention can be drawn to the characteristics of both Standard and non-standard forms.

We done that yesterday.
We was walking back from assembly.
She's like 'What you doing that for?' and I'm like 'No reason'.
I didn't say nothing.

By focusing on areas such as the use of participle forms ('done') rather than past tense forms ('did'), subject verb agreement, historic present tense and multiple negation, some sense of the differences between Standard and non-standard can be developed. Whether or not students at Key Stage 3 need to be able to linguistically describe these points is a moot point, but the social significance of these variations is something that can open up some interesting discussion, taking the study of language beyond *features* (what it is called) and into *functions* (what it means and what it is used for). While not strictly appearing under the linguistic heading of syntax or morphology, the interesting pragmatic use of 'like' as a quotative (a device to report or paraphrase others' words or actions) can also shed some light on changing speech patterns across the generations. Older speakers would be much more likely to use 'I said' or 'I went' as quotatives than younger speakers, to whom 'I was like' is almost second nature (Buchstaller 2011).

Students could be asked to think about whether or not they or their family members use these forms in speech and, if so, whether or not they would use them in formal written work as well. Some discussion about the expectations of spoken and written English, the significance of context and perhaps even the idea of linguistic register might then be introduced at this stage. Developing this into a student-led investigation about the non-standard language used in a particular area could be the next stage of such work, setting up a useful conceptual and methodological grounding for the language investigation coursework carried out at A-level by many students.

Beyond the specifics of word classes, morphology and syntax, the wider debates about Standard and non-standard English offer teachers and students a rich source of material. Between 2008 and 2013, at least five schools or academy chains have attempted to implement what have been referred to as 'slang bans'.[1] In the case of Colley Lane School in Halesowen (in the Black Country area of the British Midlands) this 'slang ban' took the form of a sheet sent home to parents, listing what were termed 'the top ten most damaging phrases' used by children, including:

> 'they was' instead of 'they were'
> 'I cor do that' instead of 'I can't do that'
> 'ay?' instead of 'pardon?'
> 'Gonna' instead of 'going to'

While some of these 'damaging phrases' fall under the remit of local dialect, others might be termed casual spoken style or simply as features of pronunciation, but none appears to be genuine slang. In discussing the efficacy or otherwise of such bans, students can start to explore the strongly held attitudes many have towards language and identity.

Hitchings (2011: 19) makes the point that 'arguments about English have always been coloured by feelings about tradition, the distribution of power, freedom, the law and identity' and this kind of discussion often sheds light on more than just the language that is under scrutiny. By assessing their own attitudes to some of these non-standard or innovative usages, and perhaps by investigating others', light can be shed on many of the links between language practice and social identity.

English beyond the UK is an area covered in the AQA English Language A-level under the topic of *World Englishes* and it is here again that the potential to explore the rich variety of the language becomes apparent. By looking at American, Australian, West African, Caribbean and Indian Englishes, students can explore not only the adaptations made to English as it has spread around the world and the new forms that have seeded in various territories, but the range of uses to which it has been put. Once again, by focusing on variation, attention can also be drawn to the norms of Standard English.

> Mi live inna Jamaica
> I like hot hot curries
> I have many informations

With examples like this, students can look at subject and object pronouns (e.g. 'I' and 'me'), reduplication for emphasis (and perhaps how Standard English might use adverbs instead) and the use of count and non-count nouns. The emphasis here is not on a 'deficit model' (for example, Bernstein 1965), where Standard English is classed as superior and non-standard as 'sub-standard', but in acknowledging variety and its use in different contexts and locations and for different functions. By focusing on world varieties, students can also learn about the past and future of English. How did it reach other countries? How has it been used? How does it relate to the different varieties spoken and written in the UK? How might it develop in the future? In more multicultural classrooms in the UK, students themselves can become resources, drawing on their parents' or grandparents' home languages to show how English is used around the world. I will return to the media discourses around World Englishes, and particularly American English, in the last part of this chapter.

Language change

The English Language is in a permanent state of change, perhaps even 'evolving at a faster rate now than at any other time in history because of social media and instant messaging' (Sutherland 2015). A report in the *Telegraph* (Anon 2015) argues that terms like 'FOMO' (Fear of Missing Out), 'On fleek' (looking perfect) and 'Bae' (either a shortening of the term of endearment 'baby' or an acronym for 'Before Anyone Else') have entered the language so quickly that they have bypassed an entire generation. New words can provide a fruitful area of study at A-level as part of a focus on Language Change, with students exploring the potential of language to reflect the changing nature of society (for example,

Ayto 1999; Green 2014) or by examining word formation processes such as combining, shifting of meaning, shortening, blending, borrowing and creating (Algeo 1991; Metcalfe 2002). But, as with language variation, concerns about change are widespread and well documented. Aitchison (2013), Hitchings (2011) and Greene (2011) all provide insightful coverage of the discourses of decline, degeneration and disease that often accompany commentaries on language change and can provide some useful starting points for work across the age range in secondary English. While the language used to promote such discourses around the topic – and the ways that students can analyse and interpret them – are something we will look at in the final part of this chapter, the ideas related to change are the key focus here.

At A-level, the nature of language change is a key topic of study across all the awarding bodies' specifications, but work on change is sparser at Key Stages 3 and 4 and often either based on the immediate language context of a studied literature text or looser project work on the history of English, with little overt linking of this to language analysis. Again, finding space for genuine language study for its own sake can be difficult but rewarding. Some more specific areas are discussed here.

Word meanings change over time, sometimes very quickly, and these semantic shifts can provide a number of different approaches to students as early as Key Stage 3. Selecting a set of words that have undergone change and tracing their etymology over centuries introduces students to the processes of pejoration and amelioration, broadening and narrowing. Choosing the right words is probably the key aspect of this; Hughes (1989) offers a useful set of words that have undergone various forms of semantic change over the centuries, including 'noble', 'gentle', 'villain' and 'slave'. Robinson (2010) provides an interesting case study on different generations' understanding of word meanings, focusing on different perceptions of the word 'awesome'. An approach such as this gives students the chance to select their own words to research (terms such as 'gay', 'sick', 'hard', 'heavy' and 'wicked' might be possible choices) and for them to carry out a similar study among their own peer groups and families. In addition, students could measure how different individuals and generations feel towards more recent meaning changes, introducing a basic insight into some of the issues explored in much more depth as part of A-level or at degree level.

For a more immediate focus on the impact of language change, resources such as Jonathon Green's piece for BBC News Magazine on slang through the twentieth century (Green 2014), Kerry Maxwell's Buzzwords archive for MacMillan Dictionaries[2] and Ayto's *Twentieth Century Words* (1999) all offer a rich and varied range of examples of new words from different years. Taking a sample of these and asking students to group them under different word formation processes and thematic links can open up both the morpho-syntactic and lexico-semantic possibilities of new words in a way that stimulates discussion about why these words come into being, what they tend to label and how they are formed. Students will be able to look at processes such as blending, compounding and affixation, applying their understanding of word formation to new words as well as being able to see such processes at work in much older forms.

Language and technology is discussed at more length in Chapter 8, but many of the recent changes to English have been driven by technology, both in its use of new terms to describe new technologies and in its function as a medium through which language changes are transmitted, often using web-based software. Hitchings (2011: 293) describes some of the language of the web as demonstrating 'creative misspellings and wilful, playful grammatical goofs, as well as multitudes of new words ... more linguistic variety, a greater degree of hybridity, a faster propagation of novelties'. For students, brought up in a time of mass web technology use – from mobile phone text messaging, to social networking such as Facebook, Twitter, Snapchat and WhatsApp through to chat via online games – language is constantly shaped by technology. Once again, teachers can draw on the language resources of students themselves to explore how language is changing and what people feel about it.

Two short activities can help illustrate the usefulness of technology in addressing this topic. The first involves a short investigation task that could be carried out with any age group from Key Stage 3 to A-level. Setting a series of short messages (as suggested below) to be conveyed from one person to another, students can look at how different age groups use a technology such as texting, comparing the differences in vocabulary and grammatical choices, as well as the use (or otherwise) of some of the affordances of the form, such as abbreviations, emoticons and emojis, and hyperlinks.

Arrange to meet a friend at 8pm outside the Arts Centre in town.
Arrange to call a friend later in the morning to discuss when you will work on your project together.
Ask how a friend is after they have got back from holiday and you have not communicated with them for a week.

A task such as this is easy to set up and could involve the participants texting or messaging an agreed telephone number or address. The messages can then be compiled and analysed.

In the second task, moving away from the words themselves and into attitudes surrounding change, the notions of prescriptivism and descriptivism can be introduced, discussed and critiqued at different stages. The simple distinction between the two positions – prescriptivism as a belief that language should be controlled and regulated and descriptivism as a belief that language usage should be described and studied rather than judged – is one that is opened up to more detailed scrutiny at A-level. At Key Stages 3 and 4 it is probably enough to introduce the competing ideas that language can be controlled and that language simply changes regardless of what some people might want to do to it.

One approach is to use a simple cline from prescriptive to descriptive, a set of statements about language change, young people's slang and regional/social variation (such as those below) and ask students to first discuss and think of examples to illustrate each statement, and then arrange the statements along the line, discussing which views are which and pointing to the language choices that help them reach their conclusions. This can be a fairly gentle introduction to discourse analysis before the more heavyweight terminology is rolled out at a later stage, but it is a simple and effective way of engaging students in thinking about how language is used to describe language.

> A changing language reflects a changing and progressing society.
> New words are helpful because they describe new objects and ways of living.
> Language change causes confusion and disruption.
> Some accents are better than others.
> Slang is a useful way of bonding with other people.
> Slang is a broken form of English and should be avoided at all times.
> Text language is quick, easy and fun.
> Text language is a threat to standards of English.

In developing these basic ideas for younger students, teachers might also be able to make use of some of the ideas put forward by Aitchison (1996) on how changes to language are viewed through a prescriptive mind-set: the models of the damp spoon, the crumbling castle and the infectious disease.

Discourse analysis

While students' own thoughts and feelings about dialect, youth sociolect and other non-standard varieties are a key component of any discussion of this topic, it is also important to look at media representations of these areas. It is here that another area of linguistic study can be brought to bear: that of critical discourse analysis (CDA). By using approaches first suggested by Fairclough (1989, 1995) and developed by (among others) Talbot *et al.* (2003) and Hyatt (2005), students can begin to use their grasp of analytical frameworks to explore the underlying positions and stances adopted by text producers, opening up the discourses around language variation to close critical scrutiny.

Media representations of youth slang, regional variation and change invariably present and contribute to discourses of decline, decay and collapse. Greene (2011) describes twin discourses of 'declinism' and 'sticklerism' manifested in many prescriptive proclamations about language change, while Barras (2014) and Trousdale (2007) identify mainstream media stereotypes in the representation of regional and social varieties.

CDA can be applied by students, at different levels of detail depending on their competence with language analysis techniques, to pinpoint and interrogate some of these stereotypes and questionable representations. In many ways, this draws together some of the 'bigger picture' topics discussed earlier in this chapter and the more detailed and finely tuned text analysis of stylistics (as discussed in more detail in Chapter 4). Two short examples serve to illustrate the power of CDA to uncover stance and positioning in texts about Multicultural London English (MLE) as identified and discussed by Torgersen *et al.* (2006) and the supposed 'Americanisation' of English.

Example one is taken from an article by Lindsay Johns (2011) from the *London Evening Standard* about the changing nature of London English and the influences of different social and ethnic groups on this change:

> The English language is an incredibly rich inheritance. Yet it is being squandered by so many young people of all races and backgrounds. Across London and other cities it is increasingly fashionable for them to speak in an inarticulate slang full of vacuous words such as "innit" and wilful distortions like "arks" for "ask" or tedious double negatives.

Example two is from an article by Matthew Engel (2010) about American English in the UK in the *Daily Mail*:

> It adds nothing to Britain's language but it's here now, like the grey squirrel, destined to drive out native species and ravage the linguistic ecosystem.

By focusing very closely on just a few short passages (and moving on to the full texts at a later stage), students can start to think about the link between the kind of language used to describe language (often their own language) and some of the wider discourses about language that have been outlined earlier. Here, for example, in the first extract, language is presented as an 'inheritance', perhaps something solid and tangible to be passed from one generation to another. Is that what language is really like? Then Johns goes on to describe the language as being 'squandered' and replaced by slang. Again, is this true? Moving to the second extract, the animal metaphor might be explored, with the presentation of the outsider destroying the native ecosystem being explored. Students can start to question the ways in which arguments about language are presented to us and begin to join the dots between wider feelings and attitudes to language and the language that shapes those views.

Notes

1 See http://englishlangsfx.blogspot.co.uk/2013/11/dialect-dissing.html for discussion
2 Available at http://www.macmillandictionary.com/buzzword/recent.html

References

Aitchison, J. (1996) *The Language Web: The Power and Problem of Words: The 1996 BBC Reith Lectures*, Cambridge: Cambridge University Press.
Aitchison, J. (2013) *Language Change: Progress or Decay?*, 4th edn, Cambridge: Cambridge University Press.

Algeo, J. (1991) *Fifty Years Among the New Words: A Dictionary of Neologisms 1941–1991*, New York, NY: Cambridge University Press.

Anon (2015) 'English language is changing faster than ever, research reveals', *Telegraph*, 1 May, www.telegraph.co.uk/news/newstopics/howaboutthat/11574196/new-forms-of-social-media-terms-which-parents-do-not-understand.html (last accessed 4 October 2015).

AQA (2015) *AS and A-level English Language*, www.aqa.org.uk/subjects/english/as-and-a-level/english-language-7701-7702 (last accessed 4 October 2015).

Ayto, J. (1999) *Twentieth Century Words*, Oxford: Oxford University Press.

Barras, W. (2014) 'Accentuate the positive? Media attitudes to accent variation', *emagazine* 65: 54–5.

Bernstein, B. (1965) 'A sociolinguistic approach to social learning', in J. Gould (ed.) *Social Science Survey*, London: Penguin.

Buchstaller, I. (2011) 'Quotations across the generations: A multivariate analysis of speech and thought introducers across 5 decades of Tyneside speech', *Corpus Linguistics and Linguistic Theory* 7(1): 59–92.

Clayton, D. and Hudson, R. (2010) 'Give us a golden age of grammar', *Times Educational Supplement*, 8 November, www.tes.com/article.aspx?storycode=6062360 (last accessed 4 October 2015).

DfE (2014) *English programmes of study: key stage 4*, London: DfE, www.gov.uk/government/uploads/system/uploads/attachment_data/file/331877/KS4_English_PoS_FINAL_170714.pdf (last accessed 4 October 2015).

Engel, M. (2010) 'Say no to the get-go! Americanisms swamping English, so wake up and smell the coffee', *Daily Mail*, 29 May, www.dailymail.co.uk/news/article-1282449/Americanisms-swamping-English-wake-smell-coffee.html (last accessed 4 October 2015).

Fairclough, N. (1989) *Language and Power*, London: Routledge.

Fairclough, N. (1995) *Critical Discourse Analysis: The Critical Study of Language*, London: Routledge.

Giovanelli, M. (2014) *Teaching Grammar, Structure and Meaning: Exploring Theory and Practice for Post-16 English Language Teachers*, London: Routledge.

Green, J. (2014) '10 slang phrases that perfectly sum up their era', *BBC Magazine*, 19 May, www.bbc.co.uk/news/magazine-27405988 (last accessed 1 October 2015).

Greene, R. L. (2011) *You Are What You Speak: Grammar Grouches, Language Laws and the Politics of Identity*, New York, NY: Delacorte Press.

Hawkins, E. (1984) *Awareness of Language: An Introduction*, Cambridge: Cambridge University Press.

Hitchings, H. (2011) *The Language Wars: A History of Proper English*, London: John Murray.

Hughes, G. (1989) *Words in Time: Social History of English Vocabulary*, London: John Wiley and Sons.

Hyatt, D. (2005) 'A Critical Literacy Frame for UK secondary education contexts', *English in Education* 39: 43–59.

Johns, L. (2011) 'Ghetto grammar robs the young of a proper voice', *Evening Standard*, 16 August, www.standard.co.uk/news/ghetto-grammar-robs-the-young-of-a-proper-voice-6433284.html (last accessed 4 October 2015).

McCallum, A (2014) 'KS4 English curriculum proposals: A backward step', 18 October, www.englishandmedia.co.uk/blog/ks4-english-curriculum-proposals-a-backward-step (last accessed 1 October 2015).

Metcalfe, A. (2002) *Predicting New Words: The Secrets of their Success*, Boston, MA: Houghton Mifflin Company.

QCA (2007) *English Programme of Study for Key Stage 4*, London: HMSO.

Robinson, J. A. (2010) 'Awesome insights into semantic variation', *Cognitive Linguistics Research* 45: 85–109.

Stubbs, M. (1982) 'What is English? Modern English language in the curriculum', in R. Carter (ed.) *Linguistics and the Teacher*, London: Routledge, pp. 137–55.

Sutherland, J. (2015) 'ICYMI, English language is changing faster than ever, says expert', *Guardian*, 1 May, www.theguardian.com/science/2015/may/01/icymi-english-language-is-changing-faster-than-ever-says-expert (last accessed 1 October 2015).

Talbot, M., Atkinson, K. and Atkinson, D. (2003) *Language and Power in the Modern World*, Edinburgh: Edinburgh University Press.

Torgersen, E., Kerswill, P. and Fox, S. (2006) 'Ethnicity as a source of changes in the London vowel system', in F. Hinskens (ed.) *Language Variation – European Perspectives, Selected Papers from the Third International Conference on Language Variation in Europe (ICLaVE3)*, Amsterdam: John Benjamins, pp. 249–63.

Trousdale, G. (2007) 'Accent and dialect – Northern English', *emagazine* 35: 31–4.

Trudgill, P. (2001) *Sociolinguistic Variation and Change*, Edinburgh: Edinburgh University Press.

Williams, A. (2007) 'Non-standard English and Education' in D. Britain (ed.) *Language in the British Isles*, Cambridge: Cambridge University Press, pp. 401–16.

Willoughby, L., Starks, D. and Taylor-Leech, K. (2015) 'What their friends say about the way they talk: The metalanguage of pre-adolescent and adolescent Australians', *Language Awareness* 24(1): 84–100.

Chapter 7

Phonetics and phonology

Ian Cushing and Sam Hellmuth

Introduction

Phonetics and phonology share a common interest in all things 'phon', that is, related to the *use of sounds in language*. This definition shows the wide scope of the subject, ranging from study of the individual vowels and consonants used to form words in a particular language or dialect, to sounds which stretch over longer chunks of speech (stress, rhythm and intonation). Phoneticians/phonologists study speech sounds in diverse contexts and for diverse reasons. How do infants develop the ability to speak their mother tongue in a few short years? How do speakers manage turn-taking in an orderly fashion in naturally occurring conversation? How are listeners able to form an opinion about where a speaker is from (and about their age and gender) from just a few seconds of speech?

In simple terms, phonetics can be defined as the actual *production and perception* of speech sounds by humans, whereas phonology is about the *systems* of sounds in use in a particular language or context. Signed languages can also be described in terms of articulatory gestures (defined in terms of hand shape or position in the signing space) which are combined in non-random, systematic ways to form meaningful units of language (signs). Although most work on phonetics and phonology operates in the speech modality, many of the basic conceptual questions can equally be asked and answered with regard to signed languages. We will focus on spoken languages here, but provide some recommended reading on the phonetics and phonology of signed languages at the end of the chapter.

The questions that phonetics and phonology allow us to explore are inherently interesting and form part of the everyday linguistic experience of all of us, including our students. More importantly, these are questions which could or should feature fairly high up on the agenda of most teachers of secondary English. The link is perhaps the most obvious at Key Stages 4/5 – since questions of this type appear on GCSE and A-level specifications, under headings such as Accents and Dialects, Child Language Acquisition and Language Change – but also at Key Stage 3, as we will demonstrate. Later on in this chapter we therefore provide an overview of some recent research in phonetics and phonology which sheds new light on common lay assumptions (or 'myths') about language in these areas.

Before that, in the next section, we suggest practical ways to introduce 'phon' concepts already in the Key Stage 3 classroom, as preparation for later stages, and in light of increasing awareness of the importance of Knowledge about Language. The National Curriculum for English refers to a number of 'phon'-related concepts: digraphs, phonemes, sound to spelling relationships, homophones, homonyms, accents, vowels and consonants.

Why bring more 'phon' into the secondary English classroom? A first strong argument is that it can be a lot of fun, if students are equipped with just a few basic tools of phonetic and/or phonological analysis. A second strong argument in favour of raising awareness of phon concepts is that it unlocks an almost unlimited resource, namely the speech patterns of those involved in the lesson. One of the great attractions about doing linguistics is that the 'data' (the raw material that research linguists analyse) is all around us, all the time (this is true for all areas of linguistics of course, and is not the preserve of phonetics/phonology). Each and every classroom in the UK is home to a group of students who i) have acquired or are acquiring English, whether as a first or additional language (and both of those are equally interesting) and ii) who differ from each other in their speech patterns (even the most homogenous classroom will reveal some sociophonetic variation). Teachers seeing students – and them seeing themselves, and each other – as a valuable and rich source of linguistic data offers limitless engaging opportunities in the classroom.

Using phonetics and phonology in the Key Stage 3 classroom

A lesson on applying phonology and phonetics in a Key Stage 3 classroom may begin in a number of ways. The following sections outline what some of these ways might look like, and they are designed to be suggestive rather than didactic – these are not 'lesson plans' as such, but ideas to adapt and explore.

Using the phonetic alphabet and transcribing speech

Objectives:

- To understand some of the differences between speech and writing
- To understand how speech sounds can be written using the phonetic alphabet

Encouraging students to think explicitly about phonetics and phonology in day-to-day environments, without necessarily the need to use any specific or new linguistic terminology, is a good way to begin exploring concepts in the classroom. Open questions, such as the following, should begin to draw out the speech/writing distinction:

- Why do accents exist and where do they come from?
- Do we write the same way we speak?

- What are some of the differences between speech and writing?
- How many different sounds are there in the English language?
- If accents are a spoken feature of language, then how could we write them down?

The final question here leads naturally on to introducing the phonetic alphabet, and the fact that there are more sounds than letters in English (which could also be an opportunity to discuss phonetic and non-phonetic writing systems). Here might be a good spot to show some very basic transcription, with an explanation (and class rendition!) of the individual phonemes, and how in some words, each phoneme is represented by a single letter:

speech   writing
[kæt]   <cat>

Next, displaying a word where the relationship between sound and spelling isn't quite so straightforward might help to illustrate the complexities of phonetic transcription – such as in:

speech   writing
[kɒf]   <cough>

Here, the idea is to elicit that English spelling is not always purely phonetic, and that often there is a mismatch between the number of letters and sounds in a word. This kind of information is useful for the next activity, when students begin to do some phonetic transcription of their own.

In the English phonetic alphabet, the (roughly) forty-four sounds each have their own symbol, just like the twenty-six letters of the written alphabet do. Students could then be given a copy of the alphabet and the chance to look over some of the more 'strange' looking symbols: [ʒ], [æ] and [ŋ] for example, and then explore some of the subtle differences in sounds, for example the voiceless/voiced differences as in pairs such as [s z] and [θ ð]. Asking students to produce these sounds whilst holding their finger and thumb on the neck where the vocal folds are and 'feel the vibration turn on and off' always produces enlightened reactions!

Students could then have a go at transcribing some individual words themselves, such as their name and their hometown. At this point, the classroom should be filled with noise – emphasis should be given to the importance of 'sounding out' the words, not thinking of the spellings. Many students will make errors, such as using two phonemes for double letters, as in [hæɹɹiː] for <Harry>, yet these can be seen as opportunities to discuss further mismatches between spelling and sound. A further activity, of students identifying the first sound in the following words: *judge, pneumonia, church, though, thought* and *yellow*, will open up further discussion for sound to spelling relationships.

Once a class has been given the tools for phonetic transcription, a suggested follow-up activity is discussing accents and how the phonetic alphabet can be used to represent these. Beginning with an example of accent variation in the UK – the north/south distinction between [ɡɹæs] and [ɡɹɑːs] (grass) is likely to be well-known, and could be a starting point for attitudes and perceptions about accents. Depending on the demographics of the class, students may well speak with a variety of accents themselves, and once again we encourage teachers to see the class itself as a rich and valuable resource.

Exploring further

- Students record a natural conversation and then transcribe the speech – what happens? For example, does the glottal stop [ʔ] replace [t] in medial and final positions? Does [f] replace [θ]? Why might these patterns emerge?
- Students research and listen to a variety of UK accents, including how world languages have influenced them. The British Library *Sounds Familiar?* archive (available at: http://sounds.bl.uk/Accents-and-dialects/ BBC-Voices) provides a rich resource for this kind of work.

Phonoaesthetics and the 'beauty' of sounds

Objectives:

- To understand that sounds can be judged to be 'pleasant' or 'unpleasant'
- To understand some of the phonetic characteristics of 'pleasant' and 'unpleasant' sounds

Phonoaesthetics is the study of inherent 'beauty' or 'pleasantness' (euphony = 'pleasant' sounds; cacophony = 'unpleasant' sounds) within speech sounds, and a lesson on phonoaesthetics would aim to answer the following question: why are certain words deemed to be more pleasant sounding than others? Teachers might ask their students to 'rate' the list of words given below (or, even better, ask them to contribute words themselves that they think sound particularly pleasant or unpleasant) on a scale of pleasantness. For the time being, phonoaesthetic judgements should disregard semantics (the meaning of words), and focus only on the phonological structure and acoustic properties.

conscience, jump, cellar, duty, jazz, chinchilla, rasp, lumpy, gravel, pomegranate, mingle

Once the scale has been made, students could think and discuss *why* they have made the decisions they have. Do they see certain phonemes appearing more regularly than others (transcribing the words phonetically and creating some numerical data will help them to spot this)? What about the number of syllables, and where the stressed syllable falls? What about the distribution and pattern of vowels and consonants? What about the frequency of voiced and voiceless sounds? What about the types and complexities of articulatory movements involved? How does the inclusion of semantics affect the rating of pleasantness?

Following on from this, introduce a piece of research conducted by David Crystal (1995) (http://www.davidcrystal.com/?fileid=-4009). Crystal analysed a corpus of words judged to be pleasant sounding and found that certain phonemes appeared more than others. The relative frequencies are shown here (where phonemes towards the left appeared more frequently):

Consonants
/l, m, s, n, r, k, t, d, f, b, v, ŋ, w, g, z, ʃ, h, tʃ, dʒ, j, θ, ʒ, ð/
Vowels
/ə, ɪ, æ, e, iː, aɪ, əʊ, ʌʊ, ɒ, eɪ, uː, ɔː, aː, ɜː, ɪə, aɪə, aʊ, ʊə/

In addition, Crystal found three further features that correlated with pleasantness: 1) polysyllabic words, 2) the stressed syllable at the beginning of a word and 3) high variance of manners of articulation. So according to the patterns in the corpus, a word such as *malleable* has a pleasing phonoaesthetic quality – because it uses conso-nants and vowels towards the more 'pleasant' end of the scale, it is polysyllabic and has different manners of articulation. Here would be a good opportunity for students to draw some comparisons between their and Crystal's findings – what similarities and differences were found – and are there explanatory reasons for these?

Exploring further

- Creating nonsense words that are phonoaesthetically pleasant or unpleasant, and using these in a creative writing activity. Using the data a class have generated from their own phonoaesthetic judgements would be particularly interesting.
- Analysing poetry for its use of phonoaesthetic sounds, thinking about why certain sounds are used and how they help to construct meaning.

Stylistic phonetics

Objectives

- To understand how stylistic phonetics can help with the interpretation and understanding of meaning
- To understand how writers use phonetics and phonology self-consciously to construct meaning

Stylistic phonetics deals with the analysis of sounds in literature, using tools and approaches from linguistics. This section brings together the classroom ideas explored earlier and although we give an extract of a poem here – *The Harvest Moon*, by Ted Hughes (2003) – it is hoped that the tools we have explored could be applied to a number of texts. This is the first stanza of the poem:

> The flame-red moon, the harvest moon,
> Rolls along the hills, gently bouncing,
> A vast balloon,
> Till it takes off, and sinks upward
> To lie on the bottom of the sky, like a gold doubloon.
> The harvest moon has come,
> Booming softly through heaven, like a bassoon.
> And the earth replies all night, like a deep drum.

As with all poetry, reading the text aloud is the most illuminating way to appreciate the sounds. Students might then begin spotting three sound patterns in the poem using different coloured pens or a similar key: **long vowels**, <u>short vowels</u> and *diphthongs*. The resulting patterns should look like this:

> The flame-red moon, the harvest moon,
> Rolls along the hills, gently bouncing,
> A vast balloon,
> Till it takes off, and sinks upward
> To lie on the bottom of the sky, like a gold doubloon.
> The harvest moon has come,
> Booming softly through heaven, like a bassoon.
> And the earth replies all night, like a deep drum.

This process enables students to do a number of things. Firstly, identifying the different types of vowels allows for a more specific analysis and interpretation. Secondly, it highlights repeating patterns and clusters of data – important for strengthening interpretative ideas. Finally, it makes them aware that different types of vowels can contribute to meanings in different ways.

'Zooming in' on the long vowels will help to put this into perspective. They are found within: *moon, harvest, balloon, doubloon, booming, through, bassoon, earth, all* and *deep*. The repeating [u:] is particularly salient. But why this sound? Here, it is important to start thinking about the bridge between sound and semantics and for students to think about *why* poets would make highly self-conscious, stylistic choices. When considering that poetry is primarily an oral tradition, the significance of sound choices in poetry becomes an important thing to explore.

Words such as *moon, bassoon, doubloon* and *booming* are all associated with large-scale objects, massiveness or loud, deep sounds. The same 'qualities' can be mapped onto the vowel sound. A vowel is a maintainable sound – one that can be lengthened for as long as the speaker's breath allows. It typically has a low resonant frequency, much like the sound of a 'booming bassoon'. These acoustic properties help to contribute to the meaning of the poem, and to create the image of a big, round, dominant moon in the night sky.

A look at the effects of certain diphthongs reveals further indication of conscious, stylistic choices. The gliding vowel sounds such as [aʊ] in *bouncing* and [əʊ] in *rolls* both indicate movement and transition – in the same way that the moon appears to move across the sky, captured through the poet's choice of verb processes.

Further phonoaesthetic judgements could be made about certain words, in what is a generally uplifting and gratifying poem, providing opportunities for exploring the relationship between sounds and semantics.

Recent research in phonetics and phonology: AS/A2 curriculum links

The primary purpose of research is to broaden our knowledge of how the world works. This often has the effect of showing that our current understanding of things, based on earlier research, needs further thought. In this section we take three generalisations related to 'phon concepts' – which are all at least partially accurate – and show how recent research sheds interesting new light on them.

'Child-directed speech is simpler than adult-directed speech.'

The phenomenon of child-directed speech (CDS) or 'motherese' is likely to feature in teaching of child language acquisition for AS/A-level English Language. It is well established that, in cultures which use it,[1] CDS differs systematically from adult-directed speech (ADS). For example, CDS is produced at a higher pitch than ADS, with shorter utterances and longer pauses (Fernald et al. 1989), and tends to contain a more limited subset of the lexicon and simpler syntax than ADS (Snow 1995). This apparent 'simplification' is usually assumed to provide the listening infant with an easier set of input data to work on, in his/her task of acquiring the sound system, vocabulary and grammar of the language they are hearing.

If this is the case, then we might also expect caregivers to simplify their speech to children by cutting out some of the sociolinguistically driven phonetic varia-tion we find in ADS. However, research on Tyneside English (spoken in and around Newcastle, i.e. 'Geordie') found a much more complex picture (Foulkes et al. 2005). The accent feature they were looking at was Tyneside 'glottalisa-tion' of [p], [t] and [k] between two vowels. A Standard Southern British English (SSBE) pronunciation of 'water' has a [t] in the middle: [wɔːtə], but in Tyneside you will hear a glottalised (t) [ʔt] in the middle: [wɔːʔtɐ]. This contrasts with complete replacement of the (t) with a glottal stop in 'Cockney' English and now also in many urban British accents: [wɔːʔə] (Watt and Allen 2003).

In their ADS data, the researchers found 90 per cent local (t) and 10 per cent standard (t). In the CDS data this changed dramatically to just 36 per cent local (t) and 59 per cent standard (t). A closer look showed that mothers used more standard (t) with younger children and more local (t) with older children, suggesting that CDS becomes more adult-like over time. Why would early CDS be produced with *more* variation in it than is found in ADS? This does not fit with the idea that the goal of CDS is to be simpler than ADS.

A possible answer lies in another finding of the study, which was that mothers used much more standard (t) if their child was a girl (70 per cent); mums of boys used standard vs local (t) roughly equally (48 per cent vs 45 per cent). This makes sense if set alongside the fact that, in adult Tyneside speech, women generally use less local (t) than men do (Foulkes and Docherty 2006); the variation in CDS resembles the sociolinguistic variation children need to learn to handle in the future. A similarly complex picture was found in research on CDS in Scottish English in relation to content and context (Smith et al. 2007). They looked at the diphthong [au], pronounced as standard (house) [haʊs] vs local (hoose) [huːs], and found that the local variant (hoose) was used by parents more during playtime (78 per cent) than in more formal contexts such as when trying to discipline the child (31 per cent) or teach something (19 per cent).

Overall, these results suggest that children acquire sociolinguistic properties of language alongside strictly grammatical or structural properties (Foulkes 2010): a child doesn't just need to learn how to pronounce (t), she also needs to learn when to produce which sort of (t) in her community.

Exploring further

Identify examples of CDS in transcriptions/recordings from CHILDES (e.g. data from Manchester: http://childes.talkbank.org/browser/index.php?url=Eng-UK/ Thomas/) or obtain some recordings from family members. Are there any dialect-specific features in the CDS?

'All children produce the same sounds in babble.'

In the early stages of phonological development, the majority of children go through roughly the same stages of development, from babble, through the one-word stage, on to longer utterances, as is widely taught. In the case of babble, the production of repetitive rhythmic vocalisations emerges at around the same time that children start to display other repetitive rhythmic movements, such as kicking (Thelen 1981). The consonant sounds that are easiest to produce in this way are 'stop' sounds (in English: [p b t d k g m n ŋ]) which require only an opening/ closing jaw movement. It turns out that the first words children produce generally feature the same sounds that the child has been using in babble. But how does the child know which words to try to say first? Does the child actually know which words will be too hard for him/her?

A recent study (DePaolis et al. 2011) tested the possibility that the sounds used most often in a child's earliest babble (in the sounds they *produce*) will also be the sounds that the child pays most attention to in words that they hear (in the sounds they *perceive*). First, the babble in recordings of twenty-eight children (average age ten months) was phonetically transcribed. The researchers then identified each child's preferred stop consonants: most used [t]/[d], but others used [b]/[p] or [k]/[g]); some children were more advanced and had mastered more than one of these pairs of sounds. Next, the children came into the baby-lab for an experiment. The child sat on the mum's lap, in a sound-proofed booth. The researchers played recordings of different children's 'stories' made up of five sentences, each with one or two invented 'nonsense' words in them. There were four different stories, each containing lots of occurrences of one pair of stop consonants (only one of which the baby would already be producing) or [f]/[v]. The recordings were played through a speaker to the child's left or right, changing the side at random each time a new story started, and the child's reactions were recorded on video. Each time a new story started the child generally turned towards the source of the sound, so this was known as a head turn preference task. The researcher counted how many seconds the child kept his/her head turned towards the source of the sound as a measure of attention to the type of sound featured in that story.

The researchers found that the children who were only using one consonant type with high frequency in their babble tended to listen more to the story with that sound in it, whereas those who were more advanced in their development and already using more than one consonant type paid attention longer to stories containing the stops that they were *not yet* producing. The researchers interpret this as the child with more diverse babble experience being ready to listen to what is new, while the child just beginning to use a single consonant frequently finds it exciting to hear it in the speech he or she hears. Overall, this suggests that children are not just learning to *produce* sounds during the babble stage. Instead, during this stage the child is picking up on the match between the sounds she produces and the sounds she perceives in the speech around her – and what she perceives is affected by what she is able to produce.

Exploring further

Find some babble in transcriptions/recording from CHILDES or obtain recordings from family members. Try transcribing a short section of babble using the IPA: how easy/difficult is it? Are there any group(s) of sounds that the child uses more than others? Read more about this study at http://www.yorkphondev. org/projects/current-projects/production-and-perception/

'You can identify an individual speaker's voice using software.'

In *Goldeneye* (1995), James Bond is hiding at the entrance to a Russian military base. We see an officer approach and speak his name into a voice-activated door access system. A speech waveform flickers across the access screen, then a matching waveform is found and the door slides open.[2] Scenes like this create the impression that individuals can be automatically identified from a 'voiceprint' – just like fingerprints – but this is not (yet) how things work in real forensic cases.

Some portrayals in fiction are closer to the truth though. In a recent episode of the US legal drama 'The Good Wife' (Season 6, Episode 9), a legal firm obtains a leaked copy of a FBI wire tap (covert recording) in which a suspect is heard to say he wants one of the lawyers killed, within the week. The clock is ticking. Is the threat real? Or has the FBI faked the wire tap to persuade the frightened lawyer to hand over privileged information? The firm's investigator offers to get the wire tap checked out – she will ask one of her 'sound guys' to take a look. First, he performs an authenticity check and confirms that the recording doesn't contain any edits; the FBI hasn't just taken bits of other recordings and edited them together to say something different. This is a reasonable approximation of the type of work that can be carried out using speech analysis software (such as Praat, http://www.praat.org). Now, the lawyers want to know if the person on the tape is really who the FBI says it is. The sound guy says he can do it if they provide some sample recordings of the suspect's voice for comparison. The task thus becomes speaker *comparison*, rather than speaker *identification*, which is indeed how such cases are analysed: known samples of speech from the suspect are compared to the disputed samples of speech and a conclusion reached as to how likely it is that the recordings are of the same person. In 'The Good Wife' the 'sound guy' came up with a conclusion (it *was* the suspect in the wire tap) within an hour or so – which isn't completely realistic – but how did he do it?

How do forensic speech experts work in cases of speaker comparison? It is as yet very rare for experts to rely purely on an automated system (French and Stevens 2013); most international experts use a combination of acoustic analysis (using speech software such as Praat) and the auditory impression of the forensic expert, and this combination is the currently recommended norm in the UK.

So what are the experts listening out for? Current UK practice advises that the analysis must determine not only the degree of *similarity* between the known and disputed samples of speech by looking at a range of features, but also how *distinctive* the features are that are found in both recordings (French and Harrison 2007; French et al. 2010). The two speech samples may contain features that are very similar, but if these are all features that almost anyone of that age/gender/ dialect would produce in their speech, the evidence does not provide strong support that the samples are likely to have been produced by the same person.

Although some of the features in a particular case may relate to a speaker's habits of grammar or lexis, very often the key features in a case relate to phonetics and phonology. It is vital in such cases to be able to establish what dialect is being spoken in both samples and, if they are found to be in the same dialect, to know what the 'typical' features are in that dialect. This is where the study of accents and dialects hits harsh reality: in criminal cases. The basic task of identifying the typical features of regional accents (as in the Key Stage 3 activities described above), lies at the heart of all UK forensic speaker comparison work. Automated voice-matching software is as yet only found in fiction – instead, we use trained linguists with skills in phonetics and phonology for this task.

Exploring further

Set up a dummy speaker comparison case by creating samples from same/different speakers (e.g. edit speech from different parts of the same recording vs different recordings). Students can work through the steps: i) what dialect does the speaker have in each sample? ii) are the two samples similar (if not, what is different? e.g. is the pitch higher/deeper?); iii) if the samples are similar, what features of speech in the samples are typical of the speaker's dialect and which are not? Overall, students could reflect on how good they were at identifying when it was/wasn't the same speaker, and what factors might lead to a 'bad decision'? (e.g. think about size of the available speech samples). Read some real forensic speaker comparison case studies here: www.york.ac.uk/language/postgraduate/taught/forensic-speech-science/#tab-4

Recommended reading and resources

Useful tools

- Phonetic symbols for use in documents: http://ipa.typeit.org/ or http://weston.ruter.net/projects/ipa-chart/view/keyboard/
- A phonetic chart for English: http://learnenglish.britishcouncil.org/en/apps/sounds-right

Further reading

- Recommended introductory texts are: Ogden (2009), McMahon (2002) and Knight (2012).
- There is a useful two page summary of the phonetics of signed languages (based on American Sign Language) in the chapter on phonetics in Fromkin *et al.* (2013). A recent article on child language acquisition of BSL phonology is Morgan (2006): http://openaccess.city.ac.uk/364/
- Summaries of recent research on English Language can be found on the following blogs:
  - http://linguistics-research-digest.blogspot.co.uk/
  - http://languagelog.ldc.upenn.edu/nll/

Sources of spoken language data

- British Library *Sounds Familiar?* archive: http://sounds.bl.uk/Accents-and-dialects/BBC-Voices

- International Dialects of English Archive (IDEA): www.dialectsarchive.com/
  - Designed as a tool for actors to hear how different dialects sound, this archive provides downloadable sound files of dialects of English from all over the world.
- Intonational Variation in English (IViE): www.phon.ox.ac.uk/IViE
  - Recordings with adolescent speakers of English from nine locations in the UK. The 'free conversation' and 'narrative' recordings are probably the most useful.
- Speech Accent Archive: http://accent.gmu.edu/
  - Recordings of the same text read by second-language learners of English from all over the world and also by speakers of different dialects of English. Useful 'generalisations' highlight the errors/features found in each recording.
- Child Language Data Exchange System (CHILDES): http://childes.talkbank.org/browser/
  - This site is aimed at researchers, so is not as user-friendly as the other sites, but it does contain a large volume of transcripts of child data. Click on one of the 'Eng-UK' transcripts to see what is available; some transcripts have accompanying sound files. Some CDS data can be found in and around the children's speech.

Notes

1 CDS appears only to be observed in cultures in which children are 'expected to be active communicators early in life'; lack of CDS does not delay acquisition of grammatical competence (Ochs and Schieffelin 1995: 80).
2 You can see the scene at about 3.54 in this YouTube clip: www.youtube.com/watch?v=ToWUx1cfDgU

References

DePaolis, R. A., Vihman, M. M. and Keren-Portnoy, T. (2011) 'Do production patterns influence the processing of speech in prelinguistic infants?', Infant Behavior and Development 34: 590–601.

Fernald, A., Taeschner, T., Dunn, J., Papousek, M., de Boysson-Bardies, B. and Fukui, I. (1989) 'A cross-language study of prosodic modifications in mothers' and fathers' speech to preverbal infants', Journal of Child Language 16: 477–501.

Foulkes, P. (2010) 'Exploring social-indexical knowledge: A long past but a short history', Laboratory Phonology 1: 5–39.

Foulkes, P. and Docherty, G. (2006) 'The social life of phonetics and phonology', Journal of Phonetics 34: 409–38.

Foulkes, P., Docherty, G. and Watt, D. (2005) 'Phonological variation in child-directed speech', Language 81(1): 177–206.

French, P. and Harrison, P. (2007) 'Position Statement concerning use of impressionistic likelihood terms in forensic speaker comparison cases', with a foreword by Peter French and Philip Harrison, International Journal of Speech Language and the Law 14: 137–44.

French, P. and Stevens, L. (2013) 'Forensic speech science', in M. J. Jones and R. A. Knight (eds) The Bloomsbury Companion to Phonetics, London: Bloomsbury, pp. 183–97.

French, P., Nolan, F., Foulkes, P., Harrison, P. and McDougall, K. (2010) 'The UK position statement on forensic speaker comparison; a rejoinder to Rose and Morrison', International Journal of Speech Language and the Law 17: 143–52.

Fromkin, V., Rodman, R. and Hyams, N. (2013) An Introduction to Language, Boston, MA: Cengage Learning.

Knight, R. A. (2012) Phonetics: A Coursebook, Cambridge: Cambridge University Press.

McMahon, A. M. (2002) An Introduction to English Phonology, Edinburgh: Edinburgh University Press.

Morgan, G. (2006) '"Children are just lingual": The development of phonology in British Sign Language (BSL)', Lingua: International Review of General Linguistics 116: 1507–23.

Ochs, E. and Schieffelin, B. (1995) 'The impact of language socialization on grammatical development', in P. Fletcher and B. MacWhinney (eds) The Handbook of Child Language, Oxford: Wiley-Blackwell, pp. 73–94.

Ogden, R. (2009) An Introduction to English Phonetics, Edinburgh: Edinburgh University Press.

Smith, J., Durham, M. and Fortune, L. (2007) '"Mam my trousers is fa'in doon!": Community, caregiver, and child in the acquisition of variation in a Scottish dialect', Language Variation and Change 19: 63–99.

Snow, C. E. (1995) 'Issues in the study of input: Finetuning, universality, individual and developmental differences, and necessary causes', in P. Fletcher and B. MacWhinney (eds) The Handbook of Child Language, Oxford: Wiley-Blackwell, pp. 180–93.

Thelen, E. (1981) 'Rhythmical behavior in infancy: An ethological perspective', Developmental Psychology 17: 237.

Watt, D. and Allen, W. (2003) 'Tyneside English', Journal of the International Phonetic Association 33: 267–71.

Chapter 8

Technology and language

Dan Clayton

Introduction

Anyone who possesses just a nodding acquaintance with twenty-first-century classrooms will be aware that technology permeates the lives of the young people we teach. From student presentations that rely almost entirely on Wikipedia to frantic messaging under the desk during lessons, and from student emails opening with 'Hey' to the apparent proliferation of online punctuation and spelling conventions in written work, technology can be a distraction and a hurdle to concentration, written accuracy and learning. But in many ways it can also prove to be one of the most fruitful and dynamic areas for language study.

While concerns about young people and perceptions of declining standards are addressed (among other things) in Chapter 4, what I would like to focus on here is the potential for the study of language and technology to open up work in the English classroom across the age ranges and offer students and teachers the chance to explore their own and others' language use. By looking at how language is used in various social media environments, such as Twitter, Facebook, web discussion forums and online gaming chats, we can consider some of the core language issues of individual and group style, variation and change, and by using some of these technologies we can also collect data in ways that weren't available to language students and their teachers just a decade ago.

Technology itself is a term that can be used fairly loosely to include such *writing technologies* as the pencil and pen, *printing technologies* as the printing press and photocopier, *telephonic technologies* such as the home and mobile phone and text messaging, up to the more recent *web-based technologies* of email, social media and online discussion. Baron (2009: xi) refers to all of these as 'writing technologies' but it is this last group of digital technologies that I will concentrate on here, while making reference to some of the older technologies as points of comparison.

In the first part of this chapter, I will look at where the study of language and technology sits in the existing English curriculum, before moving on in the second part of the chapter to examine work that has been done on digital technologies and which explores the ways that computer-mediated communication

(CMC) – defined by Herring (1996:1) as 'communication that takes place between human beings via the instrumentality of computers' – straddles the traditional categories of speech and writing. In looking at ideas around mode, I will offer some ideas about how English students can make use of the language around them. As part of this, I will concentrate on social media, such as Twitter, to look at ways in which English teachers can draw on students' own language use and that of those around them to establish a linguistic foundation for studying apparently ephemeral texts and build on them to help students focus on more canonical texts, too. In the third and final part of the chapter I will focus on the notion of performance in language and how ideas drawn from the work of Goffman (1959) can be applied to the creation and performance of online identities, both in helping young people understand more about how language functions in different settings but also how they might learn to decode the ways others use language to represent themselves, their views and their relationships with others.

Language, technology and the curriculum

The 2013 Department for Education *GCSE English Language Subject Content and Assessment Objectives* document spells out its intentions for English Language study unequivocally:

> GCSE English language is designed on the basis that students should read and be assessed on high-quality, challenging texts from the 19th, 20th and 21st centuries. Each text studied must represent a substantial piece of writing, making significant demands on students in terms of content, structure and the quality of language. The texts, across a range of genres and types, should support students in developing their own writing by providing effective models. The texts must include literature and extended literary nonfiction, and other writing such as essays, reviews and journalism (both printed and online). Texts that are essentially transient, such as instant news feeds, must not be included. The number and types of texts, and their length, are not prescribed.
>
> (DfE 2013: 4)

The penultimate sentence is particularly telling, appearing to single out for proscription what might be termed 'technology texts', but hardly surprising, given the political climate at the time of its production and the then Secretary of State for Education, Michael Gove's, dislike of non-canonical texts and spoken language study (caricatured in one speech [Gove 2011] as 'listening to tape recordings of Eddie Izzard and the Hairy Bikers'). Online essays, reviews and journalism are described as legitimate texts for study however, so there is perhaps some wriggle room if teachers want to study not just the structural, linguistic and generic conventions of these forms but also the affordances of online publication: hyperlinks, interactive pages and readers' comments, for example.

Again, it is A-level English Language that offers the most natural setting for the study of language and technology as a topic. Until 2015, the AQA B English Language AS-level offered Language and Technology as one of its three *Language and Social Contexts* options on the ENGB1 paper. The specification outlines it thus:

> In preparing for this topic area candidates should study how varieties of language are shaped by the medium of communication, for example telephone, radio, television, computer. Candidates should also study the social practices that surround these forms of communication, for example conventions for using mobile phones, aspects of netiquette, conventions of radio and television programmes etc.
>
> (AQAa 2015)

In the nine series (or sittings) of the ENGB1 examination since May 2010, a range of texts was set for examination, including Twitter feeds, email and text message exchanges, blogs, podcast transcripts, newspaper and charity websites and transcripts of radio broadcasts. In Principal Examiner reports (drawn up each series by senior examiners to comment on the performance of candidates in the paper and to highlight areas of strong and weak performance) reference was made (between 2010 and 2014) to the good work done by students in discussing (among other things) the visual design of technology texts, the construction of identity online, the changing nature of online language and the interactional possibilities made available through the affordances of CMC.

Elsewhere, technology appeared on the smaller AQA A English Language AS-level specification as part of ENGA1: *Language and Mode*. Here it was situated in a different context, not foregrounding technology *per se*, but rather the potential of electronic texts to be 'multimodal' and analysing how 'the texts' language is affected by their mode and context' (AQAb 2015). As well as more traditional written and spoken texts, ENGA1 presented students with web pages offering advice and charity appeals along with discussion forums. Both the AQA A and B specifications provided online texts (website match reports and text updates, as well as a range of online articles) to analyse as part of the A2 *Language Change* topics in ENGA3 and ENGB3, here considering technology as a driver of language change and a source of material to discuss abbreviation, new words for new inventions, word formation processes (such as the *Tw-* element with new Twitter words, or the *i-* element of iPad and iPod), along with the different expectations for language practice in online and electronic environments.

In the new AQA English language A-level (introduced for first teaching in September 2015 and first examination in May 2016), technology is an element of Component 1 where it can be relevant to both the mode and language change strands of the course, as well as in Component 2 where it again appears as part of *Language Change* (and Diversity). Another area of both the legacy (2009–15) and current A-level English Language specifications is the student-led *Language Investigation* coursework unit which allows A-level students to choose a topic of their own and to set research questions, gather data, analyse it and report back on their findings in a substantial piece of project work. In my capacity as a moderator for this unit, I have come across a rich and fascinating range of work on technology, including work on text messaging, online gaming, Twitter and Facebook, much of it at the very top end of the mark range and demonstrating exactly the kind of analytical rigour that the new GCSEs would suggest might be applied to literature texts, but demonstrating – crucially – a precise and detailed knowledge of how language works, not through the study of literary texts but through the study of the language itself.

Despite the appeal of technology to students, the topic was not always as popular with teachers of the AQA B specification. Examiner reports often mentioned that it was the least popular of the three topic areas, in terms of numbers of student responses to the three optional topics. One possibility is that, being a relatively new topic, the body of linguistic knowledge and range of scholarly reference available to teachers is not as developed as for the alternative topics of *Language and Power or Language and Gender*. While *Language and Gender* can boast a string of studies and ideas from language study to refer to (common researchers used include Lakoff, Tannen, Coates, Butler, Fishman, Cameron), technology has often fallen back on just two or three A-level reference works (usually Shortis 2000; Crystal 2006; and Goddard and Geesin 2011).

Having said this, the high quality of responses to *Language and Technology* exam questions and the increasing popularity of technology-based *Language Investigations* show that students can write extremely well and exhibit detailed and insightful knowledge of technology texts. There is also a growing body of work on Language and Technology accessible to teachers of English, some of it aimed at the non-specialist. So, text messaging is addressed by Tagg (2012, 2015), Crystal (2006) and Thurlow (2003), instant messaging by Tagliamonte and Denis (2008) and a good general introduction to the whole topic by Goddard and Geesin (2011).

Mode, modes and multimodality

Work on the similarities and differences between the modes of speech and writing, such as that by Biber (1991) and Biber and Conrad (2001), establishes that the historical dichotomy between the two modes is not as fixed as some might have us believe, with some spoken texts often showing quite complex syntax and higher lexical sophistication, while certain written texts display almost the opposite.[1] The advent of CMC has led to the boundaries becoming yet more blurred. Leech *et al.* (2006: 151) refer to mode as 'a continuum from "typical" speech to "typical" writing' with electronic forms such as email or text messages somewhere in between. Baron (2008: 48), referring to her own previous study of bulletin boards, email and computer conferencing, describes CMC as

> resembl(ing) speech in that it was largely unedited; it contained many first- and second-person pronouns; it commonly used present tense and contractions;

it was generally informal ... At the same time, CMC looked like writing in that the medium was durable, and participants commonly used a wide range of vocabulary choices and complex syntax.

Crystal (2006: 47), on the other hand, and some years later than Baron's survey of CMC – perhaps a significant time gap, because of the rapid development of so many other forms of CMC in the intervening period – refers to these electronic texts as using 'netspeak': 'better seen as written language that has been pulled some way in the direction of speech than as spoken language which has been written down'.

At A-level, these ideas and discussions are a useful part of the coverage of the topic of *Language and Technology, Language Change* and/or *Language and Mode*, because they can inform a close focus on the ways in which language is used and how language practices are shaped by and through technology. Teachers can examine a range of CMC texts from Facebook status updates and comments, Twitter 'conversations', online message board posts through to email and text message exchanges, encouraging students to apply frameworks of linguistic analysis and interpretation to the language in front of them. While these are hardly canonical texts, and studying such ephemeral and apparently banal texts might run counter to certain educational agendas, A-level English Language has always made use of a huge variety of texts; a quick look at any ENGB1 paper from 2010–15 can reveal just how wide that range is. What's more, for students between eleven and eighteen years of age, so much life is now spent online that it seems perverse not to study the kind of language many of them use on a daily (and sometimes semi-permanent) basis. Indeed, I would argue that these short, rich texts offer students some of the most accessible and focused ways for them to apply their growing understanding of language.

For example, looking at the opening sequences of text messages, emails, postcards and letters can offer some insight into the different linguistic and social (and sometimes changing) conventions of these sub-genres. Are formal salutations such as 'Dear Sir/Madam' or 'Dear Mr Burroughs' used in some emails and letters? If so, why? Why are they absent in so many CMC messages? Is there a cline of formality evident in salutations used in other CMC messages ('Hi', 'Hey', 'Hello', 'Yo', etc.)? By looking at some relatively simple language features in quite small sections of short texts such as these, teachers can draw students' attention to the intersection of language and context. The technological aspect of such analysis is not necessarily the primary focus here, but forms part of the context to each act of communication. Who are the text producer/s and text receiver/s? Where are they, physically, in relation to each other? What is their social relationship? What mode of communication is being employed and how does this impact on the language styles used?

Alternatively, a cue could be taken from work by Tagliamonte and Denis (2008) on the ways in which a non-verbal feature of language such as laughter is represented in CMC. For example, is laughter signified by 'LOL', 'haha', 'hehe' or some other graphical form of communication (such as a smiley or emoji)? Students could carry out their own studies to see if there are differences across particular age groups and/or genders or social groups in particular forms of CMC (Instagram versus Twitter, for example) and to explore why these differences might exist. These digital forms could then be compared to more traditional written forms of correspondence to see if similar patterns exist in older texts. Articles such as Larson (2015) and Parkinson (2015) can provide useful classroom stimulus materials for students and can easily be converted into activities and class research mini-projects. For teachers or students interested in the potential of new technologies for data gathering and research in the field of language study, Zimmer (2011) is a good starting point.

Another approach used for A-level English Language (and which could be used with younger students) is to consider why certain modes of communication might be judged to work better than others in some situations. One way of approaching this is to give students a list of tasks to perform and messages to convey. Using a simple worksheet format, students are asked to pick the most and least appropriate form of communication from a pre-selected list for each of the tasks they have to perform (for example: face-to-face spoken, text message, email, Twitter, written letter, voice call, Facebook status update, Snapchat/ Instagram message) and to explain why. The tasks might be drawn from the following list:

1   Arrange to meet a friend.
2   Tell a friend you are going to be late for a lesson that has already started.
3   Contact a teacher to tell them that you are going to be late for a lesson that day.
4   Split up with a girlfriend/boyfriend.
5   Let others know that you are now in a relationship.
6   Tell a family member that a pet has died.
7   Tell friends that you have a new job.
8   Tell a friend that a family member is seriously ill.
9   Let a grandparent know about your week at school.

From quite simple beginnings, a wider discussion of the affordances and constraints of each form of technology can then be explored. Drawing on the ideas of Goffman (1959), Sellen and Harper (2011: 16–18) discuss the notion of the 'affordances' of different forms of communication, something that can be applied to different digital technologies too. As they explain:

> … people "pick up" information about their environment and the objects in it largely by attending to what these objects *afford*. An affordance refers to the fact that the physical properties of an object make possible different functions for the person perceiving or using that object. In other words, the properties of objects determine the possibilities for action.

Writing well before the advent of CMC, Goffman's ideas are rooted in face-to-face interaction, but Danet and Herring (2007) adapt them for a more technological context, as explained in Goddard (2012: 109–10):

> Her framework splits analysis into aspects of the tool being used – for example, whether it's synchronous or asynchronous – and aspects of the social context – for example, whether you are chatting with friends or planning a work project with colleagues ... Goffman's (1981) view of communication was that it could be split into 'system constraints' (the nature of any technology used) and 'ritual constraints' (the conventions of the language community in question). The idea that lies behind the work of both the scholars mentioned above is that the available technology does shape our language use, but so does the communication context – who we are communicating with, why we are communicating, and so on.

These are particularly useful ideas for teachers to develop with secondary English students because they lie at the heart of so many different kinds of writing. Learning to shape language to match the demands of different audiences (and here, by extension, different modes of communication used to reach those audiences) is a core skill, and with so many different forms of communication available to young people, the ability not only to use language but analyse it linguistically and comment on its appropriateness seems an important part of English teaching at this level.

By considering the nature of the message to be communicated and the pros and cons of the chosen forms, students can start to assess the affordances of each form of technology (e.g. Twitter's ability to communicate instantly with multiple audiences, to embed hyperlinks and to categorise its messages through hashtags) along with its constraints (e.g. Twitter's 140-character limit and reliance on a WiFi or 3G signal). By evaluating the different ways in which technology can not only shape the language they use but how they themselves shape their language for the particular form they are using, students are doing more than simply learning about the technology but studying how language and technology combine in new and varied forms.

A follow-up activity to this kind of task can focus more on students' own creative and re-creative writing. Selecting one of the example scenarios from earlier, students can be asked to write the message in a written letter form before transforming the text into a range of other forms. For example, students might be able to rewrite the letter as a Tweet using only 140 characters (with appropriate hyperlinks and hashtags), an email, a voicemail message to be left on an answerphone, etc. At this stage, teachers might also decide to introduce more linguistic metalanguage to allow students to describe and analyse the changes they are making and what is driving these changes. For example, on a word level, students might be asked to comment on the registers they have used, the level of formality in their vocabularies or the assumptions made about their audience's knowledge through shared understanding of abbreviations. On a phrase level, students could look at how much, or how little, detail they have included, in the form of modification using adjectives and/or adverbs. At the clause level, there is scope to explore how elliptical sentences are often a staple feature of CMC and how that can potentially lead to multiple interpretations of messages and a degree of ambiguity. For more able students, it might also be useful to explore the ways in which some forms of CMC employ more speech-like structures (coordination of clauses, preposing[2] of clause elements or a lower density of phrase modification) while others mirror traditional syntactic patterns of formal, written English. In this way, the technology itself does not become the primary focus of the activity but a means to explore language in a range of contexts.

Identity and performance

As outlined in previous parts of this chapter, the study of Computer-Mediated Communication can shed light on a range of language practices, but perhaps one key area in recent years is how identity is constructed online. For many young people, living more and more of their lives online, language is part of a growing repertoire of resources being used to communicate with others, to project aspects of individual and collective identity to the outside world and enact relationships in a wider range of ways than simple face-to-face speech or traditional pen-on-paper writing. But how is language being used in CMC to present and manage identities?

Some of the surface features of social networking technologies, such as their use of abbreviated forms of language, emoticons and emojis, elliptical grammar and non-standard spelling and punctuation have been commented upon unfavourably in many mainstream media reports (summarised extremely effectively for teachers in Goddard and Geesin 2011: 79), often presenting the public with a negative, 'deficit' view of online communication styles. Students themselves will often refer to their formal written work as in 'proper English' while their messaging is done in 'slang' or 'bad English', but the close study of some of these forms of non-standard English and creative forms of visual design can reveal much more about language than any tabloid scare story about illiterate texters.

When considering how language is employed in CMC, students can begin to explore areas of vocabulary (e.g. different levels of formality and abbreviated forms), syntax (use of ellipsis and different clause functions) and, perhaps most significantly, pragmatics. This is an area (no doubt familiar to A-level English Language teachers) that is new to many teachers of GCSE English, but one that can be introduced as part of a focus on implied meanings and how language and context intersect. For example, when looking at how feelings and tone are conveyed through CMC, students might be asked to imagine the different ways that emotions such as surprise, happiness, sadness and irony/sarcasm can be produced through different types of language.

Zappavigna (2012: 11) makes the point that

> the language used in social media … is under significant interpersonal pressure. On the one hand, it is deployed in a modality where interpersonal meanings that might otherwise be expressed paralinguistically might be expressed via other means. On the other hand, it is bound by the need for linguistic economies arising from the character constraints imposed upon microposts.

Zappavigna's observations about the tensions between expression and economy are interesting ones to develop with students, particularly at A-level where these concepts match some of those suggested by Deutscher (2006), especially his focus on economy and expressiveness as driving forces of change.

Again, the work of Goffman is helpful here. As outlined earlier in this chapter, while Goffman's focus was on spoken language and unmediated interaction, some (including Danet and Herring 2007) have usefully applied his concepts to mediated forms of interaction such as text messaging (Rettie 2009) and Twitter (Murthy 2013), along with a wider perspective on varied forms offered by Knorr Cetina (2009). According to Goffman, interactions between speakers are a form of dramaturgical self-presentation, a 'performance' of language carried out through a range of resources, both verbal and non-verbal, available to the participants. Online, the technology allows an even greater range of resources, or 'Bricoleur's Webkit' as Chandler (2006) refers to it, described as a form of 'creative tinkering' with online identity by Goddard (2012: 107). In terms of what students can do with these ideas, it is useful to look at how different forms of CMC allow users to express identity. As an example, students could look at a selected range of Facebook pages and Twitter profiles and ask students to think about all of the different elements of each that might convey meaning and express identity.

For example, teachers could ask students to consider the choice of image used in each Twitter user's avatar or profile picture and what the image might signify. Is it a straightforward picture of the person? If so, is it posed in a certain way to portray the user in a certain light: silly, serious, engaged in an activity, with others? If it is not a picture of the user, what have they chosen to use instead? Is it an image of a celebrity or something more abstract? These graphological signifiers are as much part of language analysis as the words themselves. With the Facebook pages, the range of pictures grows but other factors come into play as well, with identity being expressed through the language of status updates, the decisions to *like* or *share* certain posts and, more recently, to show a wider range of feelings through different facebook emojis, and even the actual *friends* who have been chosen. Combined with some of the elements of text analysis described earlier, students can apply quite detailed language analysis frameworks to familiar but demanding texts.

Technology allows us to communicate in many new ways, but at the heart of all 'writing technologies' are the communicators themselves, shaping language to express themselves, communicate ideas and make connections with others. I see no reason why these technologies should not be at the heart of the English curriculum – alongside the study of traditional and literary texts, of course – not consigned to the periphery and judged as worthless or ephemeral.

Notes

1 Others such as Kress and van Leeuwen (2001) have argued that mode consists of more dimensions than just speech and writing, and can include images and gestures.
2 *Preposing* and *postposing* are explained with corpus examples on the University College London Survey of English Usage Englicious site, a really useful resource for teachers of secondary English: http://www.englicious.org/lesson/preposing-and-postposing

References

AQAa (2015) *A-level English Language B*, www.aqa.org.uk/subjects/english/as-and-a-level/english-language-b-2705 (last accessed 9 October 2015).

AQAb (2015) *A-level English Language A*, www.aqa.org.uk/subjects/english/as-and-a-level/english-language-a-2700 (last accessed 9 October 2015).

Baron, D. (2009) *A Better Pencil: Readers, Writers, and the Digital Revolution*, Oxford: Oxford University Press.

Baron, N. (2008) *Always On: Language in an Online and Mobile World*, Oxford: Oxford University Press.

Biber, D. (1991) *Variation Across Speech and Writing*, Cambridge: Cambridge University Press.

Biber, D. and Conrad, S. (2001) *Variation in English: Multi-dimensional Studies*, London: Longman.

Chandler, D. (2006) 'Identities under construction', in J. Maybin (ed.) *The Art of English*, Maidenhead: Open University Press, pp. 303–11.

Crystal, D. (2006) *Language and the Internet*, Cambridge: Cambridge University Press.

Danet, B. and Herring, S. (eds) (2007) *The Multilingual Internet: Language, Culture, and Communication Online*, Oxford: Oxford University Press.

Deutscher, G. (2006) *The Unfolding of Language*, London: Arrow.

DfE (2013) *GCSE English Language Subject Content and Assessment Objectives*, London: DfE, www.gov.uk/government/uploads/system/uploads/attachment_data/file/254497/GCSE_English_language.pdf (last accessed 9 October 2015).

Goddard, A. (2012) 'Language and Technology', in D. Clayton (ed.) *Language: A Student Handbook on Key Topics and Theories*, London: English and Media Centre.

Goddard, A. and Geesin, B. (2011) *Language and Technology*, London: Routledge.

Goffman, E. (1959) *The Presentation of Self in Everyday Life*, London: Penguin.

Goffman, E. (1981) *Forms of Talk*, Philadelphia, PA: University of Pennsylvania Press.

Gove, M. (2011) 'Michael Gove to Cambridge University', www.gov.uk/government/speeches/michael-gove-to-cambridge-university (last accessed 4 October 2015).

Herring, S. C. (1996) *Computer-Mediated Communication: Linguistic, social, and cross-cultural perspectives*, Amsterdam: John Benjamins.

Knorr Cetina, K. (2009) 'The synthetic situation: Interactionism for a global world', *Symbolic Interaction* 32(1): 61–87.

Kress, G. and van Leeuwen, T. (2001) *Multimodal Discourse: The Modes and Media of Contemporary Communication*, London: Bloomsbury.

Larson, S. (2015) 'Hahaha vs. Hehehe', *New Yorker*, 30 April, www.newyorker.com/culture/cultural-comment/hahaha-vs-hehehe (last accessed 4 October 2015).

Leech, G., Deuchar, M. and Hoogenraad, R. (2006) *English Grammar for Today: A New Introduction*, London: Palgrave Macmillan.

Murthy, D. (2013) *Twitter: Social Communication in the Twitter Age*, Boston, MA: Polity.

Parkinson, H. (2015) 'No more LOLs: 50% of Facebook users prefer "haha"', *Guardian*, 10 August, www.theguardian.com/technology/2015/aug/10/lol-facebook-haha (last accessed 4 October 2015).

Rettie, R. (2009) 'Mobile phone communication: Extending Goffman to mediated interaction', *Sociology* 43(2): 421–38.

Sellen, A. and Harper, R. (2011) *The Myth of the Paperless Office*, Cambridge, MA: MIT Press.

Shortis, T. (2000) *The Language of ICT: Information Communication Technology*, London: Routledge.

Tagg, C. (2012) *Discourse of Text Messaging: Analysis of SMS Communication*, London: Bloomsbury.

Tagg, C. (2015) *Exploring Digital Communication: Language in Action*, London: Routledge.

Tagliamonte, S. and Denis, D. (2008) 'Linguistic ruin? LOL. Instant messaging and teen language', *American Speech* 83(1): 3–34.

Thurlow, C. (2003) 'Generation Txt? The sociolinguistics of young people's text-messaging', http://extra.shu.ac.uk/daol/articles/v1/n1/a3/thurlow2002003-paper.html (last accessed 9 October 2015).

Zappavigna, M. (2012) *Discourse of Twitter and Social Media: How We Use Language to Create Affiliation on the Web*, London: Bloomsbury.

Zimmer, B. (2011) 'Twitterology: A New Science?', *New York Times*, 29 October, www.nytimes.com/2011/10/30/opinion/sunday/twitterology-a-new-science.html (last accessed 7 October 2015).

Chapter 9

Cognitive linguistics

Graeme Trousdale

Introduction

This chapter provides an overview of some of the ways in which principles and methods associated with cognitive linguistics may be of use to English teachers working on language topics. In this introductory section, I provide some brief information regarding some general properties of cognitive approaches to language, but the majority of the chapter is dedicated to showing how particular principles of cognitive linguistics may be applied in the teaching of certain aspects of language structure and use.

Croft and Cruse (2004: 1) identify three features of cognitive approaches to language which distinguish them from other ways of thinking about how language works. The first concerns language in relation to other aspects of cognition. Cognitive linguists work from the assumption that our linguistic system is not fundamentally different from any other human cognitive system; in other words, the skills we use to produce and process language are used beyond language. These skills involve, among other things, our ability to categorise, to generalise, and to reuse material that we have previously learned. This can apply within language (how we know which of the words *beautiful*, *merriment* and *clarify* is a noun, and which of the made-up words *scropful*, *scropment* and *scropify* is most likely to be classified as a noun) and outside (how we know which of three animals is a cat, or why we classify a Manx cat as a cat and not a beaver). Furthermore, this non-modular approach suggests that we learn about various aspects of language form (for instance, how words are structured) in ways similar to how we learn about language function (for instance, what words mean).

This form-function connection relates to the second property of cognitive approaches to language: that grammatical structures are meaningful. By using a particular grammatical sequence, we 'select a particular image to structure the conceived situation for communicative purposes' (Langacker 1991: 12). Thus the choice between an active and a passive sentence (*Your son stole my bike* vs *My bike was stolen*, respectively) allows different participants in the process to be profiled (i.e. made more prominent in relation to other linguistic material) and backgrounded in various ways. The third feature concerns the relationship between knowledge of the structure of language and knowledge of how to use that structure. Cognitive linguists suggest that language structure and language use are linked via a feedback loop: language structure emerges across various usage events (i.e. uttered or signed tokens), and the emergent structure sanctions novel uses. These properties serve to distinguish cognitive linguistics from other models of language such as Chomskyan generative grammar.

The purpose of this chapter is not to promote, defend or critique cognitive linguistics as a model of linguistic knowledge, but instead to illustrate some of the ways in which the main ideas behind the enterprise may be used to inform and encourage discussion about aspects of language that may be relevant in the classroom. Three areas of teaching of knowledge about language (KAL) are considered. The first concerns teaching of grammar and meaning, including teaching about variation and change in language. The second and third concern KAL in relation to textual analysis. In the next section, the place of metaphor in political discourse is considered, while the final section focuses on cognitive stylistics and the language of literary texts.

Cognitive approaches to grammar and meaning

Understanding the meaning of words, their structure and how they combine to form phrases and clauses is at the heart of many English curricula. For instance, the Key Stage 3 Programme of Study for English in England and Wales (DfE 2013: 4) suggests that one of the reading skills that young teenagers should acquire concerns 'learning new vocabulary, relating it explicitly to known vocabulary, and understanding it with the help of context and dictionaries'. For grammar, students should expand and consolidate their knowledge of key grammatical terms, such as labels for parts of speech and terms for relations between words (such as head and modifier). In this section, some principles of cognitive linguistics relating to word meaning and to word class are outlined, with suggestions as to how they might be used for teaching KAL concepts in the classroom.

The linguistic study of word meaning often distinguishes semantics from pragmatics. Ask speakers of English what is meant by the word *genius*, and they will typically suggest that it means 'a person with exceptional intellectual gifts'. But imagine a context in which a man called Bob, arriving at the airport, discovers he has left his passport at home. If a fellow traveller utters something such as [1]:

[1] Bob, you really are a genius

hearers would typically understand this as ironic, and that in this context, *genius* means something like 'fool'. Thus a default meaning of *genius* would be 'a person with exceptional intellectual gifts', which may be overridden in particular instances of use. Given that the frequency of use of the more positive sense far outweighs the ironic sense, it is unsurprising that the default meaning is the positive rather than the ironic one. Furthermore, the ironic meaning is only really available in particular contexts, so it has a narrower domain of application. And if you looked in a dictionary, you wouldn't find the meaning 'fool' listed under the entry *genius*. So we might separate out a core (semantic) meaning of *genius* from a particular (pragmatic) meaning that it acquires in a particular context.

Many cognitive linguists object to this kind of compartmentalisation, however. In terms of learning word meanings, most of the words you now know are ones which you learned through experiencing them being used in a particular context, rather than having looked them up in a dictionary. The prototypical meaning of a word is one that is abstracted across usage events, and is associated with frequency of exposure. But that aspect of the meaning of the word is only a tiny part of the encyclopedic knowledge you have of that word. Consider a word like *sandwich*. A central aspect of the meaning of this word is that it is a type of food. But there are many other things which could be considered part of the meaning of the concept 'sandwich', including knowledge of its component parts, both typical (e.g. meat as a filling) and atypical (e.g. baked beans as a filling), when it is eaten (e.g. typically not at breakfast), how it is eaten (e.g. typically with the hands, rather than with cutlery), its history (e.g. its association with the 4th Earl of Sandwich), and so on. Deciding what parts of this knowledge are 'essential' for the understanding the concept 'sandwich', and which are peripheral, is somewhat arbitrary, and this undermines a sharp distinction between semantics and pragmatics.

Turning now to grammar, and returning to the word *genius*, the typical use of this word is as a noun. We know this because of properties associated with its distribution (e.g. in the expression *you really are a genius*, the position of *genius* after the article *a*, and as part of a phrase that serves as complement following the verb *you ... are*, suggest classification as a noun). But sometimes the category of *genius* is less clear. Here are some real-life examples from the *Corpus of Contemporary American English* (Davies 2008–)

[2] But her genius involves assembling these throwbacks in an utterly modern country style
[3] And what a genius plan it was.
[4] what I think is really genius is that you send two sizes

In [2], the distribution of *genius* would suggest it is a noun: again, it follows a determiner, the possessive *her*, and forms part of a phrase that functions as subject of the verb *involves*. In [4], however, the distribution of *genius* would suggest it is an adjective: for example, it is modified by the adverb *really*. We can also think about substitution. Possible substitutes for *genius* in [2] are words like *sagacity* and *skillfulness*, all of which display properties associated with nouns (such as their morphological structure, ending with the suffixes *-ity* and *-ness*). By contrast, words which can take the place of *genius* in [4] are *sensible* and *skilful*, which have properties associated with adjectives (again, the suffixes are good indicators here).

But what about [3]? How do we know whether *genius* in [3] is a noun or an adjective? Distribution doesn't help us as much here, because both nouns and adjectives can appear in this position (e.g. *what an engineering plan it was* vs *what a disappointing plan it was*). So we might say, in this construction, where the word functions as a premodifier of a noun, and is itself unmodified, that the word is underdetermined for category membership, or even that the distinction between noun and adjective is neutralised in this position. This is quite a controversial stance to take: certain theories of language structure will suggest that each word must be parsed as a member of a particular category in all cases. But from a cognitive linguistics perspective, which often foregrounds gradience in category membership, this is less problematic.

Drawing on earlier work in cognitive psychology, cognitive linguistic approaches to category membership focus on prototypes and goodness of fit of various items into particular categories. A word like *nice* is a very good fit to the category adjective, given its distribution (in e.g. *a nice hat, that hat is nice, a really nice hat*) and its capacity to mark grade inflectionally (*nice, nicer, nicest*). A word like *utter* is a less good fit (e.g. *an utter idiot* is fine, but **that idiot is utter* is not). And most crucially, as words shift over time from one category to another, they may not acquire all the properties of the new category at once (see Denison 2010 for a more detailed discussion). This gradual change may be seen in a range of words that have shifted (or are shifting) from membership solely of the category noun to dual membership of the categories noun and adjective. In addition to *genius*, there are words like *rubbish, pants, fun* and *key*, all of which show varying degrees of 'adjective-like' status: some speakers have no problem with saying *that was the funnest night out I've had in ages*, but would find *That song is much rubbisher than the last one* to be much less acceptable.

An important issue here regarding pedagogy is that many of the core issues of grammar – such as what part of speech a word belongs to, and even what we mean by 'part of speech' – can be seen as areas of investigation. This is particularly the case when understanding that some of the key issues in grammar can be enhanced by focusing on language variation and change. Dialect data can be used as a rich source of material for grammatical analysis. For example, category membership (e.g. the category of *pants* in an expression such as *'The X-Factor' is pants*) and grammatical functions (e.g. the function of *pure* in an expression such as *he's pure mental*) can both be explored using expressions that are current in a local dialect area; examples need not always refer to the standard dialect.

Metaphor and political discourse

Another important area in cognitive linguistics is the study of metaphor. For many teachers of English, the concept of metaphor is well-known, especially in its application to literary texts (consider for instance, the many metaphors associated with illness and disease in *Hamlet*, or the comparison between the beloved and a summer's day in Shakespeare's *Sonnet 18*). For cognitive linguists, the issue of metaphor goes beyond the literary and helps to reveal a great deal about how language in general works. This is because cognitive linguists see metaphor as 'a pervasive phenomenon in everyday language', one which 'represents the output of a cognitive process whereby we understand one domain in terms of another' (Coulson 2006: 32). In other words, this view of metaphor focuses on how the metaphors we use reflect some aspect of human cognitive ability. This is a fundamental issue in what has come to be known as Conceptual Metaphor Theory (CMT; see e.g. Lakoff and Johnson 1980).

An important component of CMT is that metaphorical associations are structured in a particular way so that patterns emerge across different uses of the same metaphor. Coulson (2006: 33) gives the examples in [5] to [8] below as linguistic examples of an underlying metaphorical process:

[5] The truth is clear
[6] He was blinded by love
[7] His writing is opaque
[8] I see what you mean

To this could be added examples like *Can you shed some light on this issue?* and *My view is that we shouldn't appoint him.* In all of these cases, we see a relation between the physical experience of seeing and the mental experience of knowing. Thus terms that are taken from the source domain (i.e. the domain associated with more concrete or embodied concepts) of seeing are used to express ideas associated with the target domain (i.e. the domain associated with more abstract concepts) of knowing or understanding.

Metaphor is often associated with high literary style, but by adopting this approach from cognitive linguistics we can see how widespread metaphor is in ordinary conversation. Consider, for instance, the conceptual metaphor LIFE IS A JOURNEY. (Conceptual metaphors are standardly written in capital letters, following the schema [TARGET DOMAIN] IS A [SOURCE DOMAIN].) We can see the application of this in a literary text such as Frost's *The Road Not Taken* (e.g. *Two roads diverged in a wood and I –/ I took the one less travelled by*), but just as clearly in everyday expressions such as *the baby's on its way*, *I'm at a crossroads in my career* and *she passed on last night*. Furthermore, we can see how certain aspects of a journey might be used to talk about specific aspects of life. For instance, we can talk of life's problems in terms of how motion can be impeded (*she can't get over her breakup with Tom, I feel like I'm stuck in a rut*, and *we've got a mountain to climb if we want to meet the deadline by Friday*). These conceptual metaphors are therefore hierarchised, from the more general (LIFE IS A JOURNEY) to the more specific (DIFFICULTIES ARE IMPEDIMENTS TO MOTION) (Lakoff 1993). This hierarchy involves inheritance relationships, another key property associated with cognitive approaches to language: our understanding of linguistic categories involves more specific items inheriting properties from more general ones. In terms of meaning, we can see this in a hierarchy such as 'cutlery' > 'spoon' > 'teaspoon', where 'teaspoon' inherits many of its properties from the more general category 'spoon' (e.g. has a bowl at one end of the handle, typically used with liquid or powder), while retaining some specific properties that distinguish it from other types of spoon (e.g. its size, its typical function for measuring and stirring). Similarly, impediments to motion are particular, specific aspects of a journey, just as problems are particular events in life, so this metaphorical mapping inherits the more general properties of LIFE IS A JOURNEY, while retaining some specific properties of its own (e.g. the more restricted focus on lack of motion or a difficulty involving motion, which is only a small part of the events associated with a journey).

We can see the relevance of this wider application of the concept of metaphor when we think about how metaphors work in 'non-literary' texts, e.g. political discourse. For example, topics such as asylum and immigration are often discussed in terms of natural disasters. Here are some examples from recent political statements which associate immigration and asylum with floods, tsunamis and other natural disasters associated with water:

[9]   No matter who is elected to run our police forces on November 15, Britain will be unable to stop *the tidal flood of new immigrants*

[10] Understandably, given the pressures that *this tidal wave of newcomers* has imposed on our public services, job opportunities and wage levels, the public is hopping mad about the collective failure of the political class to get a grip on our borders.

[11] *Communities in Britain are being "swamped" by immigrant workers*, Michael Fallon has said, as he confirmed that the Government will announce plans to restrict the number of foreigners coming to the UK.

[12] the wrath of those voters who expect their Representative in Congress to defend the rule of law and American exceptionalism from *the tide of illegal immigration that is drowning our country*.

This metaphor can be found in various discourse contexts. Cunningham-Parmeter (2011) reviewed the language of the US Supreme Court and found that, in addition to metaphors linking immigration with invasion, the association with floods was also attested. Here are a couple of examples, again with emphasis added:

[13] *Stemming the flow of illegal aliens* across the Mexican-American border [United States vs. Brignoni-Ponce, 422 U.S. 899, 902 (1975); Cunningham-Parmeter 2011: 1580]

[14] *With ... the facilities at Guantanamo and available Coast Guard cutters saturated ...* the Government could no longer ... protect our borders [Sale vs. Haitian Ctr. Council, Inc. 509 U.S. 155, 163 (1993); Cunningham-Parmeter 2011: 1581)]

The key issue, then, is whether it has become conventional to use this metaphor to associate immigration with excessive (and implicitly, destructive) amounts of water. Conventionalisation of original metaphorical expressions may lead to loss of figurative meaning (as is the case with *inundate* < Latin *in+undare* 'to flow into') such that earlier, more figurative senses become obscured. A focus on metaphor, understood from the perspective of cognitive linguistics, can encourage a more critical analysis of potential biases in particular kinds of discourse.

Cognitive stylistics

This final section is concerned with the more direct application of some principles of cognitive linguistics to the analysis of literary texts. Research in this field is sometimes referred to as cognitive poetics (Stockwell 2002) or cognitive stylistics (Semino and Culpeper 2002). There are many potential topics which could be addressed in this section (including the place of conceptual metaphor, discussed in section 3 above, in the analysis of literary texts); by way of illustration, however, we will explore figure-ground alignment and fictional narrative.

Like many other aspects of cognitive linguistics, figure-ground alignment has its roots in cognitive psychology, and relates to aspects of our visual perception. Our visual system allows us to pick out particular entities as more perceptually salient relative to other items which are backgrounded. Typically, if a magazine is lying on a table, we identify the smaller entity as more discrete and bounded relative to the more general, undifferentiated surface on which it is located. This has manifestations in various linguistic domains. For example, in the study of meaning, we can see that certain concepts invoke a background as part of their conceptualisation. Some examples include both technical terms like 'hypotenuse' and everyday concepts like 'lid' (see further Langacker 1987). Our understanding of the meaning 'hypotenuse' involves not only the line itself (the figure, or the part that is in profile, sometimes referred to as a trajector), but also the particular kind of triangle of which that line forms a part. The rest of the triangle forms part of the ground (sometimes referred to as the landmark). A similar relation holds for 'lid'. We recognise that a lid is a close-fitting cover, but we also recognise that it is a cover for something – a lid is a lid in relation to a container of some kind. In this case, the figure/trajector is the lid, and the ground/landmark is the container.

This relation between figure and ground has applications in the grammatical domain too. Imagine a scene in a room which contains a cat that is sleeping under a table. Imagine too that the table has some books on it. It is far more conventional to say *the books are on the table* and *the cat is under the table*, rather than to say *the table is under the books* or *the table is over the cat*. Notice that it is possible to build a context in which an utterance like *the table is under the books* would be acceptable (imagine, for instance, a very small, folding table stored in a cupboard that happens to have a pile of books stacked upon it). But typically the books are more well-defined against the less differentiate table surface, which leads us to code *the books* as the subject and *the table* as the complement of the preposition *on*, in the linguistic expression of this scene: as Schmid (2007: 131) suggests:

> As Figure entities function as anchor points of relations and subjects are known to function as starting points for clauses, this syntactic arrangement [i.e. the association of figure and subject in unmarked clauses] seems natural enough.

How can we use this distinction between figure and ground to talk about literary texts? Stockwell (2002: 13–25) provides a number of suggestions of ways in which figure-ground alignment works in a stylistic analysis of various kinds of text. For instance, he notes that characters in a novel or a play are 'figures' that operate against the 'ground' of the events of the narrative or drama. He also addresses the literary concept of 'foregrounding', suggesting that 'the literary innovations and creative expression can be seen as foregrounding against the background of everyday non-literary language. In this view, one of the main functions of literature is to defamiliarise the subject-matter, to estrange the reader from aspects of the world in order to present the world in a creative and newly figured way' (Stockwell 2002: 14). In the final part of this section, I show how figure-ground alignment and the literary notion of foregrounding can be helpful in a stylistic analysis of the opening paragraph of Aldous Huxley's *Brave New World*. This is given in [15]:

> [15] A squat grey building of only thirty-four stories. Over the main entrance, the words, CENTRAL LONDON HATCHERY AND CONDITIONING CENTRE, and in a shield, the World State's motto, COMMUNITY, IDENTITY, STABILITY.

A close reading of the text may immediately defamiliarise and estrange the reader; indeed, this may be achieved by the first sentence of the novel. First of all, there is the paradox of the association between the adjective *squat* and the noun phrase *only thirty-four stories*. While the number of floors of skyscrapers may have increased since the early 1930s when Huxley's novel was first published, even now it is peculiar to refer to a building which has thirty-four stories as squat. Notice how this links up to the earlier discussion about figure-ground alignment: a squat building invokes an image of a building (the figure) whose size and shape (squat) is relative and understood only in relation to other unexpressed buildings that form part of our background knowledge. This in turn relates to the even earlier discussion about encyclopaedic knowledge and language use. Our conceptualisation of a squat building is based on our experiences of visualising certain kinds of building in relation to others. The defamiliarisation is associated with the properties of the post-modifying prepositional phrase: the downtoning adverb *only* does not fit with our ordinary understanding of the relationship between *squat* and *thirty-four stories*. From the very first sentence of the novel, then, we are confronted with the presentation of a world whose properties differ significantly from our own.

Another significant property of the opening of the novel is the absence of verbs. Since a typical written sentence contains at least one main clause, and that main clause contains a verb often denoting a process or state, along with noun phrases which code participants engaging in that process or experiencing that state, there is something unsettling about the absence of verbs in the first paragraph of the novel. Nothing is happening. This stasis is underscored by the grammatical structures involved: we are aware of a figured entity (the squat building for which we supply a background, reimagined as described above), but it is presented more as part of a still photograph, rather than as part of a moving film.

This sensation changes subtly in the second sentence. Here we do have some sense of a relation between entities. This is coded by the prepositions *over* and *in*, so we get a sense of the spatial associations between the first set of words and the entrance, and the second set of words and the shield, but the terse nature of the style strips this spatial relation to its bare minimum. Again, the figure-ground relation is important here. The two sets of words, the first for the name of the building, and the second for the motto, are the figures, and the entrance and the shield are the ground for the first and second set of words respectively. Notice, however, that a structural device reshapes the expected figure-ground alignment. Compare the two sentences in [16] and [17]:

[16] The words are over the entrance
[17] Over the entrance are the words

This phenomenon (known as locative inversion) has a number of interesting syntactic properties (you can say *the snake might slither across the road* but not *across the road might slither the snake*; you can say *he saw that the snake slithered across the road* but not *he saw that across the road slithered the snake*); stylistically, this has the effect of foregrounding something that is typically backgrounded. While the examples in *Brave New World* are not canonical examples of locative inversion (for the very fact that there is no verb!), the patterns clearly share properties with locative inversion. This disruption to the canonical word order pattern reshapes our expectations with regard to figure-ground alignment: we are presented with the ground first, then the figure.

What we do not get, however, is any sense of how the two signs are spatially related to one another. We know that the sign for the name of the building is above the entrance, and that the sign for the motto is in the shield. But we don't know the location of the shield in relation to the entrance. We are presented with two distinct figure-ground alignments, but not the larger figure-ground alignment between the two signs. Stockwell (2002: 18) suggests that '[r]eading a literary text is a dynamic experience, involving a process of renewing attention to create and follow the relations between figure and ground'. What is so perplexing about the opening of *Brave New World* – even just the first two graphic sentences – is that we are constantly wrong-footed about the figure-ground alignment. Partly this is created by a lack of overt syntactic figures: there are no subjects, because there are no verbs. Partly this is created by the dissonance between our own experience and encyclopedic knowledge of the relative size of buildings and the depiction of the buildings in this new world. Partly this is created by the text forcing us to consider particular relations between various entities when the link between them is unstated or understated. The critical issue is that this is something we do as readers when we create the story that emerges from the narrative.

Conclusion

There are many ways in which cognitive linguistics can be of use to the teaching and learning of knowledge about language, and its application in literary and non-literary texts. Some of the terminology (such as metaphor) will be familiar to many English teachers, but typically such terms are used in a slightly different way in the cognitive linguistics literature. Like other linguistic theories, cognitive linguistics provides a framework for thinking about how language is structured. It is often this area of language structure which is a cause for concern among teachers and students alike. But modern linguistics is radically different from traditional approaches to grammar, and there are many ways in which structural properties of language may be seen as amenable to exploration and discovery. This encourages students to become critical thinkers and analysts. Many concepts in grammar, and the various theories created to explain them, are issues for debate and discussion, and this can lead to fruitful and considered analysis of both literary and non-literary texts.

There are a number of accessible texts for readers who are interested in following up some of the ideas laid out in this chapter. Particularly helpful to teachers will be Giovanelli (2014), which elaborates on many of the issues outlined here in much greater detail. A useful general introduction to cognitive linguistics is Croft and Cruse (2004), and there is a handbook (Geeraerts and Cuyckens 2007), which covers many of the major topics in the field. A clear and engaging introduction to word meaning from the perspective of cognitive linguistics is Hudson (1995). A foundational text in cognitive approaches to metaphor is Lakoff and Johnson (1980); a recent textbook which addresses metaphor, metonymy and related figures from a general cognitive perspective is Dancygier and Sweetser (2014). As mentioned above, Stockwell (2002) provides a clear introduction to the application of ideas from cognitive linguistics to literary texts; cognitive stylistics is also a central theme in Simpson (2014), and the contributions to Semino and Culpeper (2002) demonstrate the wide domain of work in cognitive approaches to literary form.

References

Coulson, S. (2006) 'Metaphor and conceptual blending', in K. Brown (ed.) *The Encyclopedia of Language and Linguistics*, 2nd edn, Oxford: Elsevier, pp. 32–9.

Croft, W. and Cruse, D. A. (2004) *Cognitive Linguistics*, Cambridge: Cambridge University Press.

Cunningham-Parmeter, K. (2011) 'Alien language: Immigration metaphors and the jurisprudence of otherness', *Fordham Law Review* 79: 1545–98.

Dancygier, B. and Sweetser, E. (2014) *Figurative Language*, Cambridge: Cambridge University Press.

Davies, M. (2008–) *The Corpus of Contemporary American English: 450 million Words, 1990–present*, http://corpus.byu.edu/coca/ (last accessed 10 March 2015).

Denison, D. (2010) 'Category change with and without structural change', in E. Traugott and G. Trousdale (eds) *Gradience, Gradualness and Grammaticalization*, Amsterdam: Benjamins, pp. 105–28.

DfE (2013) *English Programmes of Study: Key Stage 3*. London: DfE, www.gov.uk/government/uploads/system/uploads/attachment_data/file/244215/SECONDARY_national_curriculum_-_English2.pdf (last accessed 10 March 2015).

Hudson, R. (1995) *Word Meaning*, Oxford: Blackwell.

Geeraerts, D. and Cuyckens, H. (eds) (2007) *The Oxford Handbook of Cognitive Linguistics*, Oxford: Oxford University Press.

Giovanelli, M. (2014) *Teaching Grammar, Structure and Meaning: Exploring Theory and Practice for Post-16 English Language Teachers*, London: Routledge.

Langacker, R. (1987) *Foundations of Cognitive Grammar, Volume 1: Theoretical Prerequisites*, Stanford, CA: Stanford University Press.

Langacker, R. (1991) *Concept, Image and Symbol: The Cognitive Basis of Grammar*, Berlin: Mouton De Gruyter.

Lakoff, G. (1993) 'The contemporary theory of metaphor', in A Ortony (ed.) *Metaphor and Thought*, Cambridge: Cambridge University Press, pp. 202–51.

Lakoff, G. and Johnson, M. (1980) *Metaphors We Live By*, Chicago, IL: University of Chicago Press.

Schmid, H. (2007) 'Entrenchment, salience and basic levels', in D. Geeraerts and H. Cuyckens (eds) *The Oxford Handbook of Cognitive Linguistics*, Oxford: Oxford University Press, pp. 117–38.

Semino, E. and Culpeper J. (eds) (2002) *Cognitive Stylistics: Language and Cognition in Text Analysis*, Amsterdam: John Benjamins.

Simpson, P. (2014) *Stylistics: A Resource Book for Students*, 2nd edn, London: Routledge.

Stockwell, P. (2002) *Cognitive Poetics: An Introduction*, London: Routledge.

Web references for examples [9]–[12] respectively:

www.ukipmeps.org/news_642_UK-cannot-afford-Bulgarian-and-Romanian-immigrants.html (last accessed 10 March 2015).

www.conservativehome.com/platform/2015/01/owen-paterson-mp-why-ukip-is-wrong-about-immigration.html (last accessed 10 March 2015).

www.telegraph.co.uk/news/uknews/immigration/11188602/Towns-in-the-UK-are-swamped-by-EU-migrants-Cabinet-minister-warns.html (last accessed 10 March 2015).

www.conservativehq.com/article/16032-have-you-called-congress-today-oppose-amnesty (last accessed 10 March 2015).

Chapter 10

Corpus linguistics

Gavin Brookes and Kevin Harvey

Introduction

The term corpus linguistics (henceforth CL) refers to the study of machine-readable samples of spoken and/or written language that have been assembled in some particular way for linguistic teaching and research (otherwise known as a corpus, plural *corpora*). Corpora are typically very large, often amounting to millions of words in size, and are generally designed to represent a particular language or linguistic variety (McEnery and Wilson 2001). Corpora are usually examined with the help of specialised computer programs which offer a plethora of tools capable of quickly and reliably revealing linguistic features and patterns that might otherwise evade human observation.

In this chapter we focus on three staple corpus tools: frequency, keywords and concordance. Frequency displays the most frequently occurring words and phrases in the corpus, instantly revealing the linguistic landscape of the texts or type of language that it represents. The second tool, keywords, highlights the defining, most characteristic words in the corpus by comparing it with another corpus that usually represents some comparable 'norm'. The final tool we introduce here, concordance, usefully displays all the occurrences of a particular word or phrase across the corpus, along with a few words of surrounding text. This way of viewing the corpus data facilitates closer, more qualitative examination of particular words or phrases that might be of interest. In analysing large corpora we can account for a wider range of linguistic variation than might be possible through manual analyses of smaller-scale data sets. Meanwhile, sophisticated computational tools – some of which will be introduced here – can reveal interesting and unexpected insights about the kind of language under investigation, insights that might otherwise evade our attention without computational assistance (Stubbs 1997).

It is no understatement to suggest that CL has revolutionised the way that language is studied across an array of disciplines (Leech 2000). Respecting pedagogy, CL has been utilised most fervently by teachers and adult learners of additional languages, where corpora now routinely offer recourse to authentic language data, aiding in teaching, learning and material design (Baker *et al.* 1997;

Sinclair 2004). However, despite a few exceptions (Sealey and Thompson 2004, 2007; Thompson and Sealey 2007; Sealey 2011), CL has yet to make any serious contribution to educational domains *outside* language learning and higher education, particularly in compulsory and further education contexts. Sealey (2011: 94) suggests that this might have resulted from a disparity between the descriptive stance inherent in CL methods and the fundamentally prescriptive nature of traditional teaching practices, while also acknowledging the lag in the time it can take for developments in research to reach the 'chalk-face' and translate into real-world teaching practice (see also Hunston 1995; Sealey and Thompson 2007: 213).

In this chapter we argue that CL can provide a valuable method for learning about language in any educational context, but with particular emphasis on the teaching of English through Key Stages 3–4 and A-level. This chapter starts by offering some considerations for selecting a corpus. Following this, we introduce in greater detail the three aforementioned powerful but user-friendly corpus tools (frequency, keywords and concordance), providing worked examples of their use and suggesting ways in which these can innovate teaching and learning about language in classroom contexts. The chapter then concludes by offering some practical considerations regarding the integration of CL into the classroom. A list of resources, including corpora, corpus tools and useful websites, is provided at the end of the chapter.

Corpus selection

Corpora come in all shapes and sizes and so selecting one is not always a straight-forward task. The most important thing to bear in mind is that the corpus selected suits our specific needs and represents the text(s) or kind of language that we want to investigate (McEnery and Wilson 2001). For investigating many topics, existing, publicly available corpora will suffice. Corpora can be grouped, generally speaking, into two main types: general and specialised. General corpora represent language on a broad scale and so tend to be very large. For example, the British National Corpus (BNC) is 100 million words in size and contains samples of spoken and written British English across a variety of genres during the late twentieth century, including casual conversation, newspapers and maga-zines, lectures and so on. General language corpora, such as the BNC, serve myriad purposes and are particularly useful for examining how certain words or phrases are used on a general scale.

However, for learning about language in a specific text, text type or commu-nicative genre, we require a specialised corpus. Specialised corpora tend to be far smaller than general corpora and are much more abundant in number, with new specialised corpora being developed and made available to the public all the time. The variety of specialised corpora is so rich that it is beyond summation here.

Alternatively, and if there isn't an existing corpus that meets our needs, we could build our own. Corpus building can be a time-consuming and quite laborious task, littered with head-scratching decisions and frankly frustrating practical obstacles. Due to space limitations, we cannot provide extensive guidelines for building a corpus here. However, some smaller, more modest corpora are less complicated to create. For example, it would be relatively straightforward to build a corpus containing a single literary text, perhaps one which is being studied in class. This would require obtaining a digital copy of the said text, cleaning it (removing the parts that you want to exclude from the corpus analysis), and saving it, as a computer file, in a plain text format so that the corpus can be processed by the computer software. The scope and possibilities afforded by corpora do, of course, extend beyond literary texts. Whatever texts are included, it is vital that they are digitised and saved in a plain-text format. This is where building corpora of readily digitised texts (e.g. e-books, online news articles, and so forth) has the advantage over other formats, such as spoken discourse, which would need to be transcribed into a machine-readable format before it can be analysed. For more detailed guidance on corpus building, see Hunston (2002) and Reppen (2010).

In this chapter we demonstrate the efficacy of CL by examining two publicly available corpora: the general language BNC, and a specialised corpus containing William Shakespeare's play, *The Tragedy of Hamlet, Prince of Denmark* (henceforth shortened to *Hamlet*). The URLs required for accessing these corpora are provided, along with a list of other publicly available corpora, at the end of the chapter.

Corpus tools and methods

There are a vast number of user-friendly computer software programs available which allow us to manipulate and examine the language in a corpus. The majority of these programs can be downloaded from the Internet (e.g. *WordSmith Tools*), sometimes for free and sometimes for a fairly modest licence fee, or accessed via a free-to-use online interface (e.g. *AntConc*). For economy of space, we will introduce only those three tools mentioned earlier – frequency, keywords and concordance. It is worth bearing in mind, at this point, that there are many more tools available to the corpus linguist, with no one standard method or collection of tools (Thompson and Hunston 2006: 3). The aforementioned staple tools were selected as they are capable of affording intriguing and novel perspectives on the language in any corpus and are sufficiently user-friendly that they can be fairly easily incorporated into a classroom context.

Frequency

Introduced briefly earlier, frequency is arguably the most basic of corpus tools and serves as a useful starting point for any corpus analysis. As the name suggests, measures of frequency generate statistical information about the frequency of every single word (or wider phrase) that occurs throughout the corpus. Frequency information thus provides a simple yet powerful means for learning about the language in the corpus, instantly revealing the linguistic landscape of large amounts of language data, but also potentially flagging up patterns and features that might be in some way unusual or unexpected.

An intriguing example of how useful frequency patterns can be in the pursuit of textual analysis occurs in a famous study by the forensic linguist Malcolm Coulthard (1993, 1995). One evening in November 1952, police officers were called to a warehouse into which two teenagers, Derek Bentley and Chris Craig, were spotted attempting to illegally gain entry. Surrounded by police officers, Bentley gave himself up. Craig, however, resisted arrest and started firing a gun, injuring one police officer and killing another. Bentley was jointly charged with murder, even though he was under arrest and physically restrained at the time of the shooting. Following trial, both Bentley and Craig were convicted of murder. Craig, legally a minor, was sentenced to life imprisonment, while Bentley, who was nineteen at the time, was sentenced to the death penalty and was executed soon after. During the trial, Bentley claimed that his confession statement did not reflect his own words, but had actually been falsified by a police officer.

After his death, Bentley's family campaigned to overturn the guilty verdict and thirty-five years later, forensic linguistic Malcolm Coulthard was asked to analyse the statement in order to ascertain whether Bentley's claim could be substantiated. Coulthard examined the language of the statement in question in terms of a number of linguistic features, including the word 'then' (see Coulthard 1993, 1995). Coulthard compared frequency information about the words in the statement with the frequencies of words in two general language reference corpora, as displayed in Table 10.1.

These lists reveal a significant difference between the use of the word *then* in Bentley's statement (italicised in the table) and in the general language corpora, occurring significantly higher in the statement (once every 58.2 words) than would be expected compared to normal language (once every 500 words). Furthermore, Coulthard also compared the statement against two small specialised

Table 10.1 Ten most frequently occurring words in Bentley's statement compared to reference corpora of spoken and written general English

Rank	Bentley statement	Spoken language	Written language
1	I	THE	THE
2	THE	I	OF
3	AND	AND	TO
4	A	YOU	AND
5	TO	IT	A
6	WE	TO	IN
7	CHRIS	THAT	THAT
8	*THEN*	A	IS
9	WAS	OF	IT
10	POLICEMAN	IN	FOR

corpora, one consisting of other witness statements and the other of police statements, showing that the frequency of *then* in Bentley's statement was significantly higher than in the corpus of other witness statements (once every 930 words) and was, in fact, more comparable to the corpus of police statements, in which *then* occurred once in every 78 words.

With the help of corpus evidence, Coulthard was therefore able to show that the statement was unlikely to reflect Bentley's own words, but was more likely to have been written by a police officer. Thanks in no small part to linguistic evidence afforded by CL tools, the guilty verdict was eventually overturned forty-six years later, and Derek Bentley was posthumously pardoned in the summer of 1998. This case demonstrates the power of frequency measures to reveal subtle aspects of language that would otherwise evade our attention. Beyond the above example, word lists can be used to answer all kinds of questions about various aspects and varieties of language, for example to compare the features of spoken and written discourse (Adolphs 2006).

Keywords

Introduced briefly earlier, keywords are words which occur with either a significantly higher frequency (positive keywords) or significantly lower frequency (negative keywords) in one corpus compared to another that is usually representative of 'normal' language use (Scott 1997). For the purposes of this discussion, we focus on positive keywords. Keywords provide an indication of the 'aboutness' of the texts in the corpus, elucidating their defining, most characteristic words when compared to the reference or comparison corpus. To illustrate how keywords can indicate the key linguistic characteristics of the text(s) in a corpus, we have generated a set of keywords for Shakespeare's *Hamlet* by comparing the words in this play against a reference corpus containing all of Shakespeare's other plays. All of the corpora used to this end were obtained from Mike Scott's website, *Lexically.net*, the URL for which is provided at the end of the chapter.

Table 10.2 Keywords of Hamlet vs all other Shakespeare plays

BERNARDO	GUILDENSTERN	MOST	POLONIUS
CARRIAGES	HAMLET	MOTHER	PYRRHUS
DANE	HAMLET'S	NORWAY	ROSENCRANTZ
DANISH	HORATIO	NUNNERY	T
DENMARK	I	OPHELIA	THEE
E'ENIT	IT	PASTORAL	THOU
ELSINORE	LAERTES	PHRASE	THY
FOILS	LORD	PLAY	VERY
FORTINBRAS	MADNESS	PLAYERS	WITTENBERG
GERTRUDE	MARCELLUS	POLACK	WOO'T

Immediately noticeable here is the lack of grammatical and function words, which characteristically loom large in frequency lists (as Table 10.1 attests). Although such words occur with high frequency in *Hamlet*, they also occur with high frequency in the reference corpus (Shakespeare's other plays), which means that their high frequencies in this play are not marked, and so these words are not generated as keywords. Instead, we have a noticeable dominance of nouns, in particular proper nouns and their corresponding possessive forms, which represent the main characters in the play. The keyness of such words is hardly surprising, particularly the word 'Hamlet', which occurs in-text seventy-eight times in the *Hamlet* corpus, accounting for 0.26 per cent of the total words in the play, but does not occur *at all* in Shakespeare's other plays.

Other keywords reflect important themes in the play (McCarthy and Handford 2004: 174), such as 'madness', 'mother', 'nunnery', and so forth. Having read the play, it might be useful for students to classify keywords into the particular themes that they reflect. Once key themes are decided, the corresponding keywords can be used as lexical entry points into the text to explore those themes further and in greater contextual detail (Harvey 2013: 57–60).

Although lexical items tend to dominate keyword lists, it is not impossible for grammatical and function items to be keywords also. However, to be flagged as 'key', such words must occur significantly more frequently in the corpus under analysis compared to the reference corpus. The fact that the pronouns *I*, *thee*, *thou* and the possessive *thy* are all keywords in the *Hamlet* corpus suggests that, despite their being functional items, these words occur statistically significantly more frequently in *Hamlet* than if we compare this play with the language of all of Shakespeare's other plays. It seems reasonable to assume that this unexpected trend would have escaped our attention without the aid of the keywords tool. This is an intriguing trend and might be interesting for students to explore in greater detail in class, preferably through the prism of concordance.

Concordance

The concordance tool displays a list of all of the occurrences of a particular user-determined word or phrase in the corpus, with a few words of surrounding text displayed either side (Baker 2006: 71). Concordance lines afford greater sensitivity to the subtleties of meanings and patterns in language that might be obscured from view by the useful, but comparatively de-contextualised, frequency and keyword outputs (Sinclair 1996). Concordance lines are useful because they afford a more deeply contextualised, horizontal reading of interesting words and phrases, insights gleaned from which can supplement and build upon those afforded by the powerful if contextually limited measures of frequency and keywords (Barnbrook 1996).

In allowing us to inspect every instance of a particular word or phrase throughout the corpus, concordance provides an extremely useful means for pursuing specific lines of inquiry and for exploring interesting themes emergent from frequency and keyword inspection. For demonstrative purposes, and in keeping with our Shakespearian theme, we have generated a concordance output for the word 'Ophelia' in the *Hamlet* corpus. To provide an example of how concordance lines typically appear on-screen, we have reproduced a screenshot of these concordance lines which have been generated using *WordSmith Tools 6.0*.

As can be seen above, the search word – in this case 'Ophelia' – is conveniently located in the middle of each line, and so runs down the centre of the computer screen. Admittedly, the span of the concordance line can be relatively short compared to the size of the text from which it is taken. We therefore recommend that concordance lines be examined in greater detail in their original textual environments. There is no need for the user to return to the corpus file or dig out the original text to do this; many corpus software programs allow users to access the original text from which each concordance line derives, usually through a simple double mouse click of the concordance line in question.

Lines are typically listed in the order in which they occur in the corpus data, which is useful for learning about how the use of a particular word, representing, in this case, a particular character, develops throughout the course of the text(s) represented. The concordance lines above, however, have been sorted alphabetically according to the word immediately preceding the search word. We can describe this word as being in the L1 position (one position to the left of the search word). Alphabetical sorts are useful because they afford rapid assessment of the linguistic patterns in the text immediately surrounding the search word, with

```
        by accident, may here Affront Ophelia. Her father and myself,
        soul's idol, the most beautified Ophelia.—" That's an ill phrase,
    heals a stone. O, ho! Nay, but Ophelia,— Pray you, mark.
      But never doubt I love. O dear Ophelia! I am ill at these
    of action. Soft you now! The fair Ophelia! Nymph, in thy orisons
    thou liest howling. What! the fair Ophelia? Sweets to the sweet:
    go, your servants tend. Farewell, Ophelia; and remember well
    Than may be given you: in few, Ophelia, Do not believe his vows
    unmaster'd importunity. Fear it, Ophelia, fear it, my dear sister;
    . O my son! what theme? I lov'd Ophelia: forty thousand brothers
    honours. Madam, I wish it may. Ophelia, walk you here.
    , my lord. Farewell! How now, Ophelia! what's the matter?
    majesty of Denmark? How now, Ophelia! How should I your true
    from neglected love. How now, Ophelia! You need not tell us
        obey you. And for your part, Ophelia, I do wish That your
hugger-mugger to inter him: poor Ophelia Divided from herself and
        Never departed more. Pretty Ophelia! Indeed, la! without an
    Dear maid, kind sister, sweet Ophelia! O heavens! is't
the key of it. Farewell. What is 't, Ophelia, he hath said to you?
```

Figure 10.1 Screenshot of concordance lines of 'Ophelia' in Hamlet

the most frequent patterns and chains of words instantly rendered more observable (O'Keeffe 2012: 123–4). Presented with the above list of concordance lines, students could explore the various ways in which the character Ophelia is represented in the play by looking at the words in the L1 position (for example, 'beautified', 'dear', 'fair', 'poor', 'pretty' and 'sweet'). Of course, concordance is a flexible tool which allows us to investigate how any word (or phrase), and so any character of our choosing, is represented across the corpus, by examining every in-text occurence.

We envisage the role of concordance lines as bridging the gap between the quantitative insights provided by frequency and keywords and more traditional, qualitative close reading of the data. While significant themes and patterns can be identified through frequency and keyword lists, concordance lines provide a greater sense of how those words function in situ (Conrad 2002). Concordance can therefore be usefully combined with measures of frequency and/or keywords to develop practical exercises which involve synthesising multiple perspectives on the corpus data. It is possible, for instance, to present students with a series of keywords, from which they can discern themes or highlight important characters which can, in turn, be explored in more detail through concordance lines. Alternatively, presented with a select number of concordance lines relating to the representation or dialogue of a particular character, students could identify recurring patterns and themes which might only become observable when such aspects of the text(s) are isolated and presented in this format.

Conclusion: bringing CL into the classroom

This chapter has provided a brief introduction to CL, focusing on a small and select collection of staple corpus tools capable of innovating teaching and learning by providing an array of different perspectives on language as it is used in a variety of contexts. We envisage CL as contributing to learning about language in two main areas. First, teachers and instructors can consult corpora in the design of materials and lesson tasks. Second, corpus information can be used by students to investigate language in hands-on, practical activities. The basic tools that we have introduced here are fairly easy to use and do not require a sophisticated knowledge of corpus software or of the workings of computer programs more generally. CL can be liberating and empowering for students, affording them the exciting possibility of independently generating their own insights and conclusions about language based on corpus data, rather than relying entirely on what they are told by their teacher (Sealey and Thompson 2004: 89–90).

Despite the enthusiasm with which we have described CL in this chapter, there are a couple of caveats that are worth bearing in mind. First, although linguistic corpora represent authentic language use, there are some important differences between how texts look in their original contexts compared to when they are rendered into a corpus. Examining texts in plain-text format (a requirement of using corpus tools) means sacrificing non-verbal modes of communication, such as fonts, images and layouts (Widdowson 2000). While this might not present much of an issue for the analysis of mono-modal texts, such as many novels and play scripts, it is more problematic when examining semiotically rich, multi-modal genres of communication, such as advertising discourse, where meaning is conveyed through a variety of semiotic means (Kress and van Leeuwen 2006).

While ever-continuous developments in CL methodology endeavour to chip away at such issues, for now at least, an appreciation of such multi-modal aspects of texts must be sought through non-corpus means, with extra-corpus observations about text layouts, fonts, colours, sounds, etc., augmenting and enriching corpus-derived knowledge. Another important factor to bear in mind is that CL is not a human-less process. Although computers can undertake highly sophisticated statistical calculations, the human must select *which* tasks the computer will undertake and then, most importantly, interpret the significance of the results (Stubbs 2005). The role of the computer in CL is to provide different *perspectives* on language. How these perspectives are utilised and interpreted is entirely down to the human user. For more discussion of the limitations of CL and how these might be refuted and overcome, see Baker (2006).

Notwithstanding these and other potential issues with the use of corpora, CL remains at the heart of cutting-edge developments in linguistics, as well as an increasing number of other academic disciplines. The power of CL to offer fresh and invigorating perspectives on vast amounts of textual data means that it can tell us things that we never knew, and confirm or refute those things that we *thought* we knew, about language in a variety of contexts and text types. As such, we believe that CL can play an important role in the development of English language teaching materials and in practical, hands-on independent learning, allowing students and teachers alike to look at language from different angles, undoubtedly enriching their knowledge of it. Future challenges lie in fully exploring the ways in which CL methods can be incorporated into teaching practice, ideally with the eventual aim of CL being used by students working independently on research projects and assignments.

Further reading

In addition to the work cited throughout this chapter and listed in the references, readers should consult the following titles for further guidance on using CL:

Cheng, W. (2012) *Exploring Corpus Linguistics: Language in Action*, Abingdon and New York, NY: Routledge.

McEnery, A., Xiao, R. and Tono, Y. (2006) *Corpus-Based Language Studies: An Advanced Resource Book*, Abingdon and New York, NY: Routledge. (An accessible and comprehensive introduction to the field of CL, including hands-on tasks and thought-provoking discussion points; a treasure trove for teachers and instructors thinking about incorporating CL into their materials.)

O'Keeffe, A. and McCarthy, M. (eds) (2010) *The Routledge Handbook of Corpus Linguistics*, Abingdon and New York, NY: Routledge.

Corpora, programs and other useful resources

A selection of publicly available corpora

- American National Corpus: www.americannationalcorpus.org/
- Bank of English: www.titania.bham.ac.uk/
- British Academic Spoken English (BASE) corpus: www2.warwick.ac.uk/fac/soc/al/research/collect/base/
- British National Corpus (BNC): www.natcorp.ox.ac.uk/
- Brown Corpus: http://khnt.hit.uib.no/icame/manuals/brown/index.htm
- Cambridge International Corpus (CIC): www.cambridge.org/elt/corpus/
- Corpus of Contemporary American English: www.americancorpus.org/
- International Corpus of English (ICE): http://ice-corpora.net/ice/
- Longman Corpus Network: www.pearsonlongman.com/dictionaries/corpus/index.html
- Oxford English Corpus: www.askoxford.com/oec/
- Vienna-Oxford International Corpus of English (VOICE): www.univie.ac.at/voice/page/index.php

Corpus tools and interfaces

- AntConc: www.laurenceanthony.net/software.html
- BNCWeb: http://corpora.lancs.ac.uk/BNCWeb/home.html (see Hoffmann *et al.* 2008)
- BYU-BNC: http://corpus.byu.edu/bnc/
- Compleat Lexical Tutor: www.lextutor.ca/
- ELAN (linguistic annotator): www.mpi.nl/corpus/html/elan/
- Sketch Engine: www.sketchengine.co.uk/
- WebCorp: www.Webcorp.org.uk/
- WordSmith Tools: www.lexically.net/wordsmith/
- Wmatrix: http://ucrel.lancs.ac.uk/wmatrix/

Other useful websites and resources

- Englicious Grammar for Schools: online data-driven grammar-learning interface developed by University College London which makes use of the ICE-GB corpus and is aimed at students in Key Stages 1–5: www.englicious.org/
- Lexically.net: useful resource for corpus software and corpora developed by Mike Scott: www.lexically.net/wordsmith/
- Project Gutenberg website: hosts thousands of free e-books, downloadable in corpus-ready, text-only format: www.gutenberg.org/
- Tim Johns' Data-Driven Learning Page: http://archive.ecml.at/projects/voll/our_resources/graz_2002/ddrivenlrning/whatisddl/resources/tim_ddl_learning_page.htm

References

Adolphs, S. (2006) *Introducing Electronic Text Analysis: A Practical Guide for Language and Literary Studies*, Abingdon and New York, NY: Routledge.

Baker, P. (2006) *Using Corpora in Discourse Analysis*, London: Continuum.

Baker, P., Wilson, A. and McEnery, A. (1997) 'Teaching grammar again after twenty years: Corpus based help for grammar teaching', *ReCALL* 9(2): 8–16.

Barnbrook, G. (1996) *Language and Computers: A Practical Introduction to the Computer Analysis of Language*, Edinburgh: Edinburgh University Press.

Conrad, S. (2002) 'Corpus linguistic approaches for discourse analysis', *Annual Review of Applied Linguistics* 22: 75–95.

Coulthard, R. M. (1993) 'On beginning the study of forensic texts: corpus concordance collocation' in M. Hoey (ed.) *Data Description Discourse: Papers on the English Language in Honour of John McH Sinclair*, London: HarperCollins.

Coulthard, R. M. (1995) 'Questioning Statements: Forensic Applications of Linguistics', text of inaugural lecture, Birmingham, English Language Research.

Harvey, K. (2013) *Investigating Adolescent Health Communication: A Corpus Linguistics Approach*, London and New York, NY: Bloomsbury.

Hoffmann, S., Evert, S., Smith, N., Lee, D. and Prytz, Y. B. (2008) *Corpus Linguistics with BNCWeb: A Practical Guide*, Frankfurt: Peter Lang.

Hunston, S. (1995) 'Grammar in teacher education: The role of a corpus', *Language Awareness* 4: 15–31.

Hunston, S. (2002) *Corpora in Applied Linguistics*, Cambridge: Cambridge University Press.

Kress, G. and van Leeuwen, T. J. (2006) *Reading Images: The Grammar of Visual Design*, Abingdon and New York, NY: Routledge.

Leech, G. (2000) 'Grammars of Spoken English: New Outcomes of Corpus-Oriented Research', *Language Learning* 50(4): 675–724.

McCarthy, M. and Handford, M. (2004) '"Invisible to Us": A Preliminary Study of a Corpus of Business Meetings', in U. Connor, and T. Upton (eds) *Discourse in the Professions: Perspectives in Corpus Linguistics*, Amsterdam: John Benjamins.

McEnery, A. and Wilson, A. (2001) *Corpus Linguistics*, 2nd edn, Edinburgh: Edinburgh University Press.

O'Keeffe, A. (2012) 'Corpora and Media Studies', in K. Hyland, M. H. Chau and M. Handford (eds) *Corpus Applications in Applied Linguistics*, London: Continuum

Reppen, R. (2010) 'Building a corpus: What are the basics?', in A. O'Keefe and M. McCarthy (eds) *The Routledge Handbook of Corpus Linguistics*, London: Routledge.

Scott, M. (1997) 'PC Analysis of Key Words – and Key Key Words', *System* 25(1): 1–13.

Sealey, A. (2011) 'The use of corpus-based approaches in children's knowledge about language', in S. Ellis and E. McCartney (eds) *Applied Linguistics and Primary School Teaching*, Cambridge: Cambridge University Press.

Sealey, A. and Thompson, P. (2004) '"What do you call the dull words?" primary school children using corpus-based approaches to learn about language', *English in Education* 38(1): 80–91.

Sealey, A. and Thompson, P. (2007) 'Corpus, concordance, classification: young learners in the L1 classroom', *Language Awareness* 16(3): 208–23.

Sinclair, J. McH. (1996) 'The search for units of meaning', *Textus* 9(1): 75–106.

Sinclair, J. McH. (2004) *Trust the Text: Language, Corpus and Discourse*, London: Routledge.

Stubbs, M. (1997) 'Whorf's children: Critical comments on critical discourse analysis', in A. Wray and A. Ryan (eds) *Evolving Models of Language*, Clevedon, OH: Multilingual Matters.

Stubbs, M. (2005) 'Conrad in the computer: Examples of quantitative stylistic methods', *Language and Literature* 14: 5–24.

Thompson, G. and Hunston, S. (2006) 'Introduction System and Corpus: two traditions with a common ground', in G. Thompson and S. Hunston (eds) *System and Corpus: Exploring Connections*, London: Equinox.

Thompson, P. and Sealey, A. (2007) 'Through children's eyes?: Corpus evidence of the features of children's literature', *International Journal of Corpus Linguistics* 12(1): 1–23.

Widdowson, H. (2000) 'On the limitations of linguistics applied', *Applied Linguistics* 21: 3–25.

Chapter 11

Forensic linguistics

Willem B. Hollmann

Introduction

Forensic linguistics is a very broad field. It encompasses all areas in which linguists may use their expert knowledge in relation to law enforcement. It is important to note that a lot of research in forensic linguistics is not directly related to any specific court case or instance of law enforcement, but rather aims to shed light on *possible* cases. Thus, teachers might initially be concerned that drawing on forensic linguistics in the classroom will be difficult, as authentic data from police interviews or court cases is difficult to obtain. To some extent this is undeniably true, which is why the main discussion in this chapter is focused on a case for which data are readily available in the public domain. I will also try to offer some suggestions as to how teachers may find – or even better, *create*, together with their students – data that they may use in exploring some aspects of forensic linguistics. Such data, devised purely for the purpose of research, are actually similar in kind to those used by some professional forensic linguists and psychologists, so there are real opportunities to give one's students an accurate sense of some of the sorts of research carried out in this fascinating area.

To give a more concrete, albeit not comprehensive, idea of the broad range of this field, forensic linguists may work on questions of author and speaker identification; the discourse used by law enforcement professionals (e.g. police officers or lawyers) or institutional jargon associated with other powerful organisations (e.g. corporations or hospitals); the meaning of texts, such as witness or suspect statements, laws or user manuals; trademarks; verbal lie detection; national origin determination (in the context of immigration and applications for residence permits); cryptography (code-breaking); handwriting analysis and graphology.

Most of these areas can be fruitfully linked to language teaching. The focus of this volume is on Knowledge About Language, which to a large extent covers terms and concepts related to grammar. Support for teaching grammar and interesting materials for students to engage with are difficult to come by, so this chapter will concentrate on possible links between forensic linguistics and especially this aspect of the curriculum. More specifically, the area which I will use to illustrate possible links to the requirements of grammatical knowledge through the key stages is authorship attribution.

The fundamental idea that underlies forensic authorship analysis is that speakers differ from one another in terms of how they use language, i.e. choose and combine words, build sentences, and so on. In technical terms, this individual use of language is often referred to as someone's *idiolect*. (Alternatively, forensic linguists sometimes use the term *linguistic fingerprint* in this context. Olsson [2008: 25–32] strongly objects to this notion in his popular textbook on forensic linguistics but what he criticises is a very direct comparison between idiolect and biological fingerprints. In reality, though, when experts use the term 'linguistic fingerprint', they do not wish to suggest an exact parallel with a biological fingerprint. In particular, although biological fingerprints always allow one to distinguish between two people, the idiolects of two speakers could in some cases be so similar that this would be difficult. Still, there are enough similarities between biological fingerprints and idiolects that the notion of the linguistic fingerprint may be useful.)

I begin with an extended discussion of a classic case study in forensic linguistics, which is particularly useful as the data are available on the Internet. Having elaborated, in that discussion, on the fundamental idea of idiolects and idiolectal differences, which I introduced above, I will then offer some additional suggestions concerning authorship attribution, particularly in the context of social media. I wrap up the chapter by drawing some conclusions and offering another idea for language teaching inspired by an aspect of forensic linguistics: verbal deception detection.

Authorship attribution: Timothy Evans, the abolition of capital punishment and the foundation of forensic linguistics

There are many cases of disputed authorship, sometimes involving the works of well-known authors, ranging from Shakespeare to Dan Brown. Below, I discuss a case in which the term authorship attribution has a rather broad meaning. The document in question is a statement written down by the police, based on an oral confession. The question is whether the style of statement is internally sufficiently consistent that it may indeed be considered to be wholly based on the confession. Socially and historically, the case contributed to the abolition of capital punishment in the UK (as a punishment for murder in 1965 in most of the country, although only in 1973 in Northern Ireland, and actually as late as 1998 for all possible crimes). It has been the subject of a major film production, which may be drawn on in class. The case is the tragic story of Timothy Evans (†1950) and his young family.

The major miscarriage of justice of which Timothy Evans became the victim has been described in many places, starting with the (1961) book *Ten Rillington Place* by the investigative journalist Ludovic Kennedy. This was turned into the film *10 Rillington Place* (1971). Although the film offers a powerful portrayal of the events as they may have happened, and as such may be a useful tool in engaging students' interest, one must bear in mind that it is based on Kennedy's reconstruction. As for the specifics of the case, since helpful summaries can be found on the Internet (e.g. Wikipedia), I restrict myself here to the main facts, so as to get to the relation with forensic linguistics as quickly as possible.

A young couple, Timothy (b. 1924) and Beryl Evans (b. 1929), live with Timothy's family, but when they discover that Beryl is pregnant, in 1948, they move into a flat on 10 Rillington Place in Notting Hill, London. Their downstairs neighbours are John and Ethel Christie. Baby Geraldine is born later that year. However, when Beryl finds out that she is expecting again, one year later, it appears that she wants to terminate the pregnancy.

A few weeks later, Evans turns up at the police station in Merthyl Tydfil, in Wales, where he was born, and states that his wife has died after drinking the contents of a bottle he had received from a stranger in a roadside café, with whom he had happened to discuss the unwanted pregnancy. The first of many questions arises when police in London try to find Beryl's body where Timothy said he had left it: in a drain outside his front door. They find nothing, and note that as many as three men are needed to lift the manhole cover.

Evans then changes his statement and now incriminates his neighbour Christie. Evans suggests that Christie had told him that he has a medical background and had offered to abort the baby. Evans is away when Christie attempts this, but when he comes home Christie informs him that his wife is dead. He persuades Evans that it best for him to leave London and assures him that he will see to it that Geraldine is looked after.

The police carry out another search, and this time they find both Beryl and Geraldine. They fail to find two earlier victims of Christie's, who are buried on the same premises.

Following this, Evans is taken to the Notting Hill police station, where he makes two further statements, confessing to the murders of both his wife and their daughter. Based on these, Evans is convicted and is hanged in 1950.

Three years later, however, a new tenant discovers three bodies in what used to be Christie's kitchen pantry, with three more bodies found in a further search by the police, including Christie's wife, as well as the two in the yard that had already been there when Beryl and Geraldine's corpses were found. Christie confesses and is hanged in 1953.

In light of Christie's guilt, several investigations are launched into the possibility that the conviction of Evans might have been an error, and eventually, in 1966, a royal pardon is granted to him. The pardon to some extent brings closure to this case, but for the field of forensic linguistics, in a way it is where the story begins.

A committee that critically investigates the case against Evans invites the Swedish linguist Jan Svartvik to make use of his expertise in analysing Evans's statements. Svartvik's report is submitted to the 1965–66 public inquiry that precedes the posthumous pardon, mentioned above. The title of Svarvik's published (1968) study, which is based on his report, represents the first ever use of the term *forensic linguistics*. It is available for download (see references, below), and contains a wealth of information about the case, including all four of Evans's statements to the police. Since Svartvik's analysis mainly involves grammar and uses notions that are taught as part of the National Curriculum, it may be valuable to teachers who wish to get their students to engage with grammar in a very real world context.

In his grammatical analysis Svartvik targets the second statement Evans made at the Notting Hill police station (henceforth NH2), in which Evans confesses to having murdered his wife and child. Svartvik is particularly interested in the relation between the two discontinuous parts of the statement in which Evans specifically describes the murders and disposing of the bodies (henceforth: parts ii and iv, again following Svartvik) and the surrounding three parts (i, iii, v) in which he provides more general background, much of which is about their strained marriage and about Evans's work routine. A small snippet of each is given below for illustration:

> I was working for the Lancaster Food Products of Lancaster Road, W. 11. My wife was always moaning about me working long hours so I left there and went to work for the Continental Wine Stores of Edgware Road. I started at 8 a.m. and finished at 2 p.m, and the job was very nice there. In the meanwhile my wife got herself into £20 debt so I borrowed £20 off the Guvnor under false pretences, so he give me the £20 which I took home and gave it to my wife. … I was doing quite a lot of overtime for the firm working late, which I used to earn altogether £6 to £7 a week. Out of that my wife used to go to the firm on a Friday and the Guvnor used to pay her £5 what she used to sign for.
>
> (extract from NH2, part i)

> I come home at night about 6.30 p.m. my wife started to argue again, so I hit her across the face with my flat hand. She then hit me back with her hand. In a fit of temper I grabbed a piece of rope from a chair which I had brought home off my van and strangled her with it. I then took her into the bedroom and laid her on the bed with the rope still tied round her neck. Before 10 p.m. that night I carried my wife's body downstairs to the kitchen of Mr. Kitchener's flat as I knew he was away in hospital. I then came back upstairs. I then made my baby some food and fed it, then I sat with the baby by the fire for a while in the kitchen. I put the baby to bed later on. I then went back to the kitchen and smoked a cigarette.
>
> (extract from NH2, part ii)

The reason why Svartvik divided up the statement into these parts is that Evans himself later claimed i, iii and v to be accurate, but that parts ii and iv had been coerced out of him when he was upset as he had not known that Geraldine was dead as well, and that he was afraid that the police would beat him up (1968: 46).

It is thus conceivable that the police manipulated these parts of his statement, and then forced Evans to sign it.

Before zooming in on Svartvik's clause type analysis, let me note that Svartvik's study may also provide material to teach other aspects of the language curriculum. Svartvik mentions certain patterns of lexical selection and co-selection in Evans's statement that may or might not be expected from an illiterate person (1968: 19, 22–4). Compare the two snippets above from NH2 parts i and ii. The latter, which may not have been Evans's own words, contains less colloquial language and non-standard grammar than the former (e.g. *Guvnor; … what she used to sign for*). Contrasts such as this, which are quite apparent between parts i, iii and v on the one hand, and parts ii and iv, on the other, may be explored in lessons about formality, language and social class, regional variation, and/or Standard English.

Svartvik's grammatical analysis of Evans's statement focuses on the structure of and relation between clauses. He distinguishes between six different clause types:

A. free, independent clauses (e.g. *She then hit me right back with her hand*);
B. clauses linked by a 'mobile' connective, such as *then*, which is considered mobile as it may occur in different positions, e.g. clause-initially (e.g. *then I sat with the baby*) or after the subject (e.g. *I then came back upstairs*);
C. clauses linked by connectives *and, but, or* or *so*, which have a fixed position (e.g. *Out of that my wife used to go to the firm on a Friday and the Guvnor used to pay her £5 …*);
D. linked clauses with subject omission (e.g. *I then made my baby some food and Ø fed it*, where Ø represents the missing subject; compare *… and I fed it*);
E. subordinate clauses (e.g. *… as I knew he was away in hospital*);
F. relative clauses (e.g. *… which I had brought home off my van*).

Clause structure, clause combining, word classes (e.g. conjunction) and grammatical functions (e.g. subject) are of course all part of the curriculum. I will discuss below how teachers may wish to explore Evans's and Christie's statements and/or pieces of writing produced by the students themselves in terms of these aspects of grammar.

The hypothesis underlying Svartvik's analysis is that the authentic parts may display differences in terms of clause types from the coerced and/or manipulated parts. Underlying that hypothesis is the general notion that every speaker to some extent has their own, individual style of choosing and combining words into phrases, sentences and longer stretches of discourse; recall the notion of idiolects or linguistic fingerprints from the introduction, above.

An important note is that British police at the time were allowed to take two sorts of statements from suspects, either by interview, which required simultaneous and comprehensive transcription of questions and answers, or by a statement, in which case police officers were not allowed to ask any substantive questions. This second option could involve the suspect writing down the statement or dictating it to the police.

Table 11.1 Distribution of clause types A–F in NH2

Clause type	Parts i, iii, v ('true')	Parts ii, iv ('coerced')	Total
A	92 (37.1%)	10 (20.0%)	102
B	17 (6.9%)	15 (30.0%)	32
C	30 (12.1%)	1 (2.0%)	31
D	50 (20.2%)	17 (34.0%)	67
E	45 (18.1%)	5 (10.0%)	50
F	14 (5.6%)	2 (4.0%)	16
Total	248 (100%)	50 (100%)	298 (100%)

For NH2, it was the second protocol that the police adopted. Evans was illiterate, so the statement would – or rather *should* – have been based on an accurate transcription of the way he dictated his statement.

Svartvik's grammatical analysis consists of three steps. First, he performs frequency counts of clause types A–F in the 'authentic' parts i, iii, and v combined and the 'coerced' parts ii and iv taken together. His findings are presented in Table 11.1.

Visual inspection of the figures in Table 11.1 reveals substantial differences between the 'authentic' and 'coerced' parts. However, from a statistical point of view we would like to know whether the differences in distribution might not simply be the result of chance. Therefore, Svartvik performs a second step: he subjects the frequency differences to a simple statistical analysis, i.e. a chi-square test. (This test can easily be performed in programmes such as Excel or SPSS and is explained in any introductory textbook on statistics, e.g. Oakes 1998, Field 2013. However, teachers may decide that it would not add very much to a grammar lesson inspired by Svartvik's study and thus leave it out.) The test shows that the probability that the difference is due to chance is less than 0.002 per cent.

In order to lend even more support to his suggestion that there are considerable differences between the 'authentic' and 'coerced' sections of NH2, Svartvik also tests the grammatical internal consistency of the statement given by Christie, when he eventually confesses to having killed Beryl Evans. This statement does not have any parts that were produced under duress, so Svartvik simply divides it up into three parts of forty-four sentences each.

Table 11.2 Distribution of clause types A–F in Christie's confession

Clause type	Part i	Part ii	Part iii	Total
A	45 (43.7%)	45 (42.1%)	44 (40.4%)	134 (100%)
B	1 (1.0%)	2 (1.9%)	0 (0%)	3
C	9 (8.7%)	8 (7.5%)	13 (11.9%)	30
D	3 (2.9%)	14 (13.1%)	14 (12.8%)	31
E	37 (35.9%)	32 (29.9%)	28 (25.7%)	97
F	8 (7.8%)	6 (5.6%)	10 (9.2%)	24
Total	103 (100%)	107 (100%)	109 (100%)	319

The distribution of clause types here clearly looks a lot more consistent across the statement, and indeed a chi-square test reveals that the probability that the differences are due to chance is relatively high: at least twenty per cent. Social scientists usually consider any probability higher than five per cent too high for a difference to be considered significant, so the conclusion is that the small amount of internal variation in clause types observed in Christie's statement is just random. (For readers with a statistical background I note that Svartvik did not apply Yates's correction in either of his calculations. If one does apply it, the p-values rise to .00002 for Table 11.1 and to .48 for Table 11.2. Clearly, the conclusion still stands: the difference is highly significant for Evans's statement, but not for Christie's.)

Svartvik does not directly accuse the police of having falsified parts of Evans's statement. He subtly notes that the contrasts between the parts cannot be coincidental, but instead of offering an explicit explanation, he chooses to discuss some limitations of his study.

One important limitation he notes is that the data set was only small: 107 sentences. For this reason he actually had to exclude the first statement Evans made in the police station in Notting Hill. In it, Evans confesses the two murders as well, but the whole statement amounts to only three sentences, with the background taking up only half a sentence (*She was incurring one debt after another and I could not stand it any longer* ...). In this context, grammatical comparison would clearly be meaningless.

The relative brevity of NH2 also sheds light on Svartvik's decision to consider clause types, as opposed to other possible markers of style (see section 3, below, for some examples): obviously, every sentence in the statement contains one or more clause types, which means that there were enough data for the chi-square test to be meaningful. As a rough guideline, statistical significance analyses are usually only possible if there are at least thirty observations; here, instances of clause types A–F. There are other considerations as well, such as the number of observations per category, e.g. clause type A, B, or whatever, but it is beyond the scope of this chapter to go into such issues.

Teachers may wish to use Svartvik's study as a model for clause type analysis, either using the Evans and Christie statements themselves or other texts; for example, getting their students to compare the internal consistency of several pieces of their own writing and investigating to what extent the distribution of patterns is similar to or different from that of other students. An activity closer to forensic authorship attribution might be to compile a pool of student writing, with each student contributing two pieces. The teacher could select both pieces from one student, holding up one as the mystery text, whose author should be identified. In addition to the student's other text, two or three more might be added, and students could be asked to work out the degree of relative similarity between the mystery text and each of these three or four texts. These activities could also be done with existing texts (e.g. short stories by well-known authors, which would provide a useful way to link language and literature).

Authorship attribution in social media

Whereas Svartvik's analysis focused on clause types, cases of author identification often consider other possible idiolectal features, such as average sentence length or lexical richness. Svartvik in fact analyses sentence length as well but problematises its value in relation to the Evans statements: 'With a corpus of material as small as ours, too much importance cannot be attached to variations in sentence and clause lengths' (1968: 30). Nonetheless, there are also many instances of convincing analyses: see for example Coulthard and Johnson (2007: 164–7) and references cited therein for a few examples. However, the linguistic features used in these studies are often less clearly linked to terms and concepts that the National Curriculum considers as essential knowledge about language.

In addition, there are a number of methods of stylistic or stylometric analysis involving advanced techniques such as Burrow's Delta: see for example Juola (2006) for a useful summary of this and other methods. These methods often do involve grammatical concepts that are included in the National Curriculum, but they rely on a considerable understanding of statistics as well as on computerised ways of carrying out statistical and linguistic analyses.

Instead, teachers may wish to draw inspiration from authorship analysis in modern social media, as students are likely to engage with them in their daily lives. Texts of this kind dealt with by forensic linguists may be threats conveyed by instant messaging platforms (e.g. WhatsApp, SMS), offensive tweets, etc. Here, the question is often whether a victim and/or suspect has or has not composed a (set of) message(s), and the method involves comparison of the message(s) in question with messages known to have been authored by them. The problem of brevity, introduced above, is often particularly serious here, as there may not be enough material for statistical comparison of features which tend to discriminate well between speakers in general, such as sentence length, lexical richness or indeed distribution of clause types.

In practice, forensic linguists requested to offer expert advice in cases such as this often take an approach that might be characterised as opportunistic, or (at least partly) inductive. That is to say, rather than approaching the data from the knowledge that clause types or sentence types may help to distinguish between individuals, forensic linguists may start their work by simply exploring the data to see if any patterns might emerge. Of course, they will typically still be led by certain hypotheses as to what features might be relevant. In the case of instant messages these may be certain abbreviations, deletions, creative spellings or misspellings, the use of punctuation and capitalisation, or the use of emoticons such as smilies and kiss signs (see for example Grant 2013: 481 for some concrete examples and helpful discussion of an actual court case).

The number of possible classroom applications is again considerable. Students could describe their own instant messaging style as compared to that of others, and tasks could be designed around a message whose author is unknown to the class but only to the teacher. One consideration here is that in order for identification and comparison of instant messaging habits to be effective, one needs a reasonably large number of messages. Another issue is that when using private text messages, appropriate ethical approval must of course be sought and obtained.

In transferring this aspect of forensic linguistic practice to the classroom, teachers will want to focus on the correct use of linguistic terminology. For example, if a set of WhatsApp messages commonly features the omission of *I have* or *I've* (e.g. *Just been to the gym*), students should ideally describe that as deletion of the first person singular subject pronoun and the perfect auxiliary *have*, possibly its contracted form - *'ve*.

The extent to which teachers may expect this kind of analysis will of course depend on the key stage and year the students are in. Thus, the term *singular* should be introduced in Year 1, but *pronoun* follows only in Year 4, and *subject* in Year 6. The suggestion here is of course not that students should be asked to analyse WhatsApp messages in terms of pronoun use as early as Year 1 – although one recent study suggests that the age at which at least some children get their first mobile phone may be as low as five![1] Teachers will be the best judges as to the exact stage at which they may begin exploring such data.

As for the terms *perfect* and *auxiliary*, although the National Curriculum specifies that students should be taught how to use the present perfect in contrast to the simple past in Year 3–4, the technical terms themselves are not part of the statutory requirements. They are both included in the (non-statutory) Glossary, and teachers may perhaps decide to introduce them only to high attainment pupils.

The requirements for Key Stages 3 and 4 are considerably less specific. However, as students are supposed to consolidate and build on their knowledge from Key Stages 1 and 2 it would appear that this fairly detailed kind of grammatical analysis may now be attempted also by lower attainment pupils, possibly preceded by a teacher-led introduction of relevant grammatical terms.

It seems slightly curious that contracted verb forms (e.g. - *'ve*) or negators (*not* in, for example, *don't*) are not mentioned in the National Curriculum, either for primary or secondary English. The reason may be the focus on Standard English. If so, that would be slightly misguided as in spoken Standard English contractions are in fact by no means unattested or rare and they are even starting to occur in written academic prose, thought of by experts as being a highly formal text type. Whatever the reason for the omission, contractions are such a salient aspect of English grammar that teachers will probably decide to discuss them anyway, and explain when they may occur, especially in the context of lessons on modal and/or other auxiliary verbs.

Concluding remarks

This chapter has attempted to demonstrate how teachers may draw on the scientific study of authorship attribution in order to support especially their classes on grammar and possibly also formality as well as social and regional variation. It has also suggested that authorship analysis may allow for helpful connections between language and literature to be made. The discussion has only introduced a few examples and contexts of authorship identification, but at least the references provided will allow further exploration of other intriguing and often tragic cases, such as those of Derek Bentley (discussed in Chapter 10) or the Unabomber (see for example Coulthard and Johnson 2007; for Bentley, note that there is also a reasonably accurate film production, *Let Him Have It* [1991]).

One aspect of authorship analysis that was only hinted at by the mention of Dan Brown is plagiarism. Plagiarism is in fact not only an issue in the literary world, but in academia as well. Students who go on to pursue a university degree will all come across it, receive elaborate instructions on how and why to avoid it, and their writing will almost certainly be systematically checked by dedicated plagiarism detection software. Given the importance of plagiarism to students, teachers may find it appropriate and/or useful to include this dimension of the field of authorship attribution in their classes (for an overview of types of plagiarism and detection methods see Alzahrani *et al.* 2012).

Another area of forensic linguistics that relies heavily on an understanding of grammar is that of verbal deception detection. Proper discussion of this area would require another chapter. However, I encourage teachers to explore and exploit it for their purposes, not least because there are also films and television shows that feature verbal and non-verbal lie detection. Admittedly, these are usually based rather loosely on the actual research and practice, see for example the drama series *Lie to Me* (2009–11). The most authoritative overview of verbal lie detection methods is offered by Vrij (2008). Unfortunately, the most systematic and solid methods are not very easily related to standard grammatical terms, as they rely on notions such as amount of temporal or spatial information, or worse – from a National Curriculum grammar teaching perspective – clarity or realism. Teachers may prefer to look to some more eclectic studies for inspiration instead, such as Newman *et al.* (2003) or Villar *et al.* (2013), as these are based on more immediately usable terms such as the frequency of pronouns or adjectives.

This chapter has hopefully shown that forensic linguistics offers many potential applications for teachers. Yet forensic linguistics is a young field. Its analytical methods and the range of types of data to which they are applied are still expanding. As the field continues to develop, the possibilities for teachers to draw on them will multiply as well.

Note

1 See www.uswitch.com/mobiles/news/2013/08/one_in_ten_british_kids_own_mobile_phone_by_the_age_of_five/ (last accessed 16 September 2015).

References

Alzahrani, S. M., Salim, N. and Abraham, A. (2012) 'Understanding plagiarism linguistic patterns, textual features, and detection methods', *IEEE Transactions on Systems, Man, and Cybernetics – Part C: Applications and Reviews* 42: 133–49.

Coulthard, M. and Johnson, A. (2007) *An introduction to forensic linguistics: language in evidence*, London: Routledge.

Field, A. (2013) *Discovering Statistics using IBM SPSS*, 4th edn, London: Sage.

Grant, T. (2013) 'TXT 4N6: method, consistency, and distinctiveness in the analysis of SMS text messages', *Journal of Law and Policy* 21: 467–94.

Juola, P. (2006) 'Authorship attribution', *Foundations and Trends in Information Retrieval* 1: 233–334.

Newman, M. L., Pennebaker, J. W., Berry, D. S. and Richards, J. M. (2003) 'Lying words: Predicting deception from linguistic styles', *Personality and Social Psychology Bulletin* 29: 665–75.

Oakes, M. P. (1998) *Statistics for Corpus Linguistics*, Edinburgh: Edinburgh University Press.

Olsson, J. (2008) *Forensic Linguistics*, London: Continuum.

Svartvik, J. (1968) *The Evans Statements: A Case for Forensic Linguistics*, Gothenburg: University of Gothenburg Press, www.thetext.co.uk/Evans%20Statements%20Part%201. pdf (last accessed 16 September 2015) and www.thetext.co.uk/Evans%20Statements%20 Part%202.pdf (last accessed 16 September 2015).

Villar, G., Arciuli, J. and Paterson, H. (2013) 'Linguistic indicators of a false confession', *Psychiatry, Psychology and Law* 20: 504–18.

Vrij, A. (2008) *Detecting Lies and Deceit. Pitfalls and Opportunities*, 2nd edn, Chichester: Wiley.

Part 3

Linguistics, teacher knowledge and professional development

Chapter 12

Using silence

Discourse analysis and teachers' knowledge about classroom discussion

Victoria Elliott and Jenni Ingram

Introduction

Classroom discussion has been the subject of much pedagogic research and advice in recent years, particularly in terms of the focus on dialogic classrooms, which promotes real dialogue, as opposed to the 'overwhelmingly monologic' teacher discourse in some classrooms (Alexander 2004: 10). The advice provided by authors such as Robin Alexander and Neil Mercer (e.g. Mercer and Littleton 2007), and in the drive for formative assessment spearheaded by Paul Black and Dylan Wiliam (Black and Wiliam 1998), has tended to consider the nature of tasks and questions asked – that is the content of what is being said, rather than the surrounding structures that enable that content. In this chapter we argue that silence is important in enabling true dialogue and in producing an environment in which students have the opportunity to extend their reasoning and responses. In this chapter we will consider research from the fields of discourse and conversation analysis on silences in classrooms, and use that to consider how teachers can influence the nature of classroom discussions by manipulating silence. Many teachers already think carefully about the content of their talk, but this may not have its full effect if their use of silence and turn-taking does not support their intentions.

The generic advice given to teachers on silence in classrooms is to leave three seconds 'wait time' after asking a question (DfES 2004: 8); this is as far as it goes in most cases, without consideration of whether that is always appropriate, or what the desired effects are. This does not take into account the different types and positions of silence in talk, such as the silence that follows a student's turn. In this chapter we will explore the consequences of different types of pauses in classroom discussions, and how teachers and students can manipulate silences and pauses to influence the nature of these discussions.

Silence can occur in the middle of a person's turn or between two people talking. In the classroom this could be during the teacher's turn, when the turn changes from teacher to student, during the student's turn and when the turn changes from student to teacher, or when the turn changes from one student to another student. But the length, role and consequences of these silences differ depending on when they occur. In an English classroom, to give a simple example, when reading aloud from a text a teacher might pause for dramatic effect, or to stress an important feature, or to mark a change from reading to discussion.

In the research literature, silence in classroom discourse is given various names: the most common is wait time, the term used in the original research (Rowe 1974), which is the source of the recommendation to wait three seconds. Other common terms include *thinking time* (e.g. Morgan and Saxton 2006), *think time* (Alexander 2004), *gaps, lapse and pauses* (Sacks *et al.* 1974) or *waiting time* (mostly in the literature on Teaching English as a Foreign Language, e.g. Phillips [1994]). *Thinking time* is more popular in the recent pedagogical literature because it emphasises the purpose of leaving a gap, although it can also be used to refer to practices such as giving students time to talk briefly in pairs before answers to questions are required. The situation is complicated further by the fact that the term 'wait time' is used in different ways. Rowe's highly cited research (1974) focused only on the pauses preceding a teacher's turn, such as when a teacher asked a question but didn't get an answer, or following a student's answer. More recent research (Heinze and Erhard 2006; Maroni 2011) also looked at the pauses between a teacher's turn and a student speaking. Our own research in addition included pauses within a student's turn (when theoretically the teacher could have spoken) and the pauses after a student's turn when another student begins to speak (Ingram and Elliott 2015). In this chapter we will talk mainly of 'silence' but for us 'wait time' is any time when a teacher is deliberately not speaking.

While some research has concentrated on measuring the silences already in place and exploring their effects, some studies, such as the King's-Medway-Oxfordshire Formative Assessment Project (Black *et al.* 2003), have sought to manipulate the pauses which teachers leave in classroom discourse. They found that teachers struggled to leave pauses even when they were trying to: in normal conversational interactions, there is a maximum tolerance of one second of silence (Jefferson 1988) and this can contribute to teachers feeling that pauses are longer than they really are. Silence in interactions is usually interpreted as a sign of trouble in discourse: this is one of the features that means teachers can exploit silence to change the nature of classroom discussions.

We will first look at the structure of turn-taking in classrooms, before discussing what the research has shown about how pauses change what pupils say in classroom discussion, and then consider what the potential is for teachers to further manipulate silence, by considering it as part of a wider range of strategies for the promotion of dialogue in the classroom.

The structure of classroom interactions

There are a variety of structures of interactions which occur in classrooms. The most dominant one, in most classrooms, is often referred to as the three-part turn, IRF or IRE (initiation-response-feedback/evaluation) sequence (identified by Sinclair and Coulthard 1975). The teacher asks a question, a student gives an answer and then the teacher gives feedback on that answer (see Extract 1 below). This structure is rarely found in conversations outside of classrooms. Opinion on the role and impact of this structure has changed and developed over the years; for some, the focus has been on moving away from this structure because of concerns over teacher dominance and power (e.g. Barnes 1982; Wood 1992), but the sequence has remained prevalent despite many initiatives to change it. More recently, variations within this structure have been explored and, in particular, different ways of using the third turn to achieve different pedagogic goals (e.g. Wells 1993; Nassaji and Wells 2000; Cullen 2009). It is this structure, and in especially the control the teacher has over who can speak and when, which enables silences to occur in classroom discourse.

> *Extract 1:   Initiation, Response, Evaluation/Feedback*
> 1 Teacher: Kerry, what indication did you have that he might be chased?
> 2 Kerry: Because it says 'he glanced behind his shoulder but
> 3   forward'
> 4 Teacher: Okay so it's that idea that there's someone or something behind
>   him (**0**.1) good

In the three-part structure who speaks when is largely predetermined. It is always the teacher who asks the question and nominates which student can answer (whether by name or in response to students indicating that they want to speak). After a student has given their answer, the right to speak returns to the teacher. This is the 'structure of classroom interaction' which was described by McHoul (1978). Since there is no ambiguity over who should be speaking, in comparison to everyday conversation, both teacher and students can afford to leave silences after a teacher's turn, before the student starts to speak. The teacher can also leave a silence after the apparent end of a student's turn, because it is expected that they will speak next.

Other structures which are being used in classrooms, which differ from the three-part turn, such as 'basketball questioning', or 'pose, pause, pounce, bounce', still retain strong teacher control over who speaks. In these structures the teacher asks a question, a student responds and the teacher redirects the turn to another student to add to or challenge the previous student's response; even if the teacher only speaks to nominate the next student, or even simply passes the turn by gesture, the turn has still returned to them before moving to the second student. These structures can therefore differ in terms of content in the third turn (often with the evaluation or feedback still present but now in a student's subsequent turn), but still retain the teacher-student-teacher turn order, and the teacher's control over who speaks and hence the same opportunities for silences as before.

Extract 2: Redirect in third turn

1 Teacher:	… Okay – who thinks that Simon will leave his home and
2	migrate to Spain?
3 Pam:	We all agreed that he would go because he loves
4	Spanish food.
5 Teacher:	Does everyone agree with Pam? Vicky?
6 Vicky:	We agreed with that but we thought it would be more
7	important about the job. Getting a job is more important
8	than what food you like.

A structure where the teacher does not maintain control over who speaks in classrooms is one in which students respond to each other without the teacher nominating speakers, such as in a spontaneous debate or argument. This structure may occur as part of a larger interactional structure but is rarely the dominant classroom discourse. However, its features are important when considering the role of silence, as we discuss in 'Other structures of classroom talk' below, as the same opportunities as there are in the three-part structure do not exist.

As we have mentioned above, advice on classroom pedagogy recommends leaving a minimum of three seconds silence after asking a question. Rowe's original research on silence in science classroom discourse showed that most teachers leave less than one second of silence after asking a question before rephrasing or answering their own question (Rowe 1974; still found to be true in Ingram 2012), and other studies have shown teachers find it difficult to change this even when they know the recommendation for three seconds of 'wait time' and are actively trying to implement it (see for example Black *et al.* 2003).

Researching silence in the classroom

Most research exploring the manipulation of wait time has happened in artificial scenarios, such as a teacher working with one or two students. The recommendation for the three seconds comes from Rowe's research which showed that when students were left to speak they did so in bursts of three to five seconds; she argued that since children naturally left pauses of three to five seconds in conversation, it is necessary to leave gaps of at least three seconds (Rowe 1972).

The early research on wait time was conducted in science classrooms (Rowe 1972, 1974); there has been some subsequent research conducted in mathematics classrooms (Tobin 1987; Lesh and Zawojewski 2007; Ingram and Elliott 2014, 2015) and in some primary settings (e.g. Maroni 2011). Tobin (1986) also looked at 'language arts' classrooms in America, which would be the equivalent of an English classroom in the UK. The original work on the structure of classroom interactions described above was conducted in geography classrooms (McHoul 1978). Although the majority of this research was undertaken in science and mathematics classrooms, there is enough evidence to show that the findings hold true across different subjects and age ranges (and languages/countries: for example Maroni [2011] conducted her research in Italy).

In the rest of this chapter we use extracts from anonymous primary data supplied to us by teachers of English who recorded their own practice for professional development. Looking at silence needs detailed transcription where pauses are measured very tightly, which makes collecting data very time intensive, and also means that most transcriptions of classroom discourse are not useful for looking at silence in the classroom.

It is difficult to measure silence precisely in classrooms because they are noisy and busy places: it's often not easy to tell when one speaker stops talking and another begins. In addition the early researchers did not have the benefit of digital recordings and software that measures in microseconds; observers and teachers can both be inaccurate about how long a silence is, and many claim that pauses are longer than they actually are.

What silence in teacher-student interactions can do

Leaving a silence after a teacher's question

Silence after a teacher's question can occur in two places: before a student is nominated to answer (as in Extract 3), or after. In the first case the teacher has control over the length of the pause because the turn is still theirs until they pass it on to a student by nominating them (by name or in some other way). The pause after a nomination is not only the decision of the teacher however: both the teacher and the student contribute to the length of the silence. In order for the student to respond to the question, the teacher must leave enough time for them to do so, but the student also has the opportunity to wait because the turn is theirs, just as for teachers in the first case (although they must also speak before the teacher reclaims the turn). In each of these places it is the teacher's decision not to speak that creates the potential for silence. Teachers report finding it difficult to resist the urge to speak (Black *et al.* 2003); the maximum standard tolerance of silence (Jefferson 1988) means they feel the desire to speak, and it often means that individuals experience a silence as much longer than it actually is.

It is quite common for teachers to answer their own questions in the classroom, or to make the assumption that students cannot answer, simply because they have not. Studies show that when teachers actively try to leave a longer silence after asking a question, students are more likely to give some form of answer to the question and less likely to say 'I don't know' or not speak at all. They are also more likely to try out a tentative idea (Rowe 1974; Tobin 1987). This is because silence makes people feel obliged to speak, particularly if they've been nominated to speak. If the teacher does not fill that silence by rephrasing or answering their own question, then students will do so. The silence also gives students the opportunity to think about and formulate their response, so they are more likely to have a response to give (Ingram and Elliott 2014, 2015). This is why many writers refer to this silence as 'think(ing) time'. Leaving the silence before nominating a student to answer also has the advantage that every member of the class is encouraged to think, because they don't know who will be chosen to respond!

Extract 3:   *Pause before nomination*
1 Teacher: ... So what do we mean by first and third person
2   writing (1.1) what's first person ((*inaudible*)) go
3   on Ian
4 Ian: Them saying it
5 Teacher: So (.) if you did it from your perspective Ian yes I
6   isn't it (.) or we, but normally I. what about third
7   person (1.1) yep Ann
8 Ann: Like if I were saying I said Daniel (.) was

In Extract 3, in the teacher's first turn, a pause of 1.1 seconds is left before the question is rephrased and a student is nominated to answer; in the teacher's subsequent turn, he simply leaves the pause. In both these cases the pause is longer than the maximum standard tolerance of silence, but it does not need to be as long as three seconds, because the questions themselves are relatively simple. One study found that if students can answer the question but have too long a silence imposed on them, then they get bored (Kirton *et al.* 2007). There is therefore an art to how much 'thinking time' is appropriate for a question.

Extract 4:   *Pause after teacher question*
1 Teacher: So this was forty what?
2 Taylor: Per- (3.7) yeah how long it took (0.4) like
3   four (2.7)
4 Teacher: How long it took

In Extract 4, the context of the interaction means the student who should answer has already been nominated (the teacher is asking a follow-up question to an answer they have already given). It shows an example where a student initially has difficulty answering the question but after a pause of 3.7 seconds is able to respond, and give the response which the teacher was looking for (in that it is accepted by the teacher in line 4). This illustrates the way in which silence can reduce the likelihood of a non-response and support the student in making an answer.

When teachers changed their practice to extend the time they left after asking a question, over time they gradually also changed the types of questions which they asked, moving naturally to asking for explanations and reasons (Rowe 1986). Many approaches to improving classroom interactions have focused on the design of questions (e.g. Black *et al.* 2003; Alexander 2004; Mercer and Littleton 2007), trying to stimulate these types of classroom interactions. The results of Rowe

(1986) suggest that it might be possible (and perhaps easier?) to achieve this through concentrating on silence, rather than the contents of questions.

Leaving a silence after a student's response

The other occasion where silences can occur is after a student's response. This silence has received far less attention, both in the research literature and in the pedagogical recommendations. However, the effects of manipulating this silence have been shown to be more wide ranging (Tobin 1987). As we mentioned before, Rowe's first research (1972) into 'wait time' showed that when children were left to talk freely they often expressed ideas in bursts of three to five seconds and would leave gaps of up to five seconds between these bursts. In classrooms, these gaps are often filled by the teacher offering feedback or another response and therefore treating the student's response as finished. Leaving a silence enables students who don't think they have finished to do so!

However, leaving a silence can also stimulate the student to speak through another mechanism. If a student thinks they have finished speaking, then the turn (both the right and the obligation to speak) returns to the teacher. If the teacher does not speak, this creates some ambiguity about who should be speaking. In everyday conversation this type of silence would usually indicate that there was some type of 'trouble' (Seedhouse 2004) or problem, such as a misunderstanding. A student may therefore feel the need to clarify, expand or alter what they have previously said to resolve the issue. This is known as a *repair* (Schegloff *et al.* 1977). Consequently, studies that have explored extending the silence following a student's response have reported that students' answers are longer, more likely to contain an explanation or an alternative interpretation, and less likely to be inflected, that is to feature the rising inflection that usually indicates a question (Rowe 1974; Tobin 1987). If the student does not take the opportunity offered by the silence, a teacher may choose to use a continuation marker such as 'okay' or 'right' which acknowledges what the student has already said but also clearly returns the turn to the student.

> *Extract 5:*   *Pauses after (during) a student turn*
> 1 Teacher: What is this?
> 2 Sarah: Pathetic fallacy (0.4) because of the weather (2.0) it
> 3   reflects the mood (0.8)
> 4 Teacher: Well done, it is pathetic fallacy

In Extract 5 after each silence the student adds further detail to their response, although it would have been possible to interpret their turn as being complete at the end of any burst. This shows how the teacher refraining from speaking and being aware of silence can help to develop student contributions to classroom discussion, in terms of both quality and length, as advocated in approaches like dialogic teaching.

Since lengthening the pause following a student's turn leads to some ambiguity over who should be speaking, the opportunity for other students to interject arises. They may intervene to repair the trouble in the interaction, if they do not perceive the original speaker as being about to take the turn (Ingram and Elliott 2014). Although the standard maximum tolerance of silence is one second, different people feel uncomfortable at different points, so the amount of time a teacher needs to wait will depend upon the students with whom they are working. This also explains why some teachers find it harder than others to extend pauses in the classroom. Students may also, in this scenario, be responding to something that the original answerer said, that is listening to their classmates and potentially building on what was said. Conversely, Rowe found that where teachers do not extend silence in any way, 'children "stack up" waiting to tell the teacher. There is very little indication that they listen to each other' (Rowe 1972: 8). In the same way, teachers who left longer pauses after student responses also demonstrated that they listened more to those responses, as their follow-up comments related to what the student had said, rather than directly back to the question they themselves had asked.

Rowe (1972) also described an increase in the number of student questions when pauses were extended, after either a teacher's question or a student's answer. Students might, when faced with a silence after a teacher's question, be more likely to ask for clarification because they cannot rely on the teacher answering their own question; equally with the opportunity to extend their response, they may have time to think deeply enough about a topic to come to an interesting question. They may also be simply using the opportunity to speak, in a situation where there is rarely a chance to self-nominate, to ask a question which they have been unable to ask before.

Silence changes teaching

Black and Wiliam (1998) suggested that the kinds of questions which teachers ask when they are not in the habit of using silence in the classroom tend to be simple ones, because those are the kinds of questions it is possible to answer instantly. Rowe (1972) found that when teachers deliberately extend the time they wait after asking a question, they also naturally change the types of questions they ask, to ones which require explanation, reasoning, or other more thought out responses. These kinds of questions and answers are desirable in the context of dialogic teaching, but also in other approaches to teaching. Where questions are simple and instantly answerable, the response is anticipated (not necessarily consciously) by the teacher, so teachers do not need to listen to the response, they only need to recognise it as the one they wanted. In these situations pupils are constrained to predict what the teacher wants, Black and Wiliam (1998) argue; the lack of a genuine discussion, in which the teacher engages with what pupils have to say, means that pupils may therefore reduce their engagement with the topic. Increasing the use of silence, therefore, indirectly causes a change in the nature of communication between teachers and students.

In addition, teachers' expectations of students change. Teachers in a study carried out by Kirton et al. (2007) reported re-evaluating their expectations of students as being not less able, but just needing more time to answer (a finding also in Rowe 1974), if they allowed all students more time to answer.

Other structures of classroom talk

Some classrooms or types of classroom dialogue are more like ordinary conversation in terms of their structure (rather than their tone): for example, an argument or a debate where two or more students are presenting different views and the interaction resembles that of an argument outside the classroom (i.e. where it's not contrived). This might equally apply to most sixth form classes or any classroom involved in the in-depth discussion of a text, or a classroom engaged in collaborative creative work such as shared creative writing. Here the structure of the interaction does not allow for pauses between turns and it is much harder to leave silence; however, silence in this context may not be desirable. If there is an argument or debate going, or students are already engaged in thinking deeply and justifying their points, then the benefits of extending silence are already in place. This is one of the reasons why a blanket recommendation to leave three seconds of silence is problematic: teachers need to think about why they are leaving silence, what kind of interaction they are encouraging, and what their desired outcome is, rather than simply obey a rule.

Conclusion

So, while 'wait time' has become a byword in teaching advice, and absorbed into a range of dialogic and formative assessment strategies, the context, intention and type of interaction all make a difference to whether teachers should be leaving silence, and for how long they should be leaving it. The effects of extending pauses in classroom dialogue have been shown by various researchers to be wide-ranging, and it is clear that these effects can be explained through the use of some well-established linguistic norms relating to silence and turn-taking. Teachers can apply this research into silence in classroom interactions to make changes to the quality of dialogue within their classrooms, but simply leaving a standard three seconds will not have the same impact as tailoring silence to particular situations. Thinking about silence will also aid teachers who want to apply dialogic teaching approaches in their classrooms, not only because both have similar effects, but also because extending silences changes the nature of the content of teacher questions, possibly more easily than deliberately planning those questions. Silence can contribute much to learning, when its use is allied to teacher intentions and the specific classroom context.

References

Alexander, R. (2004) *Towards Dialogic Teaching: Rethinking Classroom Talk*, Cambridge: Dialogos.

Barnes, B. (1982) 'On the extension of concepts and the growth of knowledge', *Sociological Review* 30: 303–33.

Black, P. and Wiliam, D. (1998) *Inside the Black Box: Raising Standards Through Classroom Assessment*, Swindon: GL Assessment.

Black, P., Harrison, C., Lee, C., Marshall, B. and Wiliam, D. (2003) *Assessment for Learning: Putting it into Practice*, Maidenhead: Open University Press.

Cullen, R. (2002) 'Supportive teacher talk: the importance of the F-move', *ELT Journal* 56(2): 117–27.

DfES (2004) *Pedagogy and Practice: Teaching and Learning in the Secondary School Unit 7: Questioning*, London: HMSO.

Heinze, A. and Erhard, M. (2006) 'How much time do students have to think about teacher questions? An investigation of the quick succession of teacher questions and student responses in the German mathematics classroom', *ZDM Mathematics Education* 38(5), 388–98.

Ingram, J. (2012) *Whole Class Interaction in the Mathematics Classroom: A Conversation Analytic Approach*, PhD thesis: Institute of Education, University of Warwick.

Ingram, J. and Elliott, V. (2014) 'Turn taking and "wait time" in classroom interactions', *Journal of Pragmatics* 62: 1–12.

Ingram, J. and Elliott, V. (2015) 'A critical analysis of the role of wait time in classroom interactions and the effects on student and teacher interactional behaviours', *Cambridge Journal of Education* DOI: 10.1080/0305764X.2015.1009365.

Jefferson, G. (1988) 'Notes on a possible metric which provides for a "standard maximum" silence of approximately one second in conversation', in D. Roger and P. Bull (eds) *Conversation: An Interdisciplinary Perspective*, Clevedon: Multilingual Matters.

Kirton, A., Hallam, S., Peffers, J., Robertson, P. and Stobart, G. (2007) 'Revolution, evolution or a Trojan horse? Piloting assessment for learning in some Scottish primary schools', *British Educational Research Journal* 33(4): 605–27.

Lesh, R. and Zawojewski, J. (2007) 'Problem solving and modelling', in F. K. Lester (ed.) *Second Handbook of Research on Mathematics Teaching and Learning* 2, Reston, VA: National Council of Teachers of Mathematics, pp. 763–804.

McHoul, A. (1978) 'The organization of turns at formal talk in the classroom', *Language in Society* 7: 183–213.

Maroni, B. (2011) 'Pauses, gaps and wait time in classroom interaction in primary schools', *Journal of Pragmatics* 43: 2081–93.

Mercer, N. and Littleton, K. (2007) *Dialogue and the Development of Children's Thinking: A Sociocultural Approach*, London: Routledge.

Morgan, N. and Saxton, J. (2006) *Asking Better Questions*, Ontario: Pembroke Publishers Limited.

Nassaji, H. and Wells, G. (2000) 'What's the use of triadic dialogue?: An investigation of teacher-student interaction', *Applied Linguistics* 21(3): 376–406.

Phillips, D. (1994) 'The functions of silence within the context of teacher training', *ELT Journal* 48(3): 266–71.

Rowe, M. B. (1972) 'Wait-time and rewards as instructional variables: Their influence on language, logic and fate control', Paper presented at the National Association for Research in Science Teaching.

Rowe, M. B. (1974) 'Wait-Times and Rewards as Instructional Variables: Their Influence on Language, Logic and Fate Control – Part 1. Wait-Time', *Journal of Research in Science Teaching* 11, 81–94.

Rowe, M. B. (1986) 'Wait Time: Slowing down may be a way of speeding up!', *Journal of Teacher Education* 37: 43–50.

Sacks, H., Schegloff, E. A. and Jefferson, G. (1974) 'A simplest systematics for the organization of turn-taking for conversation', *Language* 50: 696–735.

Schegloff, E. A., Jefferson, G. and Sacks, H. (1977) 'The preference for self-correction in the organization of repair in conversation', *Language* 53: 361–82.

Seedhouse, P. (2004) 'The interactional architecture of the language classroom: A conversation analysis perspective', Malden, MA: Blackwell.

Sinclair, J. and Coulthard, M. (1975) *Towards an Analysis of Discourse*, Oxford: Oxford University Press.

Tobin, K. (1986) 'Effects of teacher wait time on discourse characteristics in mathematics and language arts classes', *American Educational Research Journal* 23(2): 191–200.

Tobin, K. (1987) 'The role of wait time in higher cognitive level learning', *Review of Educational Research* 57(1): 69–95.

Wells, G. (1993) 'Reevaluating the IRF sequence: A proposal for the articulation of theories of activity and discourse for the analysis of teaching and learning in the classroom', *Linguistics and Education* 5(1): 1–37.

Wood, D. (1992) 'Teaching talk', in K. Norman (ed.) *Thinking Voices: The Work of the National Oracy Project*, London: Hodder & Stoughton, pp. 203–14.

Chapter 13

Narrative interrelation, intertextuality and teachers' knowledge about students' reading

Jessica Mason

Introduction

Drawing on analysis of a 360,000-word corpus of English lesson transcripts, this chapter considers the 'class reader' as a type of reading experience. Reading a set text with a group is a major investment of time and resources and, for much of the academic year, is central to the English curriculum in many secondary schools. This chapter considers the reasons why teachers and policy-makers think reading fiction with students is a good idea, and then reflects on whether the *ways* in which fiction is read in the English classroom are likely to achieve those aims. In particular, the chapter explores the relationship between students' reading experiences inside and outside the classroom, investigating the impact, and questioning the necessity, of the divergences between studying a text and reading for pleasure.

Why read fiction in secondary school?

Why is fiction read in secondary schools at all? The answer, at least historically, is largely founded upon all the positive effects of reading for pleasure, which are well documented. Reading for pleasure is more important to a student's educational success than their family's socioeconomic status (OECD 2002). It supports healthy personal, emotional and social development as well as increasing general knowledge (Clark and Rumbold 2006). Those who read for pleasure perform better in literacy, reading and even mathematics assessments (Sullivan and Brown 2013). Reading fiction has also been shown able to make people more open-minded and empathetic (Djikic *et al.* 2013). One recent study even suggests reading *Harry Potter* results in more positive attitudes towards minority groups (Vezzali *et al.* 2015). Simply put, fiction can be a hugely powerful tool in nurturing critical, caring human beings. Fostering a population with a lifelong love of reading is thus one of the most crucial aspects of formal education, with significant social advantages. The use of a class reader, which engages students in the act of reading a complete text over an extended period, is therefore demonstrably pedagogically valuable as an activity in and of itself.

However, English lessons, the space in which most school-based reading takes place and where much of students' conceptualisations of reading will almost inevitably be formed, cannot of course be solely concerned with students enjoying the texts they read. Students must also become literate, master a technical linguistic vocabulary and formulate evidence-based and nuanced arguments. Class reader units seek to improve students' critical reading skills, to help them reflect on a text, form opinions, engage in analytical thinking and teach them about aspects of language. At the same time, there is still a desire for students to enjoy the texts themselves and to use their classroom reading experiences as a springboard to becoming avid, thoughtful, independent readers.

Unfortunately, the UK ranks consistently poorly in the Programme for International Student Assessment (PISA) tests in relation to reading for pleasure (Twist *et al.* 2007; DfE 2012), and the tendency for young people to engage in this crucial activity plummets between the ages of eleven and fourteen, i.e. over the course of Key Stage 3 (Clark and Osbourne 2008; Clark and Douglas 2011; Topping 2014). The difficulty, then, is achieving both pleasure and learning at the same time. How do teachers enable students to gain pleasure from reading whilst simultaneously making them better at it?

There is a lack of clarity about how to prioritise the various pedagogic aspirations teachers are tasked with achieving when teaching a class reader. The National Curriculum's statement regarding reading fiction at Key Stage 3 neatly demonstrates this opacity when it tells us that 'pupils should be taught to develop an *appreciation and love* of reading, *and read increasingly challenging material independently*' (my emphasis, DfE 2014: 4). The flippant coordination of these three objectives offers no indication as to the relative importance of each. It also appears to imply that 'appreciation', 'love' and a desire for 'increased challenge' are things which can be developed in students at the same time, within the same set of reading experiences.

Part of the problem is a dislocated relationship between reading inside and outside of the English classroom. As students progress into secondary school reading becomes viewed as a 'learnt skill' and encouragement to engage in reading for pleasure, both at home and in the classroom, is displaced in favour of a focus on literacy skills (Merga 2014). This dislocation is mirrored in the programmes targeted at increasing students' reading for pleasure, such as D.E.A.R. (Drop Everything and Read) or E.R.I.C. (Everyone Reading In Class), which are focused not on examining the reading teachers are already doing with students, but on reading *in addition* to class readers. The recent recommendation that every school in the UK should have a 'Reading for Pleasure policy' (Ofsted 2012) also farms out strategies for increasing reading for pleasure to other areas of the curriculum: either the library, whole-school programmes (such as D.E.A.R.) or distinct lessons within English dedicated to reading for enjoyment. This is not to suggest that any of these additional practices are a bad thing, though it is worth noting that the efficacy of silent reading programmes has been highly disputed (Merga 2013). On the other hand, collective efforts towards encouraging students to read for pleasure, at the level of both policy and practice, tend to involve delegating the task out to a separate curriculum space whilst ignoring the ways in which fiction is already being read with students in the form of class readers.

Since class readers were introduced as a school practice at the turn of the twentieth century, there has been little consideration as to whether studying a book as a group in this fashion resembles reading for pleasure at all. This, coupled with the creeping intrusion of additional learning aims, predominantly oriented around the acquisition of linguistic terminology and other speaking, listening and writing 'skills', risks moving the class reader further and further away from the kinds of reading experiences young people engage in outside the classroom. The consequences of this divergence are clearly reflected in research, which shows that students dissociate formally studying texts and reading for pleasure, viewing them as distinct, largely unrelated practices (Nash 2007; Fialho *et al.* 2011; Nightingale 2011). A clear understanding about what class readers are for, if it ever existed, appears to have been lost. As a result, reading fiction in secondary school English classrooms is in danger of becoming more to do with *learning about* books than *engaging* with them, or worse, simply using texts as vehicles to teach other (inferentially more important) things. This final scenario has significant potential to be symbiotically damaging to students' perceptions of both literature and language, as the former ceases to look anything like reading, and the latter is seen as 'the thing to blame'.

In the remainder of this chapter I will argue that this distinction between studying a text or reading for pleasure is a false binary; teachers do not need to choose between these practices: they can have both. In order to facilitate this, however, there is a need to understand exactly what uncouples the class reader from the rest of students' reading experiences. If this can be established then English teachers will be able to make informed decisions about how to shape the classroom reading experience for themselves and their students. I will posit that the isolation of the class reader from students' reading more generally is not only unnecessary but pedagogically detrimental, and I will explore some ways in which teachers could make *studying* a text feel more like *reading* it.

The 'class reader' as a type of reading experience

Reading a work of fiction with a group of students is never going to be an identical experience to picking up a book and reading it, at leisure, left to one's own devices. Nor, I think, would most teachers really want it to be (Dean 2003): studying a text *should* achieve more than the students simply having another book 'under their belt' by the end of it. In fact, by some definitions, reading for pleasure cannot be achieved in the course of studying a text as it is the practice of 'simply reading for the sake of reading' with a total absence of learning objectives or prescribed analytical aims (Laurenson *et al.* 2015: 8, following Cremin *et al.* 2008).

That said, if studying a text looks and feels *nothing* like reading for pleasure, whilst being presented to young people as the same activity, then there is a risk of misrepresenting what reading is altogether. That is, students could be concluding based on their class reader experiences, that they 'don't enjoy reading' or 'are not readers' based on a misplaced belief that studying a text and reading for pleasure independently are in essence synonymous activities.

The research

This chapter is informed by a 360,000 word corpus of classroom transcripts derived from two complete class reader units: a group of 29 mixed ability Year 7s reading *Holes* (Sachar 1999) and a 'top set' Year 9 class comprising 34 students reading *Animal Farm* (Orwell 1945). The groups were recorded from the first lesson on their respective texts through to the completion of their assessments. Roughly 25 hours of recording of each of the classes were then transcribed. The result is a rich and comprehensive picture of two typical student experiences of reading a novel in English.

Close examination of such a large body of data of 'class reader' lessons enables the identification of certain lesson designs, task types and approaches to reading fiction in school that either resemble, or depart from, other types of reading experiences (such as privately for pleasure or for a reading group). One useful way to conceptualise different types of reading is through the use of a cline, with 'authentic' reading at one end and 'manufactured' reading at the other:

> [Authentic reading] is born out of an individual's own process of unmediated interpretation [... to] have space to interpret the text, to experience it for [yourself. At the other end of the spectrum] manufactured readings are learnt, not made; they occur when readers are denied the space to engage in their own process of interpretation.
>
> (Giovanelli and Mason 2015: 42)

This distinction strikes at the heart of what can cause students to dislocate studying a text from the rest of their reading experiences. If a student perceives that interpretations of a class reader are being imposed on them, that is, if their responses are being manufactured, this is the point at which they are likely to feel that they are being taught about the text rather than being offered the opportunity to read, think about and engage with it for themselves.

Building on this definition, I will now explore how some common approaches to the class reader can be unwittingly geared towards manufacturing students' reading. In order to do this, it is necessary to briefly introduce three simple cognitive linguistic concepts (for a fuller account of these see Mason 2014):

- A *narrative schema*: This is an individual's version of a text in the mind. Additional information can be added to a schema through the process of *accretion* (Stockwell 2002: 80).

- The *mental archive*: This is the mental store of our narrative schemas accrued over time. It can be compared to 'an internal personalised library where every book, film and tale looks exactly how you remember it' (Mason 2014: 189).
- A *narrative interrelation*: This occurs when readers make links between stories. A narrative interrelation describes the mental process when a reader makes an intertextual link between two narrative schemas.

This 'narrative interrelation framework' offers a tool that can be used to describe and analyse differences between individuals' working knowledge of the same text, and to consider how readers interrelate these different versions of the stories they encounter. If two people read the same ten books and were then asked to write down a list of the last ten books they had read, their reading experiences would appear, superficially, to be identical. In reality, however, each would have different *narrative schemas* for each text. The contents and availability of the narrative schemas every reader has to form interrelations with will be different from person to person. Where one person fell asleep before the end of a film, another may have watched it fifteen times; one person skimmed a book ten years ago, another read it with great enthusiasm last night, a third may have heard about it but never read it for themselves. Parts of a narrative will be forgotten where others may be remembered in acute detail, whole passages may be memorised or complete narratives obliterated entirely. Different individuals would have accreted, thought about, retained, engaged with, ignored and forgotten different things and would be adding these reading experiences to their different *mental archives*. As a result, readers will make different *narrative interrelations* based on a combination of these, and other factors such as which stories are contained within their mental archives, how rich those narrative schemas are, how recently they have been accessed and so on. Crucially, narrative schemas can include knowledge of a text that has not come from the actual act of reading but from secondary sources such as what we have read or heard about the story ... or what a teacher has said. Thus, in a class reader unit, teacher and students may all be reading the same physical text, but each will have their own *subtly distinctive* narrative schema for that text developing in their mind.

The challenges of reading in the classroom

This cognitive framework enables description of some of the divergences between reading for pleasure, when a reader is left to their own devices, and the ways in which a text is read and discussed in a classroom. In other words, it facilitates conceptualising the English classroom as a room full of readers, all with their own narrative schema for the set text, as well as a unique mental archive comprising their personal reading histories.

The cline of authentic and manufactured reading can also be captured more precisely through the application of this framework. Knowledge about a fictional work can be accreted through a number of avenues, not solely through the direct act of reading. If a student, initially at least, predominantly accretes their narrative schema from their own reading and interpretation of a text, the resulting schema will reflect their authentic response. If, on the other hand, a student predominantly accretes their schema from discourse *about* the text, rather than from their own reading experience, the resultant reading is likely to be heavily manufactured. In other words, the student will have learnt a response rather than had one. In the class reader context, manufactured reading will result if a student accretes knowledge from what their teacher and peers say about the text, or from information they have obtained from other external sources, rather than from their own reading. Thus, class reader lessons that facilitate students authentically engaging with, reflecting upon and critically developing their own readings are more likely to result in students creating rich narrative schemas for the text. These schemas are also more likely to resemble other narrative schemas in the students' mental archives; in other words, the class reader will look and feel like their other reading experiences.

A room full of readers

Teachers have almost always read the class reader before they teach it: to not do so would likely be considered bad practice. This means, however, that teachers are always discussing the text with reference to a rich narrative schema that includes the full arc of the story, and will have a complete authentic experience of the text before they begin to teach it as a class reader. This mirrors the experiences of, for instance, members of a reading group or university students, who all read the book first and discuss and actively engage in critical interpretation second. The same is not true for secondary school students who are, or are typically assumed to be, first-time readers of the texts they study. In contrast to their teachers, students accrete text knowledge as they go and, until they reach the end, any tasks they complete, questions they answer or discussions they have are working from a narrative schema that does not include a complete version of the text.

This disjunction of text knowledge can be challenging: it is difficult to discuss a text up to chapter twenty-five when you have actually read as far as chapter fifty. Readers encounter this scenario in the course of everyday discussions all the time. Upon realising that another person has not finished reading a given text, many readers will either curtail the conversation or else carefully regulate anything else they say about the text so as to prevent spoiling the reading for the other person (consider the phrase 'I'll wait until you've finished it!'). This is because, in doing so, the reader is trying to compartmentalise off bits of their own narrative schema in an extremely unnatural manner, to talk as though chapters one through twenty-five are also their only point of reference when they probably do not remember where chapter twenty-five ends and twenty-six begins. Yet this is precisely what English teachers must do for most of a class reader unit; teachers are often positioned to draw on their superior text knowledge as re-readers. In my research, both teachers often disclosed or drew on information that could not realistically constitute part of their students' narrative schemas for the class reader at the point the discussions took place. Consider the following examples from the Year 7 and 9 transcripts respectively, both taken from points *before* the class did the day's reading of the text:

> Mrs K: At the centre of *Holes* there is a curse that's kind of like the centre of the whole novel we're going to read about that today so those of you that know the novel remember that we have to keep it zipped today okay, um, because obviously it turns, it's, an important feature.

> Miss B: If you remember Tsar Nicholas was in charge of Russia before the revolution, before Marx's idea, before Lenin, he was the one that was overthrown. He was affected by the revolution. So now that we know what Major's ideas are, you can probably predict what's going to happen in chapter two, so we'll see Mr Jones has been overthrown. The rebellion at Manor Farm taking place.

Throughout both sets of transcripts, teachers' booktalk at this stage of the lesson is often characterised by use of the future tense, indicating that they are drawing on information in their narrative schemas relating to elements of the text which are yet to be read. This suggests that when teachers are compelled to introduce or frame the day's reading, it tends to lead them to reveal some of the content of that reading ('you can probably predict what's going to happen, we'll see Mr Jones has been overthrown'), to make evaluative comments ('turns into an important feature'; 'is kind of like the centre of the whole novel'), or to make statements that can pre-empt students' interpretations of that section before they read it for themselves (Mr Jones allegorically represents Tsar Nicholas, we can tell because both get overthrown).

A lesson structure that requires teachers to discuss what the class is about to read creates the risk of accidental manufacturing of students' reading. Not only this, the nature of the student–teacher relationship predisposes the young readers in the class to view the teacher as an expert. What is also clear from the transcripts is that the typically incremental, fragmented approach to the actual reading of the class reader means that, because teachers cannot unread or unknow what happens in the rest of the text, they frequently make interpretive comments which the students could not possibly make based on their own 'reading so far'. When this happens, it positions students to accrete their narrative schemas from what the teacher says rather than from their own reading: in other words, it risks manufacturing. One such example of this can be seen in the *Animal Farm* transcripts. At this point the students are halfway through chapter two of the ten-chapter novel, and have just encountered the 'Seven Commandments' of animalism: the rules the animals have created as their guide for their fair and utopian society. Again, in the course of introducing the day's reading, the accidental imposition of interpretations, which the students could not possibly make based on their own reading, occurs:

Miss B: What we have just had then are the Seven Commandments, they are key, because what we will start to see is how they change and are amended by the pigs. The Seven Commandments are kind of the perfect ideals of animalism. However George Orwell is not going to give us a perfect ideal of animalism in the text, because he is trying to do a critique.

Miss B again shifts into the future tense ('we will start to see'; 'is not going to'). This means that she is drawing on her superior knowledge as a re-reader of the text, which is the only way she could discuss what is going to happen next. Without this richer narrative schema available to them, students are unable to assess Miss B's claims about the text making her statements, in a pragmatic sense, unchallengeable. In this way, though it was never intended, manufactured responses can be imposed upon students, who may naturally accrete their own narrative schemas from their teacher's discourse about later sections of the text, sometimes weeks before they reach that point in their own reading.

When we read

The traditionally fragmented approach to reading the text can also jeopardise students' ability to form authentic responses to a class reader. Students cannot start and stop reading whenever they wish but must read in prescribed increments, often heavily interspersed with tasks. These tasks often concentrate on very small sections of the text and often have a narrow, predetermined focus. This inserts opportunities for accidental, or even deliberate, manufacturing at every stage. Narrative schema accretion risks becoming homogenised across the class as everyone starts to learn the same reading and set of interpretations. Such a piecemeal approach also makes it difficult for students to interrelate the class reader with other texts in their mental archives because the individual links they make are rarely relevant to the specific tasks they are asked to complete. Thus, not only does the class reader feel like a completely different type of reading experience, it is potentially not being interrelated with the rest of students' mental archives, that is, with their other more authentic reading experiences.

This fragmentation is exacerbated if students are not allowed to take a copy of the class reader home with them, which offers students the chance to continue reading the text if they wish to do so. The decision not to allow students to keep a copy of the class reader for the duration of the unit is often financially driven. Either a department does not own enough copies of a text, the Tuesday group cannot keep the books because another class need to use them on Wednesday, or there is a worry that the books will get lost or damaged if the students are allowed to take them home. Sometimes this is unavoidable.

However, on an affective level, not being able to take the book home means that students are likely to have little sense of ownership of the text or the reading experience; it is something they are able to access only within the English classroom. Consider how this situates the book in the eyes and minds of the students: the text is something that they are given in the classroom and leave behind when they return to the world outside. Here the text is firmly situated as 'the thing we study' rather than 'the thing we read and enjoy'. This practice could also deny students' opportunities to immerse themselves in the world of the text which, at the same time, has been identified as one of the key things many young people enjoy about their private reading experiences (Cliff Hodges 2010).

Readers often describe feeling transported, or speak of 'losing themselves' in a book (Gerrig 1993). Most readers will have, at some stage, experienced this phenomenon either losing track of time: being suddenly startled by the presence of another person they had not observed enter the room, or even experiencing a sensation of physical immersion in the world of the text, only realised when the reader is jolted back to reality. However, if that reading experience was only allowed to occur in twenty-minute increments in prescribed slots three times a week, or perhaps, immediately after reading a section that they found deeply affecting, or enthralling, or intriguing, those readers were asked to write a paragraph about how that effect was created, it is likely this immersive sensation would be lost. It is uncontroversial to suggest that, if students are only able to interact with a text within lesson time, this is likely to result in narrative schema accretion which foregrounds the mechanics of how a text is put together but neglects the emotionally engaging aspects of the reading experience. This is not to suggest that letting students take the book home will result in every student avidly reading it cover to cover and forging a profoundly affective response; however, if students can only access the text in the classroom, it largely precludes the possibility that they might. This can also distinguish the class reader from the other reading experiences students are engaging in outside their English lessons, by making it look and feel different. In other words, it could position the class reader as an object to be studied, not as a story to be read.

Conclusion

When considered through a cognitive linguistic lens, it becomes clear that some of the most typical approaches to class readers interfere with and manufacture students' narrative schemas. In particular, the fragmented and incremental reading of the text itself creates an inevitable imbalance of text knowledge between teacher and students that is difficult to overcome. This means that teachers are frequently situated as re-readers attempting to stimulate discussions with a room full of readers who may not be in a position to form meaningful responses on topics.

Applying knowledge of cognitive linguistics, in the manner demonstrated in this chapter, could support and facilitate teachers' in-lesson design. The responses a student gives in relation to a class reader can be conceived as a reflection of their narrative schema for the text. The narrative interrelation framework also offers teachers a concrete metalanguage with which to think about the disjunction of text knowledge which exists between themselves and their students. As individuals who come to the class reader unit with an authentic reading already mentally in tow, teachers possess an invaluable but potentially volatile resource: a comprehensive narrative schema for the text. This resource can help teachers to guide their students through the richest route of their own narrative schema accretion, supporting and ameliorating their students in developing authentic responses. However, knowledge of the text must also be acknowledged as a potential danger, creating the possibility of accidental manufacturing.

The research reported in this chapter suggests that the key role of the teacher within a class reader unit is to bear the burden of superior text knowledge, in order to illuminate but not impose. Active mindfulness to the fact that they, the teacher, are a re-reader teaching first-time readers, who do not yet have the same rich level of accretion in their mental versions of the text, could be advantageous to teachers when planning their class reader units. The analysis also suggests that teachers may be usefully aided in this task by contemplating their own first-time reading of the texts they teach, by asking themselves a question that resituates them alongside their students, as fellow readers: 'If this was the first time I was reading this text, at this point, which conversations would I be willing, and feel equipped, to have?'.

References

Clark, C. and Douglas, J. (2011) *Young People's Reading and Writing: An In-Depth Study Focusing on Enjoyment, Behaviour, Attitudes and Attainment*, London: National Literacy Trust.

Clark, C. and Osbourne, S. (2008) *How Does Age Relate to Pupils' Perceptions of Themselves as Readers?*, London: National Literacy Trust.

Clark, C. and Rumbold, K. (2006) *Reading for Pleasure: A Research Overview*, London: National Literacy Trust.

Cliff Hodges, G. (2010) 'Reasons for reading: why literature matters', *Literacy* 44(2): 60–8.

Cremin, T., Mottram, M., Collins, F. and Powell, S. (2008) *Building Communities of Readers*, Leicester: PNS/United Kingdom Literacy Association.

Dean, G. (2003) *Teaching Reading in Secondary Schools*, 2nd edn, London: David Fulton Publishers.

DfE (2012) *Research Evidence on Reading for Pleasure*, London: DfE, www.gov.uk/ government/uploads/system/uploads/attachment_data/file/284286/reading_for_ pleasure.pdf (last accessed 21 January 2016).

DfE (2014) *The National Curriculum in England: Key Stages 3 and 4 Framework Document*, London: HMSO.

Djikic, M., Oatley, K. and Moldoveanu, M. C. (2013) 'Opening the closed mind: the effects of exposure to literature on the need for closure', *Creativity Research Journal* 25(2): 149–52.

Fialho, O., Zyngier, S. and Miall, D. (2011) 'Interpretation and experience: two pedagogical interventions observed', *English in Education* 45(3): 236–53.

Gerrig, R. J. (1993) *Experiencing Narrative Worlds: On the Psychological Activities of Reading*, New Haven, CT: Yale University Press.

Giovanelli, M. and Mason, J. (2015) '"Well I don't feel that": Schemas, worlds and authentic reading in the classroom', *English in Education* 49(1): 41–55.

Laurenson, P., McDermott, K., Sadleir, K. and Meade, D. (2015) 'From national policy to classroom practice: Promoting reading for pleasure in post-primary English classrooms', *English in Education* 49(1): 5–24.

Mason, J. (2014) 'Narrative' in P. Stockwell and S. Whiteley (eds) *The Cambridge Handbook of Stylistics*, Cambridge: Cambridge University Press, pp. 179–95.

Merga, M. K. (2013) 'Should Silent Reading feature in a secondary school English programme? West Australian students' perspectives on Silent Reading', *English in Education* 47(3): 229–44.

Merga, M. (2014) 'Exploring the role of parents in supporting recreational book reading beyond primary school', *English in Education* 48(2): 149–63.

Nash, J. (2007) 'The attitudes of English majors to literary study', *Changing English: Studies in Culture and Education* 14(1): 77–86.

Nightingale, P. (2011) 'Now you see me, now you don't: From reader to student and back again in A Level English literature', *English in Education* 45(2): 146–60.

OECD (2002) *Reading for Change: Performance and Engagement across Countries*.

Ofsted (2012) *Moving English Forward: Action to Raise Standards in English*, London: Ofsted.

Stockwell, P. (2002) *Cognitive Poetics: An Introduction*, London: Routledge.

Sullivan, A. and Brown, M. (2013) 'Social inequalities in cognitive scores at age 16: The role of reading', *CLS Working Paper 2013/10*, London: Centre for Longitudinal Studies.

Topping, K. J. (2014) *What Kids are Reading: The Book-reading Habits of Students in British Schools*, London: Renaissance Learning UK.

Twist, L., Schagen, I. and Hodgson, C. (2007) *Progress in International Reading Literacy Study (PIRLS): Readers and Reading: The National Report for England 2006*, Slough: NFER.

Vezzali, L., Stathi, S., Giovannini, D., Capozza, D. and Trifiletti, E. (2015) 'The greatest magic of *Harry Potter*: Reducing prejudice', *Journal of Applied Psychology* 45(2): 105–21.

Chapter 14

Systemic Functional Linguistics and teachers' knowledge about students' writing

Margaret Berry[1]

Introduction

Systemic Functional Linguistics (henceforth SFL) is an approach to language study developed by Michael Halliday, who from the early days had language education centrally in mind (e.g. Halliday *et al.* 1964), and who still (e.g. Halliday 2006) regards language education as one of the most important applications of his work.

SFL is particularly relevant to students' writing in the following ways:

1   SFL regards language as a set of resources from which choices are made, rather than, as is the case with many other approaches to linguistics, a body of rules. Teachers I have worked with have been sympathetic to this view as they see themselves as extending the range of choices open to their students and helping them to make the choices appropriately. They have welcomed information from SFL on the choices available.

2   I have just mentioned helping students 'to make the choices appropriately'. As well as investigating language, SFL, perhaps more than any other approach to linguistics, also investigates the contexts of situation in which language is used and relates the different linguistic choices to the different contexts.

3   There has been a great deal of work in SFL on different genres of writing, particularly on genres of writing which students will need to be able to produce in their various future workplaces. Martin (1985: 60) argued that 'Education [ignored] almost completely the kinds of writing that would enable children to enter the workforce'. Since then he and his colleagues, particularly those in Australia, have worked to remedy the lack. The teaching of writing, he argues, needs to be very explicit teaching: 'Bright middle-class children learn by osmosis what has to be learned. Working-class, migrant or Aboriginal children, whose homes do not provide them with models of writing ... do not learn to write effectively' (Martin 1985: 61).

There will not be room in this chapter to discuss all these matters in detail. I shall be focusing on 2) and 1) above in that order. For further discussion of the general relevance of SFL, see Whittaker *et al.* (2006). For more on the work on genre, see Martin and Rose (2008).

Contexts of situation

SFL recognises three main aspects of context of situation: *field, tenor* and *mode*. Field has to do with what the language is about and what kind of social activity is being enacted in the language. Tenor has to do with the participants in the language event, the speakers, writers, hearers, readers, the roles they are adopting and the relations between them. Mode has to do with the channel of communication, for example, whether the language is spoken (i.e. by voice) or written (i.e. by marks on a page or computer screen).

In this form, field, tenor and mode are simply general headings. Work is ongoing to establish more precise categories under each of the headings (e.g. Berry forthcoming). However, even in this general form, field, tenor and mode can act as a kind of checklist, both for teachers planning an assignment and for students carrying out the assignment.

Tenor

To begin with tenor. It seems to me important that students should always know for who they are writing for – not just themselves or the teacher – and that they should have considered what kind of writing is appropriate to that readership. The teacher should be clear about this when setting the assignment. Recent students' writing I have seen included examples where students had produced information leaflets. The teacher had commented that these were 'too chatty'. But the students had obviously interpreted the leaflets as intended for their own peer group, so maybe chattiness was appropriate. I am all for teachers encouraging students to develop non-chatty styles of writing – these are certainly relevant to their future workplaces. But in that case it might have been better to set an assignment for which the readership was clearly *not* the peer group.

Hopefully in the course of a year, assignments could be set that implied a variety of different readerships. A tactic I tried which proved interesting was to get students to write about something for a particular readership and then to get them to write about the same thing for a very different kind of readership. Students seem to enjoy this kind of exercise – it is a kind of role-play in writing.

Field

The field includes the purpose of the writing. For instance, is it intended to inform or to persuade or to entertain, or a combination of these? One of the problems with the information leaflets seemed to be that the students were trying too hard to entertain and the clarity of the information suffered as a result. Again it is necessary to be precise when setting the assignment. For the Grantham Schools' Writing Competition, about which I have written elsewhere (Berry 1995), the instruction given was:

> *Pretend that a new Tourist Guide to Great Britain is being published by one of the major motoring organisations. They have asked you to write a piece of prose to attract tourists to Grantham.*

This was certainly a more precise instruction than many I have seen since, but even so it proved to be ambiguous. The first part of it suggests purely informational writing, but the last part suggests persuasive writing of a kind more suitable for a travel brochure than a guidebook. Student C, influenced by the first part, began:

> *Grantham is 108 miles north of London. It is a small town in Lincolnshire. The parish church is St. Wulframs and has a very high spire which is lit up at night to make it stand out. There are two interesting parks Dysart Park and Wyndham Park ...*

But Student D, influenced by the last part, wrote:

> *Come to Grantham ... We have excellent nightlife as in the After Eight club where you can let your real self go and boogie the night away ...*

Both Students C and D were to be commended for trying to write in the genre they interpreted the instruction to be asking for. Student A, however, clearly needed help with genre awareness. She virtually ignored the instruction and simply wrote in the personal style she was accustomed to write in. She began:

> *I think Grantham is a nice place to visit because there are some nice places to see. I have been to Belton Park and there is a big Adventure playground with lots of things to play on ...*

Again, hopefully in the course of a year it would be possible to set assignments which implied a variety of purposes, the scenario for each assignment being sketched out as precisely as possible and discussed with the students before they began writing.

Mode

Mode has to do with the channel of communication, the most obvious distinction here being between speech and writing. Chatty writing is presumably writing that is much like speech. There is in fact a cline, a continuum, between informal spoken language and formal written language, with chatty writing coming somewhere in between. Students need to consider for what readerships and for what purposes chatty writing is appropriate, and for what readerships and what purposes it is not appropriate.

In order to recognise chattiness in writing, students need to know something about the features which distinguish informal spoken language from formal written language. I suspect they may already have some ideas under this heading and, if shown a passage regarded as chatty, could point to some of the features that made it chatty. Student V, in one of the information leaflets referred to above, included a section headed *Security*. This went as follows:

> *First of all you need to understand that there is not a lot of this! There are no fences, because this is the only place for 100 miles to have water. So because of this, if you run away you will just become Buzzard food straight away – even if you think you are a fast runner! Don't worry about Mr Sir's gun, it is for yellow-spotted lizards.*

If asked to pick out indicators of chattiness, students might mention the phrases 'Buzzard food' and 'Mr Sir's', the exclamation marks, the imperative, the frequent use of 'you', the lack of explicit connection between the heading of the section and its first sentence. It would certainly be worth gathering the students' own views on all this. However, probably more formal teaching on the differences between speech and writing would be necessary if they were to progress beyond what they knew already. In the next section I shall be discussing some of the choices that distinguish informal spoken language from formal written language and so are relevant to discussions of chattiness.

To conclude the present section, I am suggesting that, when setting assignments, teachers should analyse the implied contexts of the assignments in terms of *tenor*, the readership, *field*, the purpose, and *mode*, the position on the scale from informal spoken language to formal written language, and that they should encourage their students to do likewise. Probably some teachers do this already. However, the students' writing I have been looking at recently suggests that there is room for rather more activity of this kind.

Choices

SFL discusses a very large number of linguistic choices. The most recent account of SFL, Halliday and Matthiessen (2014), runs to 786 pages. In this section I shall be discussing just two kinds of choice, these selected because they are relevant to helping students to move from the informal, personal writing that comes most easily to them to the formal, impersonal kinds of writing that they will need for their possible future careers. That way of putting it perhaps suggests that the formal, impersonal kinds of writing should replace the informal, personal kinds. This is not intended. It is more a matter of encouraging the students to add the formal, impersonal kinds to their repertoires.

Preliminaries to the discussion of choices

Before discussing the choices, it is necessary to say something about the kind of grammatical knowledge involved. For me, the most useful bit of grammatical knowledge to teach students is how to recognise a clause and its elements of structure. I am not advocating mindless parsing, but rather an ability to recognise a clause in a text and to see what its structure is contributing to the overall tone of the text and the overall structure of the text.

It may be worth here passing on some handy hints that I was taught at school at the age of twelve and which I have found helpful all my life. First, one finds a verb or verb group – SFL calls this a predicator. Then one asks questions immediately before and immediately after the predicator.

> *Little Bo-Peep **has lost** her sheep*

has lost is the predicator.

If one asks who or what immediately in front of the predicator, this gives the subject. Who or what has lost her sheep? *Little Bo-Peep* has lost her sheep. *Little Bo-Peep* is the subject.

If one asks who or what immediately after the predicator, this gives the object or complement – SFL calls this the complement. Little Bo-Peep has lost who or what? Little Bo-Peep has lost *her sheep. her sheep* is the complement.

If one asks any other question immediately after the predicator – where, when, how, why – this gives an adverbial. SFL calls this an adjunct.

> *Little Miss Muffet sat on a tuffet*

Little Miss Muffet sat where? Little Miss Muffet sat *on a tuffet. on a tuffet* is an adjunct.

Any bit of language that answers one of these test questions around the predicator is part of the same clause as the predicator.

I have been using very simple examples; now we move on to some slightly more complex ones. Earlier in this chapter, I included the clause:

> *The most recent account of SFL, Halliday and Matthiessen (2014), runs to 786 pages.*

If I want to find the subject, I again ask who or what in front of the predicator. The predicator is *runs*, so I ask who or what runs to 786 pages? *The most recent account of SFL, Halliday and Matthiessen (2014)* runs to 786 pages. *The most recent account of SFL, Halliday and Matthiessen (2014)* is the subject.

Or if we take the proverb:

> *He who pays the piper calls the tune*

and try to find the subject of *calls*. Who or what calls the tune? *He who pays the piper* calls the tune. *He who pays the piper* is the subject.

In fact the subject there has another clause embedded inside it. *who pays the piper* is a clause, but it is a subordinate clause that cannot stand alone. We can still find the complement by asking who or what after the predicator *pays*, but the subject *who* is a substitute subject rather than the kind of subject we find in a main clause.

The test questions work for most main clauses in English. However, there are a few constructions for which they are not helpful. Perhaps the most common of these are the *there is/there are* constructions.

There is a bull in that field

The function of the subject is split between *There* and *a bull*. There is a sense in which *a bull* is the notional subject, but *There* is the grammatical subject. *There* is regarded as the grammatical subject because it is the element that shows whether we have a statement or a question. In *There is a bull in that field*, *There* occurs before *is* which shows that we have a statement. If we want to turn it into a question, *There* would move to after *is*.

Is there a bull in that field?

In what follows I am going to be using the terms subject, complement and adjunct.

Choices of what to refer to in the subject

Meaning is central to SFL. Subject is a formal category, but I am here interested in it from the perspective of the meaning choices it makes available, particularly choices of what to refer to in this element of the clause. My own research (e.g. Berry 2013) suggests that informal spoken English and formal written English differ more in their subjects than in any other parts of their clauses.

Table 14.1 shows the main clause subjects of an adult speaking about a place and its history side-by-side with the main clause subjects of a passage of an adult writing about a place and its history.

Applying this same type of profiling to examples of students' writing, Table 14.2 shows the main clause subjects of Student C alongside the main clause subjects of Student A, Student C being one of the students regarded above as genre-aware, while Student A was regarded as lacking genre-awareness.

Probably just a glance at the two tables will be sufficient to see that Student A's subjects more closely resemble those of the Adult Speaker, while Student C's subjects more closely resemble those of the Adult Writer. This would seem at least in part to explain why the teachers with whom I discussed the Grantham passages felt that Student A was writing as she would speak, while Student C had

Table 14.1 Main clause subjects of an adult speaking about a place and an adult writing about a place

Adult speaker	Adult writer
my first year's apprenticeship	the county town of the merged shires of Hereford and Worcester
the second year	it
the third	the pedestrianised High Street
I	the cathedral
I	timber frame shops, an art gallery and museum
you	the canal
you	the lovely river front
you	the view of the cathedral
you	Lady Huntingdon Chapel
you	there
they	a good place to walk around, it
you	Spetchley Park, 3 miles east on the A422
you	the race course
you	Lower Broadheath, west on the B4204
they	there
it	
everybody	

Table 14.2 The main clause subjects of the passages by Student A and Student C 'Quotations from students' writing follow the spellings of the original students' texts'.

Student A	Student C
I	Grantham
I	it
there	the parish church
there	there
they	Dysart Park
I	it
there	there
there	Wyndham Park
you	it
they	Belvoir Castle and Belton House
there	The Angel Hotel
you	there
you	there
they	the Prime-Minister Margart Thatcher
there	Grantham
they	a market
there	there
he	
he	
the Prime Minister of Britain	
she	
you	
Wyndham Park	
there	

progressed further towards an understanding of the conventions of written English.

What are the choices that make the difference between the Adult Speaker and the Adult Writer, and between Student A and Student C? Probably the most obvious differences are 1) that the Adult Speaker and Student A have chosen to refer in their subjects to participants in the discourse – the *I*'s and *you*s – while the Adult Writer and Student C have not chosen these options, and 2) that the Adult Writer and Student C have chosen to refer in their subjects to aspects of the topic they are writing about, while the Adult Speaker and Student A have not done this, except in Student A's case right at the end of her passage.

The Adult Speaker, as speakers usually do, has assumed that, although he is speaking about the history of his town, what is wanted is a personal slant on that history. Student A, although she has been told to write for a guidebook to be published by a major motoring organisation, has just produced the kind of personal writing she is used to writing. The Adult Writer is aware that he actually is writing for a guidebook published by a major motoring organisation. Student C is aware that she is pretending to do so.

Informal spoken English is usually assumed to be about the people concerned and the interactions between them. Chatty writing makes similar assumptions. So it is not surprising that personal references are foregrounded. In the most formal kinds of written English however, the people, the writers and readers, are backgrounded and the emphasis is on the content and the organisation of that content.

The Adult Writer and Student C use their subjects to introduce what they regard as the main features of the place they are writing about. In each case the remainder of the clause says something about the feature introduced. The subjects of these writers show how their passages are organised: how they are moving through their topics, feature by feature. Each passage has what Fries (1981/1983) called a clear 'Method of Development'.

We need to distinguish, then, between personal references for the subjects and topical references, the latter being particularly appropriate to formal written English.

More delicate distinctions are possible for each of these kinds of reference. It is relevant to ask of the personal references: Are they references to the language producer, the speaker or writer, or to the language receiver, the hearer or reader? And are they collective references or references to individuals? Student D, the student regarded earlier as writing in a manner appropriate to a travel brochure, has the following subjects: *we, we, we, we, we, our town, our town, Belton House, our county, sailing, we, it, we, The George Hotel, Grantham*. He has for the most part chosen personal references, with only a few topical references. However, his personal references are not to himself as an individual, but collectively to a group to which he belongs. He clearly sees himself as writing on behalf of the citizens of Grantham.

It is relevant to ask of the topical references how far they are introducing new aspects of the topic and how far they are continuing aspects already introduced.

Student C's and Student D's *its*, for instance, are referring to aspects of the topic, but to aspects of the topic which have already been introduced. Student A's *hes* and *she* are of this kind. However Student A also has *theys* which appear to be continuing an aspect of the topic, but which do not have what are technically called antecedents. For instance, in *they are building a sport centre beside it*, there has been no previous reference to the group of people referred to as *they*. As a result, the reference of *they* is vague. We do not know exactly who *they* are. The Adult Speaker's subjects also include vague *theys* without antecedents, but there are no such vague *theys* in either the Adult Writer's passage or in Student C's. Student A is again following a practice which is common in informal spoken English, but which would be frowned on in formal written English.

Something which distinguishes the two students, A and C, from the two adults, is the frequency with which the students use *there* as the grammatical subject. The teachers with whom I discussed the Grantham passages criticised both Student A and Student C for overuse of *there*. Biber *et al.* (1999: 953) say that this use of *there* is most common in conversation. They add that the number of *theres* in conversation is 'sometimes quite extreme'. This would seem to be one way in which neither Student A nor Student C has yet moved from spoken mode to written mode. It should be emphasised that it is the frequency that is particularly characteristic of conversational English. The Adult Writer's passage I have been discussing includes *theres* as grammatical subjects, but only two out of fifteen subjects are *theres*, compared with Student A's seven out of twenty-four and Student C's five out of seventeen.

Figure 14.1 summarises the choices I have been discussing in this section. I have represented these first as a choice between precise reference and lack of precise reference, there being two degrees of lack of precision: the *theres* do not refer to anything at all; the *theys* without antecedents refer only vaguely. The precise references divide into personal references and topical references. The personal references may be to the language producer(s) or to the language receiver(s). They may be individual references or collective references. The topical references may be to new aspects of the topic or to continuing aspects.

Generally speaking, the higher up on the diagram, the more the option is likely to be associated with informal spoken English; the lower down, the more the option is likely to be associated with formal written English.

For more on these referential choices for the Subject, and others, see Berry (2013). I have there described subjects of the kinds associated with formal written English as 'contentful' subjects, while the kinds associated with informal spoken English are described as 'contentlight'.

Thematic choices

SFL has paid a good deal of attention to what happens at the beginning of a clause. It calls this the *theme* of the clause. The subject is the element which most

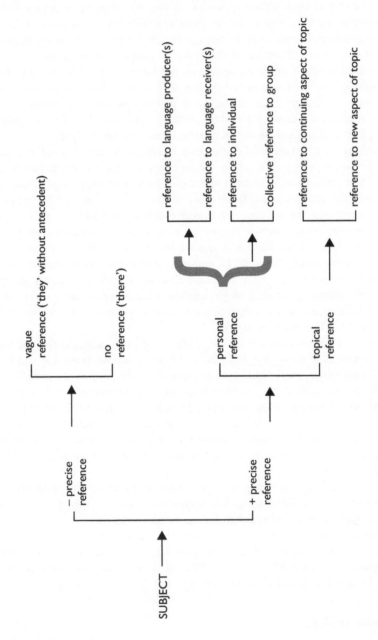

Figure 14.1 Referential choices for the subject

usually occurs at the beginning. Because the subject is the most usual theme, SFL calls this *unmarked theme*. However, it is possible to put an adjunct or a complement in front of the subject for special effects, in which case it is known as *marked theme*.

Some of the students whose work I have been studying do seem to be trying to make use of marked themes. Student A has the adjunct marked themes *A few miles out from Grantham, In Grantham, In the centre of Grantham*. However, she does not use them to structure her whole passage; the reader is not led from the surroundings of Grantham to Grantham itself and then to the centre of the town. It is not clear whether the places mentioned at the beginning and end of her passage count as in Grantham or outside Grantham.

Student D, our travel brochure writer, partially organises his passage from the point of view of different groups of readers. This is signalled by the adjunct marked themes *For our teenage visitors, For the keen golfers among you, For those who like long walks*.

Student L, aged 16, reporting on a visit to the Peak District to carry out an experiment, includes the paragraph:

> *In groups we worked out our things we needed to test to be able to use as evidence to prove our hypothesis right or wrong. Later on after having the results then we would work out the cross sectional area. The width we measured 3 times and the depth 11 times to get it accurate. The channel velocity we tested three times and used two separate experiments which were with the hydro prop and recoding the time it took for the dog biscuit to travel across 10 metres of the river at each site. We visited 4 different sites at each point of the river.*

For her subjects, Student L has chosen a personal referential option, though the collective *we* rather than individual *I*. (Whether this would be regarded as appropriate would depend on the readership and purpose of the report.) She is clearly very much aware of being a member of a group and she highlights this by using an adjunct marked theme *In groups* at the beginning of the paragraph. She also uses an adjunct marked theme to indicate a shift in time reference – *Later on after having the results then*. (Notice that this adjunct has an embedded clause inside it – *after having the results*.)

Student L also uses complement marked themes. In *The width we measured 3 times, The width* is the complement, which has been placed in front of the subject *we*. The same is true of *The channel velocity*. And if we assume that *the depth 11 times* is really a clause which has had its subject and predicator ellipted to avoid repetition – *the depth [we measured]11 times* – then the same would be true of *the depth*. In the first sentence of the paragraph, Student L mentions *things we needed to test*. In the later sentences she uses complement marked themes to highlight a list of these things.

Student L could have used passives here – *The width was measured 3 times and the depth 11 times, the channel velocity was tested three times*. This would have

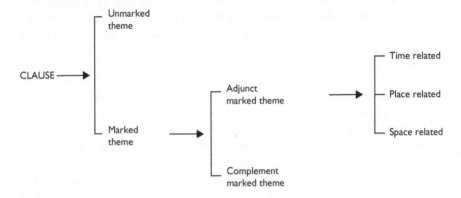

Figure 14.2 Thematic choices

made the things tested the subjects of their respective clauses. For some purposes this might have been more appropriate, but we should have lost the *we* subjects indicating the group nature of the work, which Student L clearly wishes to emphasise.

Figure 14.2 summarises the choices I have been discussing in this section: first the choice between unmarked theme and marked theme; then marked theme splitting into adjunct marked theme and complement marked theme. I have discussed a number of different kinds of adjunct marked theme, those relating to time and place and those relating to different groups of readers. There are many more kinds that there has been no room to mention.

Marked themes do occasionally occur in informal spoken English, but they are more common in formal written English, and indeed in formal kinds of spoken English such as a lecture. They are particularly useful in the more formal kinds of language as they provide indicators of the way in which the content is being organised.

For more on the thematic choices of the Grantham students, see Berry (1995). For more on thematic choices generally, see Halliday and Matthiessen (2014), Chapter 3. Or for a gentler, introductory account, see Thompson (2014), Chapter 6.

Concluding remarks

I have been suggesting that teachers can help students to extend their writing repertoires in two ways: by setting assignments that relate to a wide range of scenarios, these to be spelt out in terms of readership and purpose; and by alerting students to linguistic choices that will help them to write appropriately for the various scenarios.

It has been possible in this chapter to discuss only a few of such choices, but I have given references to works where further information is available.

Note

1 I am grateful to Sarah Mukherjee and Lindsey Thomas for sending me examples of recent students' writing, and for discussing with me points relevant to this chapter, and of course to the students who allowed me to see their work. I am also grateful to all those who helped with my earlier work on students' writing, particularly those involved with the Grantham schools' writing competition. Of course, I alone am responsible for any errors or misrepresentations.

References

Berry, M. (1995) 'Thematic options and success in writing', in M. Ghadessy (ed.) *Thematic Development in English Texts*, London: Pinter, pp. 55–84.

Berry, M. (2013) 'Contentful and contentlight subject themes in informal spoken English and formal written English', in G. O'Grady, T. Bartlett, and L. Fontaine (eds) *Choice in Language: Applications in Text Analysis*, Sheffield: Equinox, pp. 243–68.

Berry, M. (forthcoming) 'On describing contexts of situation', in W. Bowcher and J. Liang (eds) *Society in Language, Language in Society: Essays in Honour of Ruqaiya Hasan*, Basingstoke: Palgrave Macmillan.

Biber, D., Johansson S., Leech G., Conrad S. and Finegan E. (1999) *The Longman Grammar of Spoken and Written English*, London: Longman.

Fries, P. H. (1981) 'On the status of theme in English: arguments from discourse', Forum Linguisticum 6, 1–38. Reprinted 1983, in revised form, in J. S. Petöfi and E. Sözer (eds) *Micro and Macro Connexity of Texts*, Hamburg: Helmut Buske, pp. 116–52.

Halliday, M. A. K. (2006) 'Language and literacy', in R. Whittaker, M. O'Donnell, and A. McCabe (eds) *Language and Literacy: Functional Approaches*, London: Continuum, pp. 15–29.

Halliday, M. A. K. and Matthiessen, C. M. I. M. (2014) *Halliday's Introduction to Functional Grammar*, 4th edn, London: Routledge.

Halliday, M. A. K., McIntosh, A. and Strevens, P. (1964) *The Linguistic Sciences and Language Teaching*, London: Longman.

Martin, J. R. (1985) *Factual Writing: Exploring and Challenging Social Reality*, Victoria, Australia: Deakin University Press.

Martin, J. R. and Rose, D. (2008) *Genre Relations: Mapping Culture*, London: Equinox.

Thompson, G. (2014) *Introducing Functional Grammar*, 3rd edn, London: Routledge.

Whittaker, R., O'Donnell, M. and McCabe, A. (2006) *Language and Literacy: Functional Approaches*, London: Continuum.

Chapter 15

Developing beginning teachers' linguistic awareness

Issues and practice in Initial Teacher Education

Marcello Giovanelli

Introduction

In this chapter, I explore a range of issues related to subject knowledge in the context of working with pre-service teachers on teacher education programmes in the UK. Specifically, I identify some issues around the kinds of linguistic knowledge that beginning teachers[1] do, could and should know. I contextualise my discussion within the rapidly changing climate and landscape of Initial Teacher Education (henceforth ITE), arguing that there are particular issues related to subject knowledge and teacher identity of which academics, researchers, teachers, school leaders and policy-makers should be aware. In doing so, I automatically work from the assumption that knowing about language is an important asset for any English teacher (see throughout this book and particularly my discussion in Chapter 1).

The chapter begins with an exploration of the context surrounding ITE and the concept of subject knowledge. In the initial part, I outline the specific expectations in terms of subject knowledge in the National Curriculum and across other secondary programmes of study for beginning teachers. I then survey research that has been carried out on both the backgrounds of teachers coming onto ITE programmes, and how in English, historically there has been an imbalance between those with subject expertise and confidence in 'literature' and those in 'language'. I also draw attention to some other notable research on teacher identity and on teacher education and linguistic knowledge, and suggest that the shift from university-led to school-led ITE could have further consequences for subject knowledge in the future. The remainder of the chapter is then devoted to demonstrating one way that beginning teachers are supported at my own institution. Drawing on an example of a Subject Enhancement Programme to develop and support subject knowledge, I highlight how beginning teachers might be supported to increase their linguistic awareness and to feel confident and enabled to use that knowledge both to support learning and teaching in their classrooms, and to inform their own sense of professional identity.

Teachers' knowledge and backgrounds

An obvious place to start in a chapter such as this is to ask the question: 'What do those entering the profession need to know (and teach) with regards to language?'. The current Teachers' Standards document (DfE 2011) that outlines the skills, knowledge and competences for those acquiring Qualified Teacher Status (QTS) consists of two parts: teaching; and professional and personal conduct. The first part has eight distinct sections that specify attributes (although there are inevitably clear degrees of inter-relatedness and overlap). The first two characteristics of Section 3 (*Demonstrate good subject and curriculum knowledge*) are as follows:

- have a secure knowledge of the relevant subject(s) and curriculum areas, foster and maintain pupils' interest in the subject, and address misunder-standings
- demonstrate a critical understanding of developments in the subject and curriculum areas, and promote the value of scholarship.

(DfE 2011: 1)

The question of what constitutes 'English' and consequently its subject and curriculum areas has historically been seen as problematic in comparison to other school disciplines (Walmsley 1984; Protherough and Atkinson 1991), and has inevitably had the subject of literature at its heart (see Giovanelli 2014: 9–24 for detailed discussion). Although the belief that language work should be a central part of any English curriculum underpins this entire book, some appeal to an external authority might also be helpful as a way of justifying some of the arguments and examples I am putting forward. In this instance, the most sensible places to turn for what might constitute 'subject knowledge' ought to be National Curriculum documentation and any external examination specifications. Interestingly, the latest government report into effective practice in ITT (Initial Teacher Training) makes the very same suggestion:

Subject knowledge development in ITT should be sharply focused on "sub-ject knowledge for teaching"; it should focus on the content, knowledge and concepts required to deliver the national curriculum and exam syllabi where relevant, ensuring that content reflects any changes to these.

(DfE 2015a: 26)

This functional emphasis and view of the subject might be frowned upon by some but it does provide a clear direction and directive for ensuring that begin-ning teachers have a secure knowledge of language content and issues. Both the current Key Stage 3 National Curriculum (DfE 2013), which states that teachers should allow students to build on the significant work on grammar (including the learning of a substantial body of grammatical terminology) undertaken at

Key Stages 1 and 2, and the growth of A-level English Language, mean that many teachers will be expected to teach some language topics during an ITE placement and/or in their first few years of securing their first teaching post. There is every reason to argue that English teachers ought to be as secure in teaching language topics as they are teaching literature. Indeed, there are strong grounds for specialist linguistic knowledge *per se* among English teachers (Halliday 1967: 81), and at least an expectation that those from literature backgrounds develop their expertise with regards to language in the same way that there is an expectation that those primarily from linguistics backgrounds develop their own subject knowledge to ensure that they can teach literary periods and canons (Cushing 2014). In fact, recent research highlighting the positive effect of contextualised grammar teaching on children's writing (Myhill *et al.* 2012; and see Myhill, Chapter 3) identified the specific strength of teachers' subject knowledge as a crucial factor in supporting classroom practice and ensuring progress.

Despite a shift in the diversity of English provision on undergraduate programmes and the rapid rise of A-level English Language as a genuine and alternative qualification to English Literature at Post 16 (see Scott 1989; Giovanelli 2014: 19–20; and Goddard, Chapter 17 of this book for further discussion), it is still the case that the majority of teachers on ITE programmes in the UK (there were 2,262 English beginning teachers on postgraduate training courses in 2013–14 [DfE 2015b: 8]) are literature undergraduates and have studied very little language content at university level. Equally, there may still be some difference in terms of the way that those in charge of admission onto ITE programmes treat students from literature backgrounds more favourably and with less concern about subject knowledge and expertise compared to those from other 'versions' of English, including language and linguistics (Blake and Shortis 2010).

The sense of a distinctive subject identity is important for English teachers generally, and certainly for beginning teachers. The wealth of literature on teacher identity points to a clear link between an understanding of and passion for a particular aspect of one's subject and the sense of competent professionalism (see for example Beijaard 1995; Helms 1998). Once again, several studies (for example, Goodwyn 1997, 2002; Ellis 2003) have highlighted that for most teachers, this passion tends to be centred on the study of literature, and specifically reading. Literature is conventionally viewed as having a transformational effect on young people; indeed Goodwyn (2010) argues that a 'personal growth model' (DES/WO 1989) of English is something to which many teachers align themselves, maintaining this throughout their careers. In the case of beginning teachers, this strong sense of English being inherently and inextricably tied to literature forms what Goodwyn (2010: 71) terms a 'personal subject construct', an embryonic template for professional identity that emerges during a beginning teacher's formative experiences, and shapes both their personal vision for the subject and their subsequent career development.

Since there are many teachers coming into the profession with little or no exposure to language study, the role of ITE Programmes seems crucial in providing support for the kinds of knowledge and skills that teachers would need to deliver aspects of the National Curriculum that I have previously outlined. Yet language provision on PGCE programmes has been patchy (Bluett *et al.* 2004), and the increasing shift since 2013 from university-led to school-based ITE (DfE 2015a), means that it is possible that beginning teachers might well have little if any support in the pedagogy of language teaching beyond the assessment-driven resources published by examination boards. The anxieties amongst the English teaching community generally around the implementation and future impact of alternative forms of ITE on the profession have been documented in various fora. For example, Hodgson (2014), in a survey of 730 educators from schools and university education departments, found that there were significant fears regarding how schools would be able to provide the time and resources to support beginning teachers and that consequently – and inevitably – this would impact on subject knowledge.

Where national and institutional standards might expect teachers to achieve a certain level of competence, the real picture of beginning teachers and their linguistic subject knowledge and pedagogical content knowledge gives some concern. Both Cajkler and Hislam (2002) and Sangster *et al.* (2013) report on a striking disconnect between perceived and actual linguistic knowledge among beginning teachers, the latter in the context of analysis of many years of government initiatives that appear to have had minimal impact on language teaching in schools (Bell 2015; Watson 2015), and consequently have done little to enthuse those students who might well become the next generation of language teachers (see Yarrow 2007 for discussion). Watson (2012, 2015) shows how myths and fears around grammar and its perceived value can persist well into a teacher's career; even for experienced teachers, being put 'on the spot' in terms of having to deliver language content can be a difficult and terrifying experience that challenges their own identity and confidence at both personal and professional levels (Giovanelli 2015). Since a key influence on beginning teachers is their own experience as learners (Lortie 1975; Smith 2005), both in terms of their perception of the subject and the ways in which classrooms operate, it is unsurprising that there can often be such spectacular anxiety among beginning teachers.

The context

In this following section, I briefly provide the context for my subsequent description and discussion of work that has been undertaken with groups of beginning teachers. The English PGCE course at the University of Nottingham has around forty students a year and is taught by colleagues across the school with a range of specialist teaching and research interests, including multi-literacies and the discourses of place, children's literature, the sociology of reading, Shakespeare and the pedagogies associated with drama, and the philosophy of writing. I am a trained stylistician, and as such am the only academic with a background and expertise in linguistics who contributes to teaching. In terms of the yearly cohort, around sixty-five per cent of our beginning English teachers have no background in language/linguistics (that includes modern foreign languages and classics).

At the interview stage, applicants are asked to complete a subject knowledge audit that, once accepted onto the course, they review regularly both on their teaching placements and during tutorial meetings at the university. Importantly, the audit is designed and used not to make beginning teachers feel that they are weak or deficient in some way, but rather to give them an honest and realistic sense of what they need to do to develop their skillset over the PGCE year and beyond into the first years of teaching. Indeed, through initial discussions that emphasise the ongoing development of subject knowledge, we find that many beginning teachers are very honest about the fact that they were from the 'grammar vacuum' of the 1990s/early 2000s, a time when there was little explicit language work taught in English lessons in secondary schools. Historically, the course has only devoted around three to six hours a year to language topics. This has increased considerably during the last three years and has coincided with some more innovative work being undertaken with beginning teachers that reconceptualises language and pedagogy from a cognitive linguistic perspective (see Giovanelli 2014, for examples of such work). However, despite this, we find that many beginning teachers lack basic linguistic terminology, struggle to see the value in developing their own subject knowledge, and feel incredibly anxious about going into schools where they might be expected to teach language topics.

Developing a subject knowledge enhancement programme to support beginning teachers

Subject Knowledge Enhancement (henceforth SKE) programmes are common in ITE shortage subjects (e.g. mathematics, physics, chemistry, geography, computing, design and technology and modern foreign languages) either to attract those without first degrees in a subject or to re-develop skills in those who might have taken an undergraduate degree some time ago. These tend to be detailed and fairly lengthy programmes that are designed to fill significant gaps in subject knowledge for those who show promise at application and interview stage but may need to complete additional work around subject content. These are fully funded, run by universities, schools or private companies, and are flexible in terms of when they can be taken: either before an ITE programme commences or in parallel with some part of it. There is also flexibility in terms of the length of a SKE programme, with courses between eight and thirty-six weeks in length and a variety of ways of studying, for example part-time, evenings and online (DfE 2015c).

However, English has no such designation as a 'shortage subject', and consequently no formal SKE provision exists. For language work in English, where such programmes have occurred, they have tended to be driven by academics setting up their own discrete smaller-scale courses (e.g. Jeffcoate 2000), or ones that are more broadly integrated into a PGCE programme (e.g. Burgess *et al.* 2000; Turvey 2000). The description that follows is of a small-scale programme that was intended to run alongside and complement sessions that were integrated into the main PGCE timetable at Nottingham.

The rationale for this programme had several motivating factors. First, I wanted to enable beginning teachers to understand what for them were alien and difficult terms and concepts so as to feel comfortable with their own developing subject knowledge. In turn, my hope was to encourage them to see language as an interesting topic in its own right, and consequently one that they might want to share with their students. Second, I hoped that the programme would develop both what Shulman (1987) terms *pedagogical content knowledge* (the knowledge of how to frame subject material in a way to enable students to learn effectively) and *curriculum knowledge* (knowledge of the National Curriculum and awarding bodies' specification requirements). Third, and underpinning all of this, was my desire to structure the programme in a way that viewed learning as participatory; that is, I wanted to avoid mere transmission of facts and instead encourage students to undertake an ongoing process of 'becoming' (Hodkinson *et al.* 2008: 41) a language teacher, where they would be allowed to constantly reflect on, reconstruct and make sense of both subject content and themselves as learners.

The programme is offered on a voluntary basis and following an initial review of the subject audit between the beginning teacher and their university tutor. For timetabling reasons and to allow the programme to run while beginning teachers are on school placements, it operates as a series of twilights throughout the year. As I have mentioned above, the aim is to provide beginning teachers with necessary knowledge but also to provide a space for them to re-conceptualise their ideas on language work and what it can offer to their students. In doing so, it is designed to allow beginning teachers to see language as a resource that can be used by speakers and writers to achieve certain interpretative effects. That said, I wanted to impress on them the importance of terminology in descriptive analysis, and consequently how knowing even a little about the ways in which language works can be of benefit both in terms of their own teaching and presenting new topics to students, as well as opening new ways of thinking about textual analysis and representation.

The programme is based very loosely around the Kingman model of language study (DES 1988): forms/structures of English, language, communication and context, language acquisition and development, and historical and geographical variation. This enables coverage of key concepts and topics that are covered in the National Curriculum and in the various A-level English Language specifications.[2] Half of the programme is structured around the *linguistic rank scale* (Trask 2007: 242–3), which encourages students to see language as an organised system; the other half offers more conceptual topics for students to explore in the context of their own teaching. A typical programme, which covers six twilight sessions, each lasting three hours, is as follows:

1   Phonemes, morphemes and lexemes
2   Phrases and clauses
3   Text and discourse
4   Language varieties
5   Attitudes to language variation
6   Language acquisition and development

The programme is supported by readings from Deborah Cameron's *The Teacher's Guide to Grammar* (Cameron 2007), a book that provides an excellent synthesis of the theoretical and the practical in the context of supporting the kinds of work that teachers would undertake in classrooms with children. Although there is not the space in this chapter to provide a detailed description of all the sessions, one brief sketch of an activity, taken from session 2 'Phrases and clauses' should give a flavour of the kind of work that was on the programme.

In sessions prior to this one, we had discussed how lexical units formed larger structures called phrases, and how various kinds of phrases (noun, verb, adjectival, adverbial) were defined and understood in terms of their headword and other constituents. In turn we had explored how phrases could be integrated into larger structures called clauses. Through discussion, illustration and further reading, beginning teachers felt comfortable describing a sentence such as 'The young teacher loved modern novels' both in terms of word class (determiner, adjective, noun, verb, adjective, noun) and phrase constituents (noun phrase, verb phrase with an embedded noun phrase). We had looked at why text producers might want to pre-modify noun phrases in advertising, and how in literary fiction, writers might want to manipulate the presentation of noun phrases to present certain interpretative effects: the layering of noun phrases in the absence of any verbs in the opening to Dickens' *Bleak House* offers a well-tested and appealing example, and one that problematises the very notion that a sentence must contain a finite verb!

Then, following some preliminary work on the structure of clauses (making use of the terms *subject, complement, object, verb, adverbial*), we moved on to look at active and passive voice. My teaching strategy from the start had been to draw on analogies that beginning teachers would both find useful for their own learning and in the classroom with their own students. In this instance, we explored how the difference between the active and the passive voice can be viewed as one of perspective. That is, the organisation of the clausal constituents in itself is inherently meaningful as it foregrounds a particular part of the clause (either one of the participants or the event itself). Consequently, we wanted to explore how and why a language user might be motivated to choose a certain way of presenting a series of events.

To explain this, we explored some simple ways in which we can physically and visually manipulate a foreground/background relationship, for example by moving an object in front of another one to obscure it, or making a smaller object stand out (through brightness or contrast) against a larger object acting as a background. Once beginning teachers experimented with and understood this, they found it relatively straightforward to see that there are continuities in the ways that language can be organised and experience constructed. To do so, we then explored the various grammatical possibilities offered for presenting an event that we had found reported in a local newspaper. It focused on the boss of a small company firing a worker and we were able to experiment with the effects of foregrounding particular aspects:

The boss sacked the shopworker
Active voice: agency of boss foregrounded for prominence

The shopworker was sacked (by her boss)
Passive form: agency defocused (can be removed completely to foreground simply the shopworker)

Shopworker sacked!
Nominalised form: verb process reified so the process itself is foregrounded with no mention of agency

Shocked co-workers describe how their boss sacked a shopworker
Reported form: agency subordinated and delayed to foreground the reporters and the reporting rather than the event

As we explored each of the examples, beginning teachers were encouraged to think about how they might use this knowledge in the context of teaching their own students and supporting their work in English. I should add here that they were encouraged to do this by thinking for themselves and discussing with their peers and on their teaching placements. I avoided merely giving them suggestions, and instead aimed to encourage their own enquiry, and while the Cameron book offers some ideas, I wanted them to think carefully in their own terms and in the context of the schools in which they were teaching.

One way that they were enabled to do this was through the setting up of a dedicated space on the university's online learning environment, Moodle. This had a section with all programme materials (PowerPoint slides, handouts, wider reading lists, teaching resources, and so on) and separate sections designed to provide additional resources for beginning teachers to explore as and when they felt appropriate to support their teaching. These included: the *Englicious* online library of teaching resources run by the Survey of English Usage team at University College London; Dick Hudson's personal website and his collection of articles and papers on grammar teaching, *Teaching Grammar* (run with Geoff Dean); and Dan

Clayton's *EngLangBlog* for A-level English Language teachers and students. In addition, a forum was set up to allow beginning teachers to pose any questions that they might have (both theoretical or practical) that could be answered either by me or by another beginning teacher. And, a second forum operated to encourage reflection and discussion of practice, allowing beginning teachers to share and discuss a language-focused activity or a resource, some reading they had undertaken or something that had been in the news or discussed in the beginning teacher's department or school. For example, Megan,[3] who had come onto the PGCE having no background in language and linguistics whatsoever, soon became an avid poster. In the space of one post reprinted below, she shows her eagerness to experiment with her teaching, share those reflections in an open and encouraging way with her peers through the medium of the forum, and extend her thinking about the role of language and grammar work in schools more broadly.

> *Re: How is grammar taught in your SE school?*
>
> *In my school grammar is usually integrated into lessons whether they are focused on literature or language. I am trying to follow this model in my teaching of poetry to year 7 and am doing a lesson on Jabberwocky soon in which I want to get the pupils to form an understanding of a nonsense poem by using knowledge of grammar and to be able to assign nonsense words to word classes. I'm not sure of how well the lesson will work in practice though so I'll have to wait and see! Year 7 on the whole seem to have a very good grasp of grammar which the teachers at my school think is a reflection of the new tests at KS2.*
>
> *I am also teaching poetry with year 10 and wanted to do the collapsed poem technique we used at uni and other activities with a grammar focus but the teacher wasn't that keen on the idea mainly because GCSE poetry lessons in my school are taught in quite a formulaic way, probably due to the teachers' perceptions of what examiners want to see students doing in the exam. I would say that at my school grammar is taught in a much more integrated way at KS3 than it is at KS4, when it is often taught in quite a dry way through lesson starters on apostrophes and semi-colons etc.*

At the end of the programme, beginning teachers were asked to evaluate both the content and their personal stance with regards to language work. Reflecting on what she had covered, Megan was able to elaborate in more detail how her perception of the value of language work had changed, and how she saw her own shifting identity as a language teacher.

> *Grammar was situated in context and studied with reference to 'real life' texts. This enabled, then, my knowledge of terminology to develop but also, perhaps more importantly, my interest in grammar as a tool and a resource for linguistic analysis. At the same time, the session did reinforce to me the necessity of subject knowledge and made me realise that a more developed understanding of*

grammar could enable me to say what I wanted to say and teach what I needed to teach within the classroom.

The sessions also made grammar seem less unwieldy and less 'scary' as a subject area. As something that could be discussed and something that could be analysed in context, grammar came to seem less intimidating, and I began to develop an understanding of grammar [as a] tool for analysis rather than simply a daunting body of knowledge.

Conclusion

In this chapter, I hope to have highlighted some issues around the raising of linguistic awareness and the supporting of subject knowledge on ITE programmes and shown a specific example of how this has been addressed at one particular higher education institution. Indeed, given the fact that a significant number of teachers are still coming onto programmes with either little knowledge or anxieties (or both) about teaching language topics, the lack of 'official' SKE programmes in English is surprising. The renewed focus on grammatical terminology in the most recent National Curriculum and the continued growth of English Language at Post-16 make these kinds of opportunities for teachers particularly important. It also seems to me that there is a call for, as Sangster *et al.* (2013: 313) suggest, a more concerted and coherent national programme of in-service professional development for teachers to complement what ITE provision on its own can never achieve, particularly given the drive towards more school-led ITE. In addition, the recommendation that universities consider introducing modules that provide a 'bridge' from first degree to ITE programmes in the final years of undergraduate courses for would-be teachers (DfE 2015a: 7) shows a further need for some joined-up thinking. Beginning teachers clearly need to have the time and the space to develop their skills and to reflect on the importance of language work in the English curriculum. Both they, and the students they will go on to teach, deserve it.

Notes

1 I use the term 'beginning teacher' throughout this chapter to refer exclusively to those on teacher education programmes (e.g. PGCE, School Direct). I am aware that this term can also refer to teachers in their first year of teaching, and that other terms such as 'trainee teacher', 'associate teacher' and so on are used interchangeably. Equally, I prefer, both for personal and professional reasons, to use the term 'Initial Teacher Education' rather than 'Initial Teacher Training'.
2 This refers to legacy specifications rather than those from first teaching in September 2015.
3 I am grateful to Megan Mansworth for allowing me to use her Moodle post and part of her evaluation of the programme.

References

Beijaard, D. (1995) 'Teachers' prior experiences and actual perceptions of professional identity', *Teachers and Teaching: Theory and Practice* 1(2): 281–94.

Bell, H. (2015) 'The dead butler revisited: Grammatical accuracy and clarity in the English primary curriculum 2013–2014', *Language and Education* 29(2): 140–52.

Blake, J. and Shortis, T. (2010) *Who's Prepared to Teach School English?: The Degree Level Qualifications and Preparedness of Initial Teacher Trainees in English*, London: Committee for Linguistics in Education.

Bluett, J., Cockcroft, S., Harris, A., Hodgson, J. and Snapper, G. (2004) *Text: Message: The Future of A level English*, Sheffield: National Association for the Teaching of English.

Burgess, T., Turvey, A. and Quarshie, R. (2000) 'Teaching grammar: Working with student teachers', *Changing English: Studies in Culture and Education* 7(1): 7–21.

Cajkler, W. and Hislam, J. (2002) 'Trainee teachers' grammatical knowledge: The tension between public expectation and individual competence', *Language Awareness* 11(3): 161–77.

Cameron, D. (2007) *The Teacher's Guide to Grammar*, Oxford: Oxford University Press.

Cushing, I. (2014) 'Learning and teaching grammar across the curriculum: English and Foreign Languages', Paper given at Linguistics Association of Great Britain Education Committee, Oxford.

DES (1988) *Report of the Committee of Inquiry into The Teaching of English Language* (The Kingman Report), London: HMSO.

DES/WO (1989) *English 5–16* (The Cox Report), London: HMSO.

DfE (2011) *Teachers' Standards*, London: DfE, www.gov.uk/government/uploads/system/uploads/attachment_data/file/283566/Teachers_standard_information.pdf (last accessed 1 September 2015).

DfE (2013) *English Programmes of Study: Key Stage 3: National Curriculum in England*, London: DfE, www.gov.uk/government/uploads/system/uploads/attachment_data/file/244215/SECONDARY_national_curriculum_-_English2.pdf (last accessed 1 September 2015).

DfE (2015a) *Carter Review of Initial Teacher Training (ITT)*, London: DfE, www.gov.uk/government/uploads/system/uploads/attachment_data/file/399957/Carter_Review.pdf (last accessed 1 September 2015).

DfE (2015b) *Initial Teacher Training Performance Profiles: 2013 to 2014 Academic Year*, London: DfE, www.gov.uk/government/uploads/system/uploads/attachment_data/file/456186/Performance_Profiles_2014.pdf (last accessed 1 September 2015).

DfE (2015c) *Subject Knowledge Enhancement (SKE) Courses*, getintoteaching.education.gov.uk/subject-knowledge-enhancement-ske-courses (last accessed 1 September 2015).

Ellis, V. (2003) 'The love that dare not speak its name? The constitution of the English subject and beginning teachers' motivations to teach it', *English Teaching: Practice and Critique* 2(1): 3–14.

Giovanelli, M. (2014) *Teaching Grammar, Structure and Meaning: Exploring Theory and Practice for Post-16 English Language Teachers*, London: Routledge.

Giovanelli, M. (2015) 'Becoming an English language teacher: Linguistic knowledge, anxieties and the shifting sense of identity', *Language and Education* 29(5): 416–29.

Goodwyn, A. (1997) *Developing English Teachers: The Role of Mentorship in a Reflective Profession*, Buckingham: Open University Press.

Goodwyn, A. (2002) 'Breaking up is hard to do: English teachers and that LOVE of reading', *English Teaching: Practice and Critique* 1(1): 66–78.

Goodwyn, A. (2010) *The Expert Teacher of English*, London: Routledge.

Halliday, M. (1967) 'Linguistics and the teaching of English' in J. Britton (ed.) *Handbook for English Teachers: 2. Talking and Writing*, London: Methuen, pp. 80–90.

Helms, J. (1998) 'Science and me: Subject matter and identity in secondary science school teachers', *Journal of Research in Science Teaching* 35(7): 811–34.

Hodgson, J. (2014) 'Surveying the wreckage: The professional response to changes to initial teacher training in the UK', *English in Education* 48(1): 7–25.

Hodkinson, P., Biesta, G. and James, D. (2008) 'Understanding learning culturally: Overcoming the dualism between social and individual views of learning', *Vocations and Learning* 1: 27–47.

Jeffcoate, R. (2000) 'Teaching English grammar in initial teacher training: A course evaluation', *Educational Research* 42(1): 73–84.

Lortie, D. (1975) *Schoolteacher: A Sociological Study*, Chicago, IL: Chicago University Press.

Myhill, D., Jones, S., Lines, H. and Watson, A. (2012) 'Re-thinking grammar: the impact of embedded grammar teaching on students' writing and students' metalinguistic understanding', *Research Papers in Education*, 27(2): 139–66.

Protherough, R. and Atkinson, J. (1991) *The Making of English Teachers*, Milton Keynes: Open University Press.

Sangster, P., Anderson, C. and O'Hara, P. (2013) 'Perceived and actual levels of knowledge about language amongst primary and secondary student teachers: Do they know what they think they know?', *Language Awareness* 22(4): 293–319.

Scott, P. (1989) *Reconstructing A Level English*, Milton Keynes: Open University Press.

Shulman, L. (1987) 'Knowledge and teaching: Foundations of the new reforms', *Harvard Educational Review* 57: 1–22.

Smith, L. (2005) 'The impact of early life history on teachers' beliefs: In-school and out-of-school experiences as learners and knowers of science', *Teachers and Teaching: Theory and Practice* 11: 5–36.

Trask, R. L. (2007) *Language and Linguistics: The Key Concepts*, 2nd edn, P. Stockwell (ed.) London: Routledge.

Turvey, A. (2000) 'Teaching grammar: Working with student teachers 2', *Changing English: Studies in Culture and Education* 7(2): 139–52.

Walmsley, J. (1984) 'The uselessness of formal grammar', *CLIE Pamphlet 2*, London: Committee for Linguistics in Education.

Watson, A. (2012) 'Navigating "the pit of doom": Affective responses to teaching grammar', *English in Education* 46(1): 21–36.

Watson, A. (2015) 'Conceptualisations of "grammar teaching": L1 English teachers' beliefs about teaching grammar for writing', *Language Awareness* 24(1): 1–14.

Yarrow, R. (2007) 'How do students feel about grammar?: The Framework and its implications for teaching and learning', *Changing English: Studies in Culture and Education* 14(2), 175–86.

Chapter 16

Developing teachers' linguistic knowledge

Continuous professional development in schools and colleges

Felicity Titjen

Introduction: English Language teaching and CPD

The expectation for teachers to undertake continuous professional development (CPD) throughout their career is explicitly highlighted in the Teachers' Standards.

> As their careers progress, teachers will be expected to extend the depth and breadth of knowledge, skill and understanding that they demonstrate in meeting the standards, as is judged to be appropriate to the role they are fulfilling and the context in which they are working.
>
> (DfE 2011: 7)

In contextual terms, the complexity for English teaching in post-16 roles is the varieties of 'English' offered for study and examination (with English Language, English Literature and English Language and Literature all available for providers to offer as discrete options for students). In turn, these varieties offer different academic disciplines and require different approaches, knowledge and skills from a versatile English teacher. One potential dilemma that faces English teachers in meeting the DfE's expectations is that despite the growth in the student numbers taking A-level English Language alone increasing by around 10,000 between 2003 and 2013 (Clark *et al.* 2014: 5), many current teachers of A-level English Language or Language and Literature may not have either a language or linguistics background (see also Giovanelli, Chapter 15 of this book). Although the range and number of English language and linguistics courses at BA level in the UK has grown – arguably accommodating the greater interest at A-level – teachers with specific expertise in English Language may only just be embarking on their teaching careers. As a consequence of this shortfall of specific subject expertise, older professionals have upskilled and developed their own linguistic knowledge and understanding to fulfil the need created by the increasing popularity of A-level English Language.

More general forms of CPD can be provided by schools and colleges through in-house INSET programmes. These can meet the DfE's requirements for 'appropriate self-evaluation, reflection and professional development activity', something they assert 'is critical to improving teachers' practice at all career stages' (2011: 7).

However, the expectation that teachers will 'demonstrate a critical understanding of developments in the subject and curriculum areas, and promote the value of scholarship' (2011: 11) is pertinent to the discussion of A-level English Language teachers and the opportunities and routes available for developing their linguistic knowledge. Of heightened relevance now is that links between teacher standards and pay are being made explicit, with annual performance appraisals focusing on teachers evidencing how they meet, maintain and exceed the standards. The DfE's advice to educational employers foregrounds the link between performance and pay as 'an incentive for continuous improvement' (2015: 6). This link taps into two of the four key motives affecting teachers' participation (Stout 1996): firstly, gaining new skills and knowledge to boost classroom practice; and, secondly, salary improvement. These links also formalise extrinsic, external motivations that shape teachers as employees in an educational workplace; keeping knowledge and skills current becomes a requirement to meet the annual objectives set to receive financial and professional rewards. Yet these motivations can be balanced with the intrinsic and internal ones that additionally drive teachers, such as curiosity and the desire for more knowledge for both enjoyment and personal gain, what Deci and Ryan (1985) perceive as 'the most self-determined type of motivation' and that studies have found directly impact on student engagement (Demir 2011).

Yet it often seems incumbent on teachers themselves to find and exploit opportunities to extend their own knowledge and be inventive, flexible and committed in achieving this; meeting the DfE's requirement to show 'critical understanding of developments' (2011) specifically in linguistics is impossible to achieve from whole staff training activities. This chapter will focus on how teachers of English Language undertake continuous professional development formally through academic and accredited routes of study, and informally through networks and communities of practices that have formed from using the internet and social media or through such activities as external examination work. Finally, through extending the notion and application of teachers as working within communities of practice, a case study exploring an English Department's use of language and behaviours within team meetings will demonstrate how the development of linguistic knowledge as part of a teacher's CPD can have a practical application to understanding notions about professional identity and teacher discourses.

What are communities of practice?

Community of Practice (CoP) is a term to describe people coming together for a particular purpose and establishing ways of doing things and ways of interacting to achieve their shared purpose. Wenger (1998: 76–80) separates CoP into three crucial areas:

- *mutual engagement*, which involves regular interaction;
- a *joint negotiated enterprise*, an ongoing process involving the complex relationships of mutual accountability that become part of the community of practice;
- a *shared repertoire* in order to pursue a joint enterprise.

Lave and Wenger (1991) articulate membership of a CoP metaphorically, representing it as an 'apprenticeship', where new members have to learn and become competent and where part of belonging in an institution or department is learning about the ways things are done and the ways things are articulated in the appropriate jargon. For Wenger, a CoP also incorporates recognition and notions of identity and community membership, beyond active engagement, giving it real life relevance to all workplaces (educational or otherwise). All CoP share three elements: *domain*, *community* and *practice*. The *domain* is the scaffold for a joint enterprise and shared purpose, acting as the gel that holds the community together. Building the *community* together helps individuals combine both a sense of belonging and a sense of personal identity as a contributing member of the community. *Practice* is defined by Wenger *et al.* (2002: 38) as a set of socially defined ways of doing things in a specific domain: a set of common methods and shared standards that create a basis for action, communication, problem-solving, performance and accountability.

For teachers, membership of multiple CoP is the norm. Not only is there the departmental and institutional CoP, there is a broader teaching CoP and, within the discussion of linguistic CPD, the ways that teachers in their specialisms come together as CoP in real and virtual ways in order to impact their own practice and expertise in the classroom. What is different in each domain (the department, the institution, the online network) is the formalisation of the practice; for example, aspects that Wenger identifies such as 'accountability' might be very literal in academic results in the educational institution's CoP but 'accountability' may be less tangible or relevant in a looser connection between English Language teachers coming together in communities to share their knowledge.

CPD: developing 'critical understanding of developments in the subject' and 'the value of scholarship' through personal academic study

The recent growth in MA Distance Learning opportunities for English Language and Linguistics courses perhaps testifies to higher education's response to the specific CPD needs of English Language teachers. In 2008, when I was looking for a suitable course to develop and extend my linguistic knowledge, very few UK institutions were offering appropriate courses, but even then the flyers sent to schools and colleges demonstrates that they could see the potential to market these at A-level English Language teachers. Today an Internet search reveals a wider range of universities offering the academic study of English Language at a higher level and in a flexible manner to meet the needs of working and practising teachers. Indeed, online course marketing material highlights the targeting of English teachers: Lancaster University's Department of Linguistics and English Language foregrounds this by stating on their website that their distance learning MA

> is designed to appeal to a wide audience, including people who want to gain
> a further qualification in English Language or those, such as teachers of the

A-level in English Language in the UK, who have taught English Language
and want to consolidate their background
> (http://www.lancaster.ac.uk/study/postgraduate/postgraduate-
> courses/english-language-by-distance-ma/)

Likewise the University of Birmingham asserts that their
> MA in Applied Linguistics is intended for anyone interested in the application
> of language research to language pedagogy, and for teachers of English who
> wish to upgrade their professional standing.
>> http://www.birmingham.ac.uk/postgraduate/courses/
>> distance/english/applied-linguistics.aspx

Using verbs like 'consolidate' and 'upgrade' highlights unashamedly the compe-
tency and skill discourse that Appleby and Hillier (2012: 32) identify as surrounding teaching and 'supports professional identity formation and continuing
professional development'.

Distance learning is probably the delivery model most suited to practising
teachers, who are balancing work and home commitments with a desire to
undertake further study. Master's teaching usually combines some face-to-face or
residential sessions and web-based tutorials and activities, with assessment via
coursework and learning supported by an online forum – allowing a professional,
academic dialogue in addition to communicating with fellow participants.
Pamela Camm, a participant on the MA programme at Lancaster University
defines herself immediately by role as 'a teacher of A-level English Language' in
her course testimonial on the university website. She identifies some of the key
drivers for an MA as CPD, discussing its potential to 'enhance' her teaching as
well as being 'intellectually challenging and stimulating'. In a similar vein, Wendy
Archer's course testimonial also highlights her role as 'a full-time lecturer' at the
outset and her motivation as 'an aspiring researcher'.

Another motivating factor was the academics' 'enthusiasm, expertise and
professionalism' in delivering the modules. Hou's (2015) study of Chinese
student teachers using online communities found that professional support was
a crucial factor to students' online learning, as was the reliance on other peer
members. Pamela Camm articulates this in her testimonial, expressing that she
'particularly enjoyed contributing to the online discussion' and reading others'
responses to the tasks set. She points to the meeting face-to-face with other
students as 'a good experience', allowing the cohort to essentially establish itself
as a CoP. For Hou (2015: 7) the online community 'may develop a shared learning experience with a rich array of resources including meaningful stories, tools,
and possible ideas or solutions for dealing with problems' and this was one of the
key benefits of this distance learning model for me. As well as sharing our
academic responses to the tasks set, the option to network at a personal level
facilitated group cohesion, the feeling of support and academic growth within
the context of shared experiences.

Pamela Camm also highlights the pleasure in being a learner, remarking that 'it was also a nice change for me to be on the other side of the desk!'. This recognition of the process of learning and the change in roles is a common theme. Wendy Archer too expresses her appreciation of being taken out of her 'comfort zones' in some of the topics and activities, valuing this as 'a good learning experience', showing the motivation of scholarship and increasing subject knowledge in this type of CPD. Another common strand of experiences in these testimonials resonates with my own, specifically the time consumed by undertaking an MA as CPD. These are, however, presented both positively in the students' testimonials who comment on the flexibility to complete the online sessions and assessment tasks to accommodate working schedules and family commitments and, negatively, with the final dissertation element being demanding in the time needed to achieve this.

Yet CPD activities for enhancing linguistic knowledge do not have to commit teachers to MAs and PhDs. Valuable face-to-face training opportunities are provided by specialist organisations like the National Association for the Teaching of English (NATE) and the English and Media Centre (EMC), who offer workshops, seminars and conferences as formalised opportunities to offer the scope for growing linguistic knowledge and updates on current linguistic research.

Using informal CoP to gain CPD and develop linguistic knowledge

Lave and Wenger align themselves to a sociocultural perspective on learning that recognises that it also takes place outside of organised or formal learning and CPD opportunities in the linguistic field do not need to be formalised academically. Useful here is the idea of an 'affinity space' defined by Gee (2004: 73) as 'a place or set of places where people can affiliate with others based primarily on shared activities, interests, and goals, not shared race, class, culture, ethnicity, or gender'.

For many English teachers, the relevant 'affinity spaces' to affiliate and share with other professionals are accessed online. Networks and communities can be sourced and joined by using social media like *Twitter* and online teaching and learning resources are available from reputable educational sources such as the *TES*, where they are either offered free or for a small fee and can be peer assessed in reviews for helpfulness and quality; currently there are over 2,000 resources for English/Language and Linguistics available. Other alternatives for English resources are *Teachit* and *EnglishEdu*, subscription sites where teachers can share their resources with each other following a formal vetting process by the organisation. Both offer fora too, allowing teachers to discuss ideas and find inspiration from peers. Helpfully, there are also blogs aimed at English Language teachers and students such as Dan Clayton's EngLangBlog, and the *Linguistic Research Digest*. Both are orientated to A-level English Language and its teaching but each focuses on ideas about language and linguistics rather than resources.

Dedicated English Language online fora such as the subscription site *The English Language List*, allow teachers to build networks, share resources and ask questions of each other. Less public than *Twitter* and mostly advertised through professional word of mouth, it allows teachers to grow professional knowledge available in a 'risk free' forum (outside of the politics and hierarchies of the school or college institutional context) for testing ideas, gaining resources, asking questions and getting different points of view. According to Louise Astbury (personal correspondence), a former Head of English and, a long-time contributor, 'the List allows for any teacher to request very specific support and guidance on pedagogy' and cites its use by HE specialists as providing 'an opportunity for teachers to "ask the experts" particularly on more complex grammatical structures'. However, she also comments on the way 'in recent years it has morphed into a general support network for English teachers on other issues'. So, as an 'affinity space' it affords many benefits and characteristics of a CoP but in its self-mediated form has some limitations that are recognised by experienced community members.

So, as a way of developing subject knowledge, these formal or informal memberships of online communities can provide much that will help us directly in our classroom practice, as well as the scope for collaborative problem-solving where peer-to-peer contact is a valuable source for advice and assistance. For Tseng and Kuo (2014: 43) 'closer connections among online CoP members can lead to great recognition of and altruism towards others' and it is in the online communities that this altruism is most displayed through the sharing of resources and advice. As Perry *et al.* (1999) observe, the planning, enacting and reflecting on their joint enterprise serve to improve what members of a CoP do and these online communities provide an appropriate and effective platform.

Another form of common CPD joint enterprise is external examination marking. Personally this was my first CPD choice for English Language. New to A-level English Language teaching in 2000, the same time as a wholesale curriculum change to the AS and A2 modular approach, I opted to mark externally. The value of external marking at this time offered opportunities to forge links within the community of English Language teachers, in addition to developing subject knowledge. As I advanced up the examining hierarchy, I became seen as an expert, leading CPD training for teachers and writing articles and textbooks about A-level English Language that have created a responsibility to keep up to date with research and developments in language and linguistics.

Extended case study: Exploring an English department's CoP

An ethnographic study (Titjen 2013) on my own workplace and department allowed me to combine my more highly developed linguistic knowledge, gained through the specific CPD activity of an MA programme, with the very practical research methodology of ethnography to focus on teachers' professional roles, practices and interactions in a workplace context. This choice of dissertation topic afforded me the opportunity to foreground how linguistic knowledge can become central to a teacher's self-awareness of the role in other ways outside the classroom, a contrast to the more prevailing view of the role as a facilitator of other people's learning, engaging with Wenger's (1998) response to the artificiality of defining learning simply as something limited to a classroom situation. It also offered scope to apply a methodology that, to use Hymes' (1999: xxxiii) motto, involves 'feet on the ground and one eye on the horizon', by performing micro-level analysis of interaction whilst placing this in a bigger picture of communities and identities.

Exploring community membership, identity and role within an English department

The corpus was elicited from recording the same participants in consecutive meetings occurring over a two-month period and part of my research focus was on Wenger's three areas of CoP that contribute to the shared purpose of the group participants: *mutual engagement, a joint negotiated enterprise* and *a shared repertoire*. In respect of *mutual engagement*, doing things together, these meetings exemplify the regular interaction between the whole team. For *joint enterprise*, the topics and discussions in the meetings of student and course success, negotiating tasks and deadlines, alongside the emphasis on participation (standardising, open mornings, NUT demonstrations) emphasise the importance of activity to this CoP.

Shared repertoires around the challenges of teaching were most obviously centred on time. In addition, these meetings occurred in a timetabled forty-five-minute meeting slot potentially constraining discussion or acting as a point of stress when a meeting looked likely to overrun. References to time occur in all meetings and are made by all department members whatever their position and level of responsibility, showing that, unsurprisingly, time (or lack of) is a significant part of teacher discourse. For example, this interaction between the Course Leader (CL) and a teacher (T1) from the second of the recorded meetings highlights the teachers' concerns.

CL: Once Easter's over there's very little time.
T1: Yeah
CL: So it's, the danger will be that everything would be, that all the standardising would be in the same fortnight and there'd be no classes running.
T1: Well that's the first week.
CL: It's quite important to stagger that.
T1: That first week back, we've only got three days anyway haven't we?
CL: Yeah

Time references were trying to alleviate the group's fear of activities taking too much time and to acknowledge the impact of the workload created by coursework standardisation. Here adverbial intensifiers, used by both the Course Leader, 'very little time' and teacher 'only three days', also express the shared fear of time, seen when planning coursework deadlines, marking and standardisation processes. This fear is encapsulated in many speakers' talk, epitomised in time as being presented as an enemy in the declarative, 'it's the danger'.

The Head of Department's concern for the team is also time-related, as shown in her focus on key agenda items in the first meeting.

HoD: If I can just begin with, there's only a couple of things I wanted to do today. Information Morning. Obviously we need to meet today to set up as quickly as possible. If if we aim for as many people as possible to meet then at three, hopefully it won't take much longer than half an hour to get everything you know everything set up. Er I've only got a couple of other things in the agenda um and those can be done really quickly.

Here the department head also reassures participants about the length of time activities will take with the emphasis on speed shown by the repetition of the adverb 'quickly' and the attempt to minimise time commitment when discussing setting up for open morning, perhaps against the backdrop of weekend working.

References to holiday periods and specific dates occurred in all meetings, acting sometimes as possible deadlines, dates for specific events and as an orientation around which to make decisions. In Meeting 3, the English Language Course Leader outlines her message to colleagues regarding coursework deadlines and the implications for standardising these.

CL: Yeah just a reminder that the deadline's next Friday and to er be very strict about that. And will you let me know if you've got any flaky ones that are looking like they're not going to meet the deadline? I've got a couple but I do think we need to be very firm with them about it. I know this is why before we would usually have a deadline but um I'm not prepared with the flaky ones to extend it really, unless there's been illness or er genuine circumstances. Um I've given everybody their coursework cover sheets. I'll also put in for photocopying the internal mark sheets so I'll put those in your pigeon holes as well. If you remember the bit at the top, they can fill in so that saves you a lot of time ((*sounds of agreement*)).

Repetition of the noun 'deadlines' gives the decisions a finality, further modified by the adjectives 'strict' and 'firm', to influence other teachers' behaviours with their students. Additionally, her flicking of diary pages thorough her talk foregrounds the diary as an artefact that physically manifests time; commitment to deadlines will not only be ratified in the minutes but in individual diaries brought to meetings.

For this group of teachers, students seem to fall into distinct categories, either as deserving and hardworking, or in a binary construction of students as irresponsible and unreliable. One teacher tells a story of 'Carl' in the pre-meeting talk.

T1:   Carl has got in on that Cambridge thing, yeah.
T2:   What about the other girl?
T1:   No. I didn't think she would though because her parents because [her mum]
T2:   [Agh]
T1:   teaches science here. She's Dr A what's her name [isn't she]
T2:   [Oh okay.]
T1:   didn't get in really. It's good for Carl though, a good result.
T2:   He was in West Side Story last night.
T1:   Yeah, apparently yeah. He'll get in though. He's the kind of person.

From this exchange Carl seems well known within the department, contrasting to the vague identification of another Oxbridge student in 'what about the other girl'. Stating that 'Carl has got in on that Cambridge thing yeah' depicts the possible conflict between the pride at his success and an ideological view of this as an elite institution, shown in the teacher's colloquial dismissal of the event as a 'thing'. Her representation of Carl as a deserving underdog is reinforced further with the dismissal of the female student's possibility of success. The positive presentation of Carl is reinforced by repeating 'good' and confidently asserting his likely success in his Oxbridge application as 'he's the kind of person'. On the face of it, the next comment from another teacher that 'he was in West Side Story last night' is simply a factual statement, but this adds to the presentation of Carl as a good student through his willingness to participate in college cultural activities. Other positive presentations of students in other meetings also value achievement and the evaluative opinion of personality (and possibly a non-troublesome student in the classroom) of a particular student as 'a nice boy' is followed swiftly by another colleague's metaphorical assertion that 'he was our brightest hope'.

To contrast with these representations is the discussion of less favoured students. The Year 13 resit students are a main agenda item of Meeting 2 with exam entries, a procedural action, to be sorted. The language used is almost interrogational, seen in one teacher's choice of the verb 'denied' to express dismay at her students refuting their assent to a resit and the HoD's implication that she has the 'proof' as 'well I've got the signatures on the list'. Likewise, the comment 'I wouldn't chase them up enormously hard it's their funeral' also reflects metaphorically the dire outcome for those students who miss their resit. Irony concerning students is a shared way to realise the beliefs of this CoP. One teacher refers to a student's coursework as 'Sarah's masterpiece' and another comments on the brevity required for the GCSE controlled assessment coursework with 'that shouldn't be a problem with our lot' to which all laugh. This supports Holmes and Marra's (2002) findings that humour gives insights into the workplace culture of a community of practice. In these meetings the humour is often supportive and collaborative between colleagues, although in letting off steam, the students are almost always the vent. The English Language Course Leader's use of the noun phrase 'flaky ones' seen in the earlier discussion of time describes those English Language students unlikely to meet deadlines. So, as well as stories about students, the style in which the team discuss students is indicative of a *shared repertoire*.

Students are defended but only in response to an outside threat via the exam boards and the GCSE results, a big focus of the discussion in Meeting 2. However, it becomes clear that the threat is to the department, in possible underachievement and poor overall results, rather than to the student as seen in this interaction with the Head of Department (HoD) and another teacher (T3).

GCSE CL: Um what I felt slightly miffed about ((*laughs*)), erm perhaps unfairly was when I looked at the the enhanced results analysis compared to similar centres, our coursework's no better and I couldn't quite believe that I think.

HoD: (overlaps) Well this time around it's not our coursework.

T3:   We don't tend to get As and A* and there will be schools that have the whole range.

GCSE CL: Well what no? This is comparing us to similar centres, so I assume these are sixth form colleges. Yeah well done everybody. Thanks for everybody's HARD work and it is hard work, isn't it? It's gruelling, particularly the workshops. I think they're essential ((*T3 makes agreeing sounds*)) input really so…

Pronoun choices, 'our' and 'we', refer not to the actual GCSE students but to the department and college's difficulties and achievements. Indeed, the Course Leader's congratulation to the team is reinforced by reformulating the difficulty of the job, with the tag question seeking agreement from the team. Within the same utterance, her stronger, more emotive word 'gruelling' to describe the challenge of GCSE success emphasises the feelings of teaching as effort and hard work.

Stock cupboards as shared spaces are also indicators of the smaller communities of practice within the English department even in terms of language styles. Although seemingly a small point of difference, the English Language Course Leader refers to 'investigation resources', a broader term to describe the physical objects (primarily books), whereas the literature teachers refer to the 'books', by title 'Hamlet' or by writers, 'Duffys' and 'Sheers'. This links back to the initial discussion in this chapter about the complexity of teaching English post-16 in the 'varieties' of English offered, illustrating the tension between the specialisms – where the slightly different jargon represents different 'English' identities at this level and perhaps beyond in higher education.

However, my dissertation findings are already obsolete. The Head of Department featured in my data retired in 2012, and the CoP has changed considerably under new management. What this demonstrates is that at one level, a CoP cannot be seen as fixed or permanent but as shaped by its members, a critical conclusion from my research that is interesting in itself. At another level, it also highlights the idea that change is ongoing, whether in the workplace or in the roles and practices of the English teaching professional. For me, the opportunity to reflect, explore and increase my linguistic knowledge, in addition to putting this into practice, has reinforced the importance of continuous professional development in all of its many forms.

References

Appleby, Y. and Hillier, Y. (2012) 'Exploring practice: Research networks for critical professional learning', *Studies in Continuing Education* 34(1): 31–43.

Clark, B., Giovanelli, M. and Macrae, A. (2015) 'Lang-Lit from A to BA: Student backgrounds and first year content', Middlesex University Research Repository, eprints. http://mdx.ac.uk/14424/1/clarkgiovanellimacrae_2015_Lang-Lit_AtoBA.pdf (last accessed 9 March 2015).

Deci, E. and Ryan, R. (1985) *Intrinsic Motivation and Self-determination in Human Behaviour*, New York, NY: Plenum.

Demir, K. (2011) 'Teachers' intrinsic and extrinsic motivation as predictors of student engagement', *E-journal of New World Sciences Academy Education Sciences* 6: 1397–409.

DfE (2011) *Teachers' Standards*, London: DfE, www.gov.uk/government/uploads/system/uploads/attachment_data/file/283566/Teachers_standard_information.pdf (last accessed 1 February 2015).

DfE (2015) *Implementing Your School's Approach to Pay: Departmental Advice for Maintained Schools and Local Authorities*, London: DfE, www.gov.uk/government/uploads/system/uploads/attachment_data/file/452050/Implementing-your-school_s-approach-to-pay.pdf (last accessed 15 September 2015).

Gee, J. (2004) *Situated Language and Learning: A Critique of Traditional Schooling*, New York, NY: Routledge.

Holmes J, and Marra, M. (2002) 'Having a laugh at work: How humour contributes to workplace culture', *Journal of Pragmatics* 34(12): 1683–1710.

Hou, H. (2015) 'What makes an online community of practice work? A situated study of Chinese student teachers' perception of online professional learning', *Teaching and Teacher Education* 46: 6–16.

Hymes, D. (1999) 'Introduction', in D. Hymes (ed.) *Re-inventing Anthropology*, New York, NY: Randon House, pp. v–xlix.

Lave, J. and Wenger, E. (1991) *Situated Learning: Legitimate Peripheral Participation*, Cambridge: Cambridge University Press.

Perry, N., Walton, C. and Calder, K. (1999) 'Teachers developing assessments of early literacy: A community of practice project', *Teacher Education and Special Education* 22(4): 218–33.

Stout, R. T. (1996) 'Staff development policy: Fuzzy choices in an imperfect market', *Education Policy Analysis Archives* 4(2): 1–15.

Titjen, F. (2013) *An Ethnographic Study of English Departmental Meetings in a Sixth Form College*, MA dissertation, Lancaster University.

Tseng, F. and Kuo, F. (2014) 'A study of social participation and knowledge sharing in the teachers' online professional learning community', *Computers and Education* 72: 37–47.

Wenger, E. (1998) *Communities of Practice: Learning, Meaning, and Identity*. Cambridge: Cambridge University Press.

Wenger, E., McDermott, R. and Schneider, W. M. (2002) *Cultivating Communities of Practice: A Guide to Managing Knowledge*, Boston, MA: Harvard Business Review.

Websites

EngLangBlog: http://englishlangsfx.blogspot.co.uk

English and Media Centre: www.englishandmedia.co.uk

English Edu: http://english.edusites.co.uk

Linguistics Research Digest: www.linguistics-research-digest.blogspot.co.uk

National Association for the Teaching of English: www.nate.org.uk/

Teachit: www.teachit.co.uk

TES: www.tes.com/uk/

The English Language List: www.mollybleed.com

The Guardian: www.theguardian.com/media/mind-your-language

University of Birmingham: www.birmingham.ac.uk/index.aspx

University of Lancaster Department of Linguistics: www.lancaster.ac.uk/linguistics/

Chapter 17

Language and linguistics in higher education

Transition and post-16 English

Angela Goddard

Introduction

There are three distinct AS/A-levels in English available for students post-16: English Language, English Literature, and English Language and Literature. Up to the 1980s, English Literature existed alone as the only A-level English option available. Now, students can choose between distinctive types of English study. English Language continues to show steady development annually both in terms of overall entry figures for AS-level and A-level, and also in terms of gender balance (M = male; F = female, below). In 2015, English Language and English Language and Literature between them represented almost half of all the entries for A-level English nationally:

English Literature
M: 13,394
F: 37,494
Total: 50,888

English Language
M: 7,562
F: 16,325
Total: 23,887

English Language and Literature:
M: 4,217
F: 10,507
Total: 14,724

(Source: Joint Council for Qualifications (JCQ) www.jcq.org.uk)

AS/A-levels at 16–19 present students and teachers with some complex issues of transition in both directions – back to pre-16, secondary school English, and forward to degree-level study. Transition from GCSE to study at 16–19 and beyond has always represented a shift of gear, as students are expected to become more critical readers and more independent learners, able to set up and manage their own academic lines of enquiry. However, recent reforms at both GCSE and at A-level (for courses beginning in 2015, first examined in 2017) are likely to make the experience of transition much more of a culture shock for students in coming years, despite the initial aims of the reforms being 'to better prepare students for higher education' (DfE 2013a). While all students of English will be adversely affected, English Language students will be particularly hard hit, for a number of reasons.

Structural changes

A major structural change at the heart of the A-level reforms is that new A-levels will be linear, two-year courses with end of course assessments. This represents a significant move away from the structure that operated from 2000, at which point A-levels were changed from linear courses to modular, unitised ones in response to criticisms that A-levels were too specialised and narrow. The modularisation of A-levels, called 'Curriculum 2000', was a government-driven initiative to give students a more rounded experience, allowing them to take several AS-levels in their first year of study and to specialise more in the second year, but with AS-level modules counting towards the final A-level grade. In the new reformed structure, AS-levels are 'de-coupled' from A-level, which means that any credit gained from an AS-level assessment cannot be counted towards an A-level outcome. If students take an AS-level course and decide to continue to A-level, they have to take all the A-level examinations as well. On the other hand, students who fail their assessments at the end of their A-level course will have worked for two years for nothing. The system of reforms is therefore going back to the 'all or nothing' educational culture of former times.

The structural change described above applies to England only, because the Secretary of State and all the bodies associated with qualifications taken in England – the Department for Education (DfE), the examinations regulator Ofqual, and the English exam boards AQA, OCR and Edexcel (Pearson) – have no jurisdiction over how examinations are run in Scotland, Wales or Northern Ireland. Each of these parts of the UK has been given devolved powers and is currently following its own distinctive pathway in terms of educational policy. Scotland is continuing the system of Highers that has been in existence for many years, based on different curricula from those of A-levels. Wales is not reforming its English A-levels at all for its own Welsh candidates, who are obliged to take the qualifications offered by the Welsh exam board, WJEC. However, WJEC has also created a new entity called Eduqas, which is offering reformed A-levels in English to candidates in England. Northern Ireland has its own exam board, CCEA, and the current plan is not to reform. However,

CCEA only offers English Literature A-level, and not the other two 'Englishes', English Language and English Language and Literature.

It is unclear how schools and colleges will be able to advise students in this fragmented educational landscape. With some A-level subjects reformed and others not, and with some parts of the UK operating non-reformed and others reformed versions of the same subject, the picture is considerably more challenging than it was. Whereas schools across the UK are required either to take reformed A-levels or non-reformed ones (or Highers), depending on where they are located, universities have no such regional constraints, although there are complexities around tuition fees, of course. But it is unclear what difference it would make to a student's chances if he or she applied from one area to another: for example, if a Welsh student applied to an English university. In theory, universities in England should look more favourably on applicants with reformed qualifications, since they are supposed to be more rigorous and robust. However, all the qualifications, old and new, have the same names and so in reality many university admissions staff are unlikely to know the difference.

Coursework

One general way in which all the AS/A-levels in English have less continuity than before, both with GCSE and with higher education, is in the abandonment of coursework (now called non-examined assessment or NEA) at GCSE and the reduction of its importance at AS/A-level. Students coming from GCSE will from 2015 have no experience of coursework to build on, so will need to be taught what it means to ask questions of their own about aspects of English and find out answers to their questions (including the idea that there are no cut-and-dried answers). The JCQ, representing all the major UK examination boards, regularly produces guidelines for coursework supervision and the general idea is that teachers can prompt students by asking them questions but that it is not the teacher's role to micro-manage their studies. A coursework project is a valuable opportunity for students to develop research skills by setting up and following through an individual workplan, in the process showing initiative, sustained commitment and the ability to think critically, as well as the skills involved in report writing and dissemination. But understanding this way of working and developing the skills to do it cannot be learned overnight. It takes support from teachers over time to help students develop their confidence to work independently and not seek constant reassurance and guidance.

The maximum percentage allowed for coursework at A-level has been reduced from forty per cent to twenty per cent. The Department for Education subject content documents for all the Englishes make it clear that working independently is a skill that A-level specifications (as distinct from AS-level specifications) must aim to develop in students. For example, the subject content document for

English Language below begins by listing what all specifications at AS and A-level must aim to do, then describes how A-level specifications must go further:

> The aims and objectives for this subject require specifications to develop students' interest in and enjoyment of English as they:
>
> - develop and apply their understanding of the concepts and methods appropriate for the analysis and study of language
> - explore data and examples of language in use
> - engage creatively and critically with a varied programme for the study of English
> - develop their skills as producers and interpreters of language.
>
> In addition, A-level specifications must encourage students to develop their interest in and enjoyment of English as they independently investigate language in use.
>
> (DfE 2014: 1)

The requirement above, coupled with the reduction in coursework percentage, is likely to result in coursework being left to the second year of the course where AS-level and A-level students are being co-taught (which will be the case in schools and colleges that cannot afford to run separate classes for the different qualifications). It will only be in the financially better off establishments, where A-level students can be taught alone, that coursework will be able to form part of the learning from the outset. Of course, good teaching at any level encourages student independence. But the reality is that many students going on to university will only have had a single year of experiencing the form of assessment that is at the heart of university learning and teaching.

Universities have developed assignment-based coursework as a mainstream way of assessing learning because they long since realised that students' standard of intellectual performance is improved considerably if they are able to spend time planning, thinking about and directing their own enquiries. Additionally, in terms of employability skills, universities recognise that coursework assignments teach the crucial skills of independent working that are required in real-world contexts, where for most tasks we are asked to perform, we go through a process much closer to a coursework assignment than to a test under exam conditions, where we are cut off from all sources of information. In studies of transition from A-level to undergraduate study for students of English Literature (Green 2005), for students of English Language (Goddard and Beard 2007), and for students of English Language and Literature (Clark *et al.* 2015), A-level coursework was seen by higher education colleagues as the main area where students gain some experience of what university study will involve. Coursework was seen as extremely valuable in showing that students are able to demonstrate sustained commitment over time to an area of academic interest. It seems contradictory, then, that despite the claim that A-levels were being restructured in order to smooth transition to higher education, the main area that university stakeholders saw as a strong connection has been weakened.

Transitions in English Language

There are some disjunctions from GCSE to A-level in all the Englishes. For example, English Language and Literature A-level has no precursor at all at GCSE. But students transiting from GCSE to A-level English Language face more profound reorientations than their English Literature peers. There is some continuity from GCSE to A-level English Language in terms of writing skills. But in the reformed English Language A-level, writing can only be credited up to a possible maximum of fifteen per cent of the total marks. At both AS and A-level, the subject becomes primarily the study of language as a topic – for example, how it changes, how it varies, public attitudes to it, how it is acquired, how it represents people and things, how representations build into discourses that construct realities for users. Unless school pupils happen to have a teacher who is interested enough in the topic of language to include some study of it, they will not have treated language as a topic – as a phenomenon – anywhere in their English curriculum pre-A-level. There was formerly an opportunity to do this, in the GCSE 'study of spoken language', which existed for a brief time as a coursework option. But this has been abandoned, as no coursework is allowed at GCSE; and although the National Curriculum for English requires opportunities for pupils to develop their speaking and listening skills, the assessment of these skills is optional and it does not contribute to the overall GCSE mark. The current proposal is that students who are entered are graded via the categories 'distinction', 'merit', 'pass' and 'not classified'.

Digital literacies

At GCSE, then, English Language is conceived as a skill – and with the abandonment of compulsorily assessed speaking and listening, essentially a literacy skill only, and a very narrow one at that. GCSE does not recognise the kinds of 'new literacies' that academics have been commenting on for some years (see the many publications from the London Knowledge Lab, for example Selwyn 2011, 2013). Instead, the model is secretarial and distinctly pre-Internet; digital texts, initially proscribed at GCSE, have been grudgingly allowed following objections during the consultation period (DfE 2013b). Edexcel's GCSE in Digital Communication has been dropped, during the reform process. In stark contrast, the subject content for A-level English Language explicitly *requires* the study of multimodal texts, for understandable reasons: new technologies have fundamentally challenged many erstwhile concepts about language use, and have constituted an extremely fertile research area for some time, particularly around the language used by young people themselves: for example, see Thurlow *et al.* (2004); Goddard and Geesin (2011); and Gillen (2014).

At university level, multimodal communication can be studied in rich contexts of authentic language use and it has afforded new opportunities for students to collaborate across space, time and cultural boundaries (see Goddard 2011; Goddard and Henry 2013). But however imaginatively teachers of A-level frame the learning experiences for their students, assessment constraints produce some bizarre dislocations. Although most of the examination processes have now gone online (such as the production of exam papers, examiner stand-ardising, and marking), the AS/A-level student of English is invariably stuck with a paper booklet and pen, rather than screen and keyboard, in the exam room. It was probably some considerable time ago that most of us wrote in any sustained way on paper, using a pen; and even the briefest notes and memos are now often typed on our smartphone screens.

Apart from the fact that assessment contexts in the UK do not replicate the communication conditions we all use every day, there are also problems around the texts that might be set for analysis. For example, if examiners want students to analyse part of a website in exam conditions, the text has to be transformed from its original digital format and reset for paper. The student then has to analyse a paper-based text with knowledge drawn from experience of how a text such as this example might have worked in practice. The answer to this conun-drum is not to ban digital material, but to find ways to examine students that fit twenty-first-century lives. This has been happening for some time in Denmark and Norway, where students have been able to type exam answers on computers since the 1990s, and where full access to the Internet has been allowed in final-year school examinations since 2009 (Hobson 2009). Meanwhile, Finland, whose educational achievements regularly top the OECD PISA rankings for European countries, is removing cursive handwriting from their curricula from 2016 and replacing it with keyboard skills: 'Minna Harmanen from the National Board of Education told Finnish publication *Savon Sanomat* that "fluent typing skills are an important national competence"' (O'Connor 2015).

The study of digital material offers rich scope for language exploration in all phases of education; however, university courses seem to be the only providers in the UK who can offer digital texts for study in a properly situated way. In pre-16 curricula, every attempt has been made to ignore forms of new commu-nication (despite the requirement for primary age pupils to study programming); while at post-16, classroom practice can provide authentic contexts for study but assessment vehicles cannot.

Metalanguage

A further example of discontinuity within English Language study across the phases is the issue of metalanguage. Perhaps because grammar is often in the spotlight as a Shibboleth, it can seem as though grammatical terminology is the only aspect of metalanguage that there is, within English Language.

As well as seeming to overshadow other aspects of language, a further issue around the study of grammar is when grammatical terminology should be taught. For example, Richmond (2015) sees the National Curriculum requirements at Stages 1 and 2 as over-demanding and likely to lead to a situation where terminology is introduced before learners have any real understanding of language structures. He advocates a more gradual introduction through the key stages, reserving the study of more complex structures for the later key stages. Key Stage 3 currently has lighter coverage than Key Stages 1 and 2, which seems hard to fathom. This lack of cohesion means that by the time students being given the reformed National Curriculum reach the AS/A-level stage, they will have to think back to their primary school years to remember the grammatical concepts and terms they learned – if, indeed, this aspect of language made any sense to them in the first place.

Language and interdisciplinarity

Thankfully, the AS/A-level subject content is at pains to stress both the importance of other levels of language study besides grammar – for example, phonology, semantics, pragmatics, and discourse – and the importance of applying knowledge of these levels to aspects of 'historical, geographical, social and individual' contexts (DfE 2014: 2). In order to do the latter, students need more than terms and concepts about language structure; they also need ideas from – as the list suggests – history, geography, sociology and psychology. How can language change be understood without some history? How can World Englishes be understood without some geography? How can behaviour online, language acquisition or attitudes to accent be explained without some concepts from the social sciences? English Language as a subject is nothing if not interdisciplinary, and the nature of these connections is rightly made more explicit as students progress to undergraduate study.

The interdisciplinary nature of English Language was pointed up sharply in a transition study that focused specifically on the future study plans of AS-level students of English Language (Goddard and Beard 2007). When students who were planning to go on to higher education were asked what subjects they were interested in taking, a total of seventy-five different subjects or specific courses (in addition to English Language/Linguistics) were named. This shows that English Language A-level has an important role, not only in supporting transition to higher education English Language/Linguistics courses, but also to higher education in a wider sense. This picture does not seem to be repeated for English Literature A-level, which appears to have a narrower, more specialist profile with a simpler continuity between A-level and undergraduate study. However, this apparently simple continuity can hide its own complexities: as Green (2005) shows, the similarity of name can conceal some significant differences in the nature of the subject at the different levels.

What's in a name?

Who 'owns' the English subject name, and where does the subject live? This might seem to have injected a rather philosophical note into proceedings at this point, but the answers to these questions carry some very practical and profound implications for students – particularly students of English Language – who are aiming to go to university to study what they see as 'English'.

The subject of 'English' in UK universities originally meant 'English Literature'. Now there are distinctive aspects of English study with separate qualifications at A-level, the term 'English' should logically be an umbrella term that covers the whole subject, much in the way that 'Mathematics' covers 'Applied Mathematics', 'Further Mathematics', and so on; similarly, 'Geography' can be 'Human Geography', 'Physical Geography', etc. In material that comes from higher education providers – for example the pages of UCAS, the university admissions gateway for applications to higher education, 'English' sometimes does refer to a wide range of different types of courses and modules. But at other times, it means simply 'English Literature'. An example of the latter is a course entitled 'English and Advertising' where the 'English' part consists of studying 'the literary greats' (quotation from the university's own course description in 2015). Another example from 2015 is the combined course 'English and English Language', where the only possible meaning of 'English' is 'English Literature'. Examples of many such ambiguities were recorded in 2007 (see Goddard and Beard 2007: 37) and are seemingly still extant.

Sixth formers who have studied English Language (or indeed English Language and Literature) are likely to think of themselves as students of 'English'. A-level English Language is taught in school departments of English, and it can be the case that a single teacher teaches both English Literature and English Language. And although English Language A-level owes much to the academic subject of Linguistics, it also shares approaches to text analysis and production with Literary-Critical and Creative Writing fields (see Goddard 2012). When students who were planning to study English Language at university were asked what course names they would search for when applying, the top three responses were 'English Language', 'English Language and Linguistics', and 'English' (Goddard and Beard 2007: 29). It seems that students of English Language have more work to do than their English Literature peers in order to ensure that they are making the right choices.

Subject identities in higher education are not only about names; they are also about locations and intellectual 'housings'. While English Literature almost always lives in Arts schools or faculties, English Language can be found anywhere from Business (for example, offering language proficiency to non-native speakers) to Applied Sciences (for example, training speech and language therapists) to Communications (for example, teaching digital literacy skills). The way the territories of 'English' are arranged in one phase is not necessarily true for another. From the perspective of learners in transition, this can be a baffling experience, and a very expensive one if they find themselves on the wrong kind of course and want to change direction. Higher education institutions need to spell out in detail what kind of courses they are offering. Obviously, this is important in all subjects and for all students in transition. But, given that English Language has such possible breadth and so many interdisciplinary connections, it is particularly important for practitioners in this subject to offer clear descriptions of their courses.

A relatively recent addition to the complex landscape of English in higher education has been the publication of a pamphlet called *Informed Choices*, issued by the Russell Group of UK universities, a self-selected group formed in 1994 after a meeting at the Hotel Russell in London. The Russell Group promotes itself as an elite, research-intensive community. Its *Informed Choices* pamphlet, produced in 2013, identified a group of A-level subjects most often listed in entry requirements at these universities. While English Literature was listed, neither English Language nor English Language and Literature were included. It is easy to see why: English Literature courses normally expect applicants to have A-level English Literature, so it is understandable that this subject features as a requirement for those courses, while English Language and English Language and Literature courses often have more wide-ranging entry requirements. Students taking the latter A-level subjects can gain entry to diverse fields of study – remember the seventy-five courses listed by the AS English Language students in the study by Goddard and Beard (2007) – and in that sense are genuinely 'facilitating' across the whole HEI sector; however, these subjects are not necessarily explicitly required for particular courses in quite the same way as English Literature is.

Informed Choices has been perceived in schools and colleges as suggesting that it is only the listed subjects that should be taken by students if they are to gain a place at a Russell Group university. Myers (2013), who runs the biggest university Linguistics department in the UK (at Lancaster University), reports on his experiences of visiting schools where headteachers tell pupils explicitly not to take English Language if they want to go to 'good universities'. Myers concluded that his subject 'was being threatened by the offhand decisions of a club of which my university wasn't even a member' (Myers 2013: 1). But even those schools and colleges who understand the vagaries of higher education politics find themselves constrained by the new government Key Stage 5 requirement to report how many pupils in their establishments gain two As and a B grade in the Russell Group list of 'facilitating' subjects.

The fundamental problem with the pamphlet is that it is not based on any research about the subjects that students who gain places at Russell Group universities actually come with. This is somewhat ironic, given that these universities pride themselves on their research skills. McInerney (2013) accuses the Russell Group secretariat of laziness and does some research herself on the subjects that students actually gain entry with. She summarises as follows:

> The government measure has been widely criticized … as elitist, or non-creative, or boring. But the real problem with this scheme is much simpler: there is no

evidence (beyond stated prejudice) to support the claim that they actually do 'facilitate' entry to Russell group universities.

(2013: 1)

Examples of non-facilitating subjects that seem to be more successful in gaining course acceptances than any of the facilitating ones include Economics and Drama. Drama appeared high on the list for Law LLB (Hons) at three separate Russell Group universities. McInerney concludes:

> Drama, which no-one has ever mentioned to me as a 'rigorous' or 'preferred' subject actually seems quite important for law. When you think about it, this should not be a shock. Law has an enormous amount of performance to it. But if you follow league table thinking, no-one would ever advise a student of theirs who wants to do law at a Russell Group university to study drama. Instead you might pick physics, or chemistry, or one of the other subjects which – as it stands – look to have a much lower success rate.
>
> (2013: 1)

McInerney's research shows that, even if the *Informed Choices* idea of facilitating subjects is accepted, it is unwise to take three of the listed subjects at the expense of others. But the sad reality is that there are probably many students who are being persuaded to do subjects that are not their real preferences, simply because they are 'approved' subjects. In the end, students who do well are those that have a passion for their subject, regardless of which subject is on one list or another. But students are often not in a position to understand that official statements can themselves be misleading or driven by academic politics.

A possible example of the latter is given below. This is from the Russell Group's own website, and features in their FAQs list:

> *English is listed as a facilitating subject, does this mean English Literature, Language, or Language and Literature?*
>
> In our list of facilitating subjects, English refers to English Literature. However, individual universities will have their own admissions policies, and entrance requirements will vary by courses within institutions. In general, English Literature or a combined English Language and Literature course is required at advanced level for entry to study English at university. A few universities will also accept English Language without a Literature qualification. (Russell Group official website FAQs)

How might an English Language A-level student understand this response? If they want to study their subject at university and they think of that subject as 'English', what is the writer communicating to them? That 'only a few universities' will accept their subject as valid, even to study English Language?

The writer of this response realises that English Language exists, because the subject is mentioned in the final sentence. But the meaning of 'English' in the writer's mind can only be 'English Literature'. This is either careless or deliberate and, if the latter, represents an attempt to shore up English Literature and side-line English Language, which would be particularly odd given that the Russell Group universities have significant numbers of English Language courses. A more complex explanation may be that there is academic in-fighting between different areas of English study within the Russell Group university departments, with an English Literature lobby attempting to reclaim the old idea that they are the only practitioners who have a right to the subject name of 'English'. Support for this explanation can perhaps be found in Eaglestone and Kövesi's (2013) picture of English as a subject that is 'eating itself'. They warn that in light of falling numbers, the subject is 'not too big to fail' (but also see the response to this article in Clark *et al.* (2014), where some commonality across the Englishes is proposed).

While the Department for Education in England is busy narrowing the subject options available for students to take, Finland is going in the opposite direction, broadening its school curriculum by abandoning subject study altogether. Seeing academic subjects with all their self-interested disciplinary boundaries as a nineteenth-century century preoccupation, Finnish educators want to look for twenty-first-century answers to questions of skills and knowledge. This will involve teaching by topic, with subjects integrated to mirror real-world experiences:

> Subject-specific lessons – an hour of history in the morning, an hour of geography in the afternoon – are already being phased out for 16-year-olds in the city's [Helsinki's] upper schools. They are being replaced by what the Finns call "phenomenon" teaching – or teaching by topic. For instance, a teenager studying a vocational course might take "cafeteria services" lessons, which would include elements of maths, languages (to help serve foreign customers), writing skills and communication skills.
>
> More academic pupils would be taught cross-subject topics such as the European Union – which would merge elements of economics, history (of the countries involved), languages and geography.
>
> There are other changes too, not least to the traditional format that sees rows of pupils sitting passively in front of their teacher, listening to lessons or waiting to be questioned. Instead there will be a more collaborative approach, with pupils working in smaller groups to solve problems while improving their communication skills.
>
> (Garner 2015)

Such a move would solve another problematic aspect of the 16–19 curriculum diet in the UK, which is the abiding division between 'academic' and 'vocational' subjects. This chapter has concentrated on the academic curricula at AS/A-level, but of course many students go to university with other types of Level 3 qualifications, and we need a way to integrate these different routes. A topic-based starting point is by its very nature integrative. And, English Language would form a natural part of that integration. We can but dream.

References

Clark, B., Giovanelli, M. and Macrae, A. (2014) 'English, diverse but unified: Putting texts at the heart of the discipline', *Teaching English* 6: 17–19.

Clark, B., Giovanelli, M. and Macrae, A. (2015) 'Lang-Lit from A to BA: Student backgrounds and first year content', Middlesex University Research Repository, eprints. http://mdx.ac.uk/14424/1/clarkgiovanellimacrae_2015_Lang-Lit_AtoBA.pdf (last accessed 5 September 2015).

DfE (2013a) *Reforming qualifications and the curriculum to better prepare pupils for life after school*, London: DfE, www.gov.uk/government/policies/reforming-qualifications-and-the-curriculum-to-better-prepare-pupils-for-life-after-school (last accessed 22 February 2015).

DfE (2013b) *Reformed GCSE Subject Content Consultation: Government Response*, London: DfE, www.gov.uk/government/uploads/system/uploads/attachment_data/file/254513/GCSE_consultation_-_government_s_response.pdf (last accessed 22 February 2015).

DfE (2014) *Subject Content for English Language*, London: DfE, www.gov.uk/government/uploads/system/uploads/attachment_data/file/302109/A_level_English_language_subject_content.pdf (last accessed 22 February 2015).

Eaglestone, R. and Kövesi, S. (2013) 'English: why the discipline may not be "too big to fail"', *Times Higher Education*, 31 October, www.timeshighereducation.co.uk/features/english-why-the-discipline-may-not-be-too-big-to-fail/2008473.fullarticle (last accessed 22 February 2015).

Garner, R. (2015) 'Finland schools: Subjects scrapped and replaced with "topics" as country reforms its education system', *Independent*, 20 March, www.independent.co.uk/news/world/europe/finland-schools-subjects-are-out-and-topics-are-in-as-country-reforms-its-education-system-10123911.html (last accessed 2 June 2015).

Gillen, J. (2014) *Digital Literacies*, London: Routledge.

Goddard, A. (2011) '"Type you soon!" A stylistic approach to language use in a virtual learning environment', *Language and Literature* 20(3): 1847–200.

Goddard, A. (2012) *Doing English Language*, London: Routledge.

Goddard, A. and Beard, A. (2007) *As Simple as ABC? Issues of Transition for Students of English Language A-level going on to Study English Language/Linguistics in Higher Education*, Higher Education Academy English Subject Centre, Report Series 14, www.english.heacademy.ac.uk/archive/publications/reports/transition.pdf (last accessed 22 February 2015).

Goddard, A. and Geesin, B. (2011) *Language and Technology*, London: Routledge.

Goddard, A. and Henry, A. (2013) 'English language learning for international employability', in T. Bilham (ed.) *For the Love of Learning: Insights from the Higher Education Academy National Teaching Fellows*, Houndmills: Palgrave Macmillan, pp. 2477–53.

Green, A. (2005) *Four Perspectives on Transition: English Literature from Sixth Form to University*, Higher Education Academy English Subject Centre, Report Series 10, www.english.heacademy.ac.uk/archive/publications/reports/transition.pdf (last accessed 22 February 2015).

Hobson, J. (2009) 'Danish pupils use web in examinations', BBC News, 4 November, http://news.bbc.co.uk/1/hi/education/8341886.stm (last accessed 22 February 2015).

London Knowledge Lab, www.lkl.ac.uk (last accessed 2 June 2015).

McInerney, L. (2013) 'What A-Level subjects do Russell Group universities prefer?', www.lkmco.org/article/what-level-subjects-do-russell-group-universities-prefer-23092013 (last accessed 2 June 2015).

Myers, G. (2013) 'English Language, Facilitating Subjects and the review of A Levels', *The Use of English* 65(1).

O'Connor, R. (2015) 'Finland to remove cursive handwriting from education curriculum', *Independent*, 3 February, www.independent.co.uk/news/education/education-news/finland-to-remove-cursive-handwriting-from-education-curriculum-10021942.html (last accessed 1 June 2015).

Richmond, J. (2015) *English, Language and Literacy, 3 to 19: Grammar and Knowledge About Language*, Leicester: UKLA/Owen Education.

Russell Group website FAQ pages, www.russellgroup.ac.uk/faqs#7 (last accessed 2 June 2015).

Selwyn, N. (2011) *Education and Technology: Key Issues and Debates*, London: Bloomsbury.

Selwyn, N. (2013) *Education in a Digital World: Global Perspectives on Technology and Education*, London: Routledge.

Thurlow, C., Lengel, L. and Tomic, A. (2004) *Computer Mediated Communication: Social Interaction and the Internet*, London: Sage.

Index